PRA___ ___

UNDER ONE ROOF

"*Under One Roof: Creating Harmony for Multigenerational Living* is an inspiring and comprehensive read that explores the benefits, practicalities, and challenges of multigenerational living. Authors Emily K. Graham, Angel L. Vargas, and John L. Graham present compelling stories from diverse families who have found innovative ways to live together and meet the evolving needs of our society. By highlighting the advantages of living together, the authors offer a fresh perspective on fostering strong intergenerational relationships. From designing and remodeling homes to finding suitable housing, this book provides practical guidance for those considering multigenerational living arrangements. Moreover, it addresses cultural stigmas and financial concerns, offering valuable insights to overcome these challenges. With their extensive research and thought-provoking approach, the authors inspire readers to embrace the power of multigenerational living to create harmonious and fulfilling family environments. In a society facing changing needs and constraints, this book serves as a beacon of hope, encouraging readers to embrace the unity, support, and creativity that multigenerational living can provide. An excellent read for anyone interested in creating stronger family ties and finding innovative solutions to the challenges facing American families today."

—Donna Butts, Executive Director of Generations United

"This book is a guidebook to a solution that this country desperately needs—aging in place. The COVID-19 pandemic left many family members that were in nursing homes alone and without support from their families; it stressed the need for a different solution. Reading this book can help you map out the financial, emotional, and physical needs of the family when the decision is to live under one roof."

—Amy Irvine, CFP®, EA, MPAS®, CCFC, CDFA®, CFT-I™,
Certified Financial Therapist-Level I™ Professional

"Emily, Angel, and John's book is a wonderful read on the difficulties, pitfalls, and, yes, opportunities that confront families and households when generations come together under one roof (or at least neighboring roofs). The authors provide us with the facts, but perhaps more importantly, they relate the wide range of lived experiences of families past and present, from all over the world, and with a variety of household arrangements, lifestyles, and resources. Their stories and this book inspire but also advise us, wisely, sympathetically, and with practicality."

—Professor Edward Coulson, Director of the Center for Real Estate,
Merage School of Business, University of California, Irvine

"This book is a particularly valuable resource for those in the field in Intergenerational Relations. The authors have combined their expertise to produce a guide for families and professionals who are dealing with multigenerational households—e.g., living in a single home or living nearby. They provide some helpful background and historical perspectives since multigenerational arrangements were so common in earlier times . . . The writing style is down to earth and easy to understand. The concepts and principles of successful multigenerational families come to life with the many first person accounts from different generations."

—Professor Paul Roodin, SUNY Oswego,
Journal of Intergenerational Relationships, 6:2, 2008

PRAISE FOR THE PREVIOUS EDITION OF
UNDER ONE ROOF, TITLED *TOGETHER AGAIN*

"*Together Again* is a fresh, timely exploration of huge cultural and personal shifts in the choices Americans make about living with our multigenerational families. The book is magnificent in its thoroughness—first-rate social analysis, philosophical and psychological depth and sophistication, and warmth and generosity to all generations. *Together Again* is written by realists, who truly value family and do not see closeness in terms of dependency or dysfunction. The authors and I share a core belief; that generations belong together on a daily basis, and that we all benefit when we live together as complicated, loving, and caring tribes."

—Mary Pipher, PhD, author of *Reviving Ophelia* and *Another Nation*

"*Together Again* is a refreshing antidote to those who seek to divide the generations. We know from our research at AARP that all generations in America are closely connected and care deeply about one another. As society ages, more and more people will be looking for alternative living arrangements in order to stay involved in communities and out of nursing homes. *Together Again* offers readers valuable advice and choices on how to do it."

—Bill Novelli, former CEO, AARP

CREATING HARMONY *for*
MULTIGENERATIONAL LIVING

UNDER
ONE
ROOF

EMILY K. GRAHAM
ANGEL L. VARGAS
JOHN L. GRAHAM

RIVER GROVE
BOOKS

Published by River Grove Books
Austin, TX
www.rivergrovebooks.com

Distributed by River Grove Books

Design and composition by Greenleaf Book Group
Cover design by Greenleaf Book Group
Cover Images by ©Kueakoon T; ©Anastasy.a. Used under license from Shutterstock.com

Publisher's Cataloging-in-Publication data is available.

Print ISBN: 978-1-63299-759-3

eBook ISBN: 978-1-63299-760-9

Third Edition

We dedicate this book to our own extended families that have supported us in so many ways, including during the writing of this book.

Sharon Graham Niederhaus holds a special place in our minds and hearts. She was the first author of the first two editions, and we are happy to memorialize her thorough research, her always useful and often poignant interviews of Americans from around the country, and her prescient advocacy of multigenerational living.

CONTENTS

PREFACE

Harmony happens when different voices come together.
It's not always easy, but the results can rock.

This book is a third edition. The first two editions, written by Sharon Graham Niederhaus and John L. Graham, were titled *Together Again* (published in 2007) and *All in the Family* (published in 2013). Back in 2006, when Sharon and John wrote the first edition, they accurately predicted the housing price collapse and the Great Recession of 2008–2009, and the growth of multigenerational living arrangements that, we see now, are continuing into the 2020s. But much has changed since. The country has become more divided along political, racial, economic, and other ideological lines, and the COVID-19 pandemic has impacted both the world and the United States. Closer to home, sadly, Sharon herself passed away in 2021 after a long and fulfilling life. Now in 2024, we can see increasing evidence of the cracks in our social systems here in the United States. The economy and both pension and health care institutions are suffering under the weight of the baby boomer retirement tsunami.[1]

In response to the foreseeable troubles coming our way, we have now joined a new team of authors to describe how inventive, multigenerational families are now managing these challenging 2020s. Emily K. Graham and Angel L. Vargas combine their new and different perspectives with John L. Graham's longstanding expertise regarding multigenerational living. Very briefly, below, each of the three of us describes our family background relative to the creation of *Under One Roof: Creating Harmony for Multigenerational Living.*

EMILY'S PERSPECTIVE

Emily K. Graham: In the past, I lived in multigenerational households twice, once with my father and once with my mother. My parents divorced when I was three. As a child growing up, I lived with both my parents, but separately over time. For most of high school I lived with my father and his wife and their two kids. After I graduated, we all moved to Spain for a year, and I as an adult started my undergraduate studies in Madrid. The five of us shared a three-bedroom *piso* (apartment), and we had a great time. I stayed an extra year to finish a two-year degree, then moved back to San Francisco to finish my bachelor's degree at the University of San Francisco.

In 2004 I moved in with my mother in Mammoth Lakes, California. There, I held a position at the local hospital as a social worker coordinator. What a beautiful place to live and work! I knew it would be important to get an MSW, so in 2007 I moved to the San Francisco Bay Area for graduate school. I completed my master's in social work in 2009 and qualified as a licensed clinical social worker (LCSW) in 2015.

Now years later, I am facing my future. My story reflects a portion of the population little mentioned in the previous editions of the book, that of single people. Like most, I had expected that I'd grow up, meet somebody, start a family, and share my life with a partner. That didn't happen for me. I have often felt like the outlier in my family—all three of my siblings have married. But along the way, I have come across other people in my position. I am now fifty years old, never married, never have lived with a partner, and don't have children. I was born and raised in Southern California, and I live in Los Angeles about forty-five minutes from my father and stepmother, my older sister, her husband, and their son. My mother, other siblings, and other extended family are now scattered throughout California and different parts of the United States.

I have lived up and down the coastal regions of California and can say that I have probably moved about twenty times since college. At thirty-five, I made some career changes and went back to graduate school and took out loans to earn a master's degree in social work. I didn't find that path until later, and it was through experience and trial and error. Finding the right career for me took time. It wasn't as simple as "earn degree, decide on job, and get one." I tried all kinds of things to find the right match for my skills, talents, abilities, and natural propensities.

The point of sharing this story is to illustrate that not all people end up with the stereotypical, traditional, nuclear family lifestyle. I had really wanted to find a partner and life companion and to have a big family. I had watched pretty much all my friends, siblings, and cousins find partners, start families, and buy homes. I didn't have the help of carrying the load of a mortgage in California with two incomes, so I have continued to rent. I didn't have a second income or anyone else to share decision-making with and carry the joys and burdens of life. This was very difficult and at times really sad for me. At one point in my early forties I thought, *If I want children, I better do it alone.* I did all the research, I had to have a surgery because of some physical problems, and I looked into my possibilities. Between the costs, the physical and emotional stress, and the uncertainty, I reluctantly decided against that option. I didn't want to go into it with a load of stress and worry about how I'd manage a child alone, and to burden the child with that.

As I paint this picture it sounds quite sad, and quite frankly, I have spent many days crying, angry, frustrated, and dumbfounded by why this is my circumstance. So, with that said, I had to find a different path to joy. I had to find a new perspective, open my heart, and expand my perception of what life is supposed to look like. I had to come into alignment with the upsides of being single.

It took a lot of hard, emotional work. It came with an exploration on a deeper inner level. It wasn't about the outer world but how I related to myself around this issue. When you spend the amount of time I've spent on my own, you really get to know yourself well. You get to know your own inner landscape, the things that upset or trigger you, and the beliefs and attitudes acquired through your experiences. You can take one of two roads: you can complain and be quite miserable or you can find a new way. It became a matter of my spiritual path on a deep level.

So, why is this even relevant to this book? Why is sharing this story important? Data, statistics, and a real hard look at the social and support systems is necessary and critical. It helps with planning, it helps with understanding, and this book is meant to offer solutions, guidance, and assistance.

I am offering yet another perspective. This perspective comes from understanding your inner world. It comes from understanding what you believe, what misunderstandings have been developed, and what you do and don't have any control over. I have come to the conclusion that we all buy into an illusion of control, but we really have little control over so much. What is important to highlight is how you relate to yourself and others as you move through your life.

This book is meant to be a resource guide to the possibilities, a starting point of sorts. This book is more of a creative way of addressing these grander societal problems we are facing. It is a guide to help you step outside of the comfort zone, open your mind and your heart, and get creative on how to face the facts and uncertainty of the systems in place that are supposed to support us but sometimes don't. And of course, we weren't even considering a pandemic when the earlier editions of the book were published (or intense social unrest, inflation, or the possibility of a World War III scenario). So, who will support you?

Our ideas here focus on the support of the extended family. Many of the recommendations, considerations, and suggestions being made in the book can be transferable to the single person, but the playing field may look different and the social circumstances, the people you interact with, won't be family.

I have immersed myself in several small communities of people that share similar interests in one way or another. I have developed relationships with friends that might provide a lifeboat in some sort of a crunch or crisis. I have made connections with others my age who have also found themselves alone. I have begun exploring other types of communities and potential living environments where people might take care of one another.

I must admit, at this point it would be hard for me to share an apartment with someone. While independence is great, interdependence is more practical. I could be open to a compound type situation where there are several smaller dwellings with a main community gathering space for meals, movies, music, connection, and sharing of the responsibilities of pets and well-being. There are communities being developed all over the world. Expatriates moving to places like Costa Rica and building sustainable communities is one example. Communities are also springing up here in the U.S., with the intentions of land regeneration, recycling, thinking about the planet and the environment, and taking care of each other.

Relatedly, feelings and beliefs deserve attention as well. In all systems (immediate family or wider), there are multiple perspectives and perceptions of reality. Even in one family, five people may see a problem from totally different points of view. How do you get to any kind of agreement without that awareness? Especially when trying to merge homes, living environments, in-laws, children, etc., it will require flexibility. In some ways it is really simple but still not easy. It is worth exploring, especially when merging families and considering creating and building communities.

ANGEL'S STORY

Angel L. Vargas: Growing up in Indiana, I had the best of both worlds: Midwest living and close proximity to Chicago. This upbringing, and other various life events, led to my current professional and personal situation. As a second-generation American of Puerto Rican and Mexican descent who was born in the 1980s, my family upbringing and its structure shaped much of my worldviews on life and laid the foundation of how I interact with family and friends, as well as how my work ethic frames my personality.

My father and mother came from very humble backgrounds, and my grandparents even more humble. My father, who was born in Puerto Rico, never finished seventh grade, while my mother was born in America to Mexican immigrants. Both had one thing in common—families living together in multigenerational households.

My family has been and continues to be multigenerational-driven. This is true for both sides of the cultural divide. An aunt/cousin of mine, for example, lived with her parents for fifty years and then her sister for twenty years, to this day. During her career she served as a home health aide, providing high-quality care to patients in the comfort of their own homes. She often brought our multigenerational cultural perspective to her patient encounters, and she was very well received by patients. This aunt was also my babysitter and a key influence in my life while my parents worked.

Going further, until recently, my mother represented the epitome of a multigenerational family with four generations living under the same roof for almost twenty years. These generations included my mother, my sister, her children, and their children. Prior to this, my grandmother, mother, sister, and her children all lived together for several years. This structure was the foundation of my family—multigenerational levels of love, joy, support, and unity.

That said, it was not all hunky-dory or positive growing up in this environment. My immediate family, as well as other family members, struggled with gang influences, economic uncertainty, and avoidable loss. Our multigenerational family made these pains and struggles all the more visible in Chicagoland. From prison sentences to early loss of life and living uncomfortably in certain settings, we evolved as a close family to "ignore" or "dismiss" the negativities as just a part of life. Hindsight may be 20/20. I learned that despite this, our family time was still a positive marker for people and at these moments, these negative circumstances were subdued as a result.

I personally continued the tradition of a multigenerational environment when I had my daughter and lived with my parents for her first four years. It was not an experience of shame or failure but rather one of support, love, and empowerment to grow. Specifically, I was working and pursuing my degree while having full custody of my young daughter. It was an eye-opening experience for me, as my parents' support during this period allowed me to raise my daughter while maintaining some balance while in class and at work.

Speaking of work, I saw the uniqueness of multigenerational families beyond mine from my work in the home health industry. It was there that many patients lived with their children and their grandchildren during their care needs. Oftentimes, our staff would train these family members in medication management, wound cleaning, and other clinical or nonclinical support needs. This behavior mirrored my own family's and further validates how multigenerational living provides utility and value to society from a support and social determinants perspective.

In conclusion, my entire value system is based not just on my cultural or religious background but rather my exposure to a multigenerational family upbringing. The values of support came to me from multiple areas: family support, social support, clinical support, emotional support, financial support, academic support, and companionship. I would not be where I am today without this foundation!

JOHN'S STORY

John L. Graham: As my sister Sharon and I told it in the earlier editions of this book, our first story concerned our own family and the difficult death of our wonderful brother Steve in 1998. He was only forty-five.

Ours became a family of seven back in 1959. That's when our youngest brother, Bill, was born. The firstborn to our parents, John and Charlotte, was Sharon, born in 1942. Then came Mary Ellen in 1943, Johnny in 1947, Steve in 1953, and then Bill. Our parents loved all of us. But, with each birth, John and Charlotte had to move to a bigger house. Our dad was a lingerie salesman. He covered the western states for Warnaco Group, and he traveled a lot. Mom stayed at home and managed the five of us. She did the homemaking things wives did in her generation.

Dad retired at age sixty-four. He got off the road and onto the golf course. He loved the grandkids and finally had time to spend with them. Mom loved them too, but after five kids of her own, she was a bit iffy about having them around a lot. All this is pretty normal, we suppose. In fact, so was our dad's relatively sudden death in December of 1983. So many of his generation had lasted just a year or two past retirement. Mom died just nine months later, also common for her generation. She really missed her husband.

The deaths of our parents were tough on us all. They were very young—sixty-seven and sixty-nine years old, respectively. We miss them so much. But they were relatively healthy before their deaths. The five of us kids had no long parental illnesses to handle. Dad died within a month of his diagnosis of cancer, and Mom died suddenly one August night, just after meeting her new grandson, nicknamed "Jack" for her husband.

Our family travail was the illness, long-term care, and premature death of our brother Steve. In 1970 he experienced a seizure. At the time the doctors could not diagnose his problem. His case became the subject of seminars at the hospitals of both Stanford University and the University of California—San Francisco. It wasn't epilepsy; they were fairly sure of that. There weren't brain scans and MRIs to help them out back then, just fuzzy X-rays and a series of symptoms. Steve took all this uncertainty pretty well. Our parents worried about him deeply. But Steve had inherited a double dose of our father's sense of humor. He often quoted Groucho Marx, and his own jokes got him through much of the inconvenience of his affliction, whatever it was. Indeed, it's too bad Steve couldn't have made it to old age as Groucho recommends at the beginning of chapter 1!

Steve attended the Gemological Institute of America and ultimately became the manager of a very nice jewelry store in Palo Alto. Like our dad, he was a great salesman—all his customers adored him. The women in our family all loved having a jeweler in the family. Secretly, the guys did too—it saved them money! He vacationed in Kenya and Tahiti and enjoyed the good single life. He learned to live with the seizures, and the prescribed Dilantin handled them pretty well. All the while medical science was improving, and in such an odd way it slowly revealed the seriousness of Steve's illness to him.

Our parents had died not knowing what afflicted Steve, not knowing what was going to torture him beginning in the early 1990s. With the new brain-scanning technologies, the diagnosis became easy—a congenital abnormal vascular malformation. That's medical talk for bad plumbing in the head: every once in a while, a vein in his head would open; these brain bleeds caused immediate stroke-like symptoms. At first they were minor, terrible headaches. As the blood was reabsorbed into the tissue, his condition would improve surprisingly fast. But, after every bleed and recovery there was scar tissue that refused to let normal functioning return to that region of his brain.

Steve had good medical insurance and the disability insurance helped. And then in 1991, the surgeons at Stanford's hospital decided to take action. The best doctors in the world offered him an awful choice. With surgery things might improve, but untreated, the course of the disease was going to be a slow deterioration of brain functioning over a period of years. Every bleed would mean more disability. That would mean no more driving, loss of short-term memory, and speech problems. He would have to give up the job he enjoyed so much. Unfortunately, jewelers with short-term memory problems lose valuable items, such as diamonds. Steve bravely went for the surgery, and it nearly killed him.[2]

He spent the last six years of his life at the best assisted-living/skilled-nursing facility we could find in Palo Alto. Steve started out with his own apartment there—he had made an unpredicted good recovery from his first deathbed at Stanford University's hospital and was able to walk, talk, and even cook for himself—with a great amount of effort. His independence was important to him. During those six years there was a series of medical incidents that took more of his brain away from him. Perhaps not being able to talk was the worst. Not being able to swallow ice cream was bad, too—our mom had taught us all to love hot-fudge sundaes. The decisions about stomach tubes and such during the medical events and hospital stays were awful for us all.

Sometimes, siblings are a lot of trouble. Lucky for the four of us, we all did our part in managing Steve's care. Bill and Sharon lived close by, giving them the bulk of the frequent visits. Mary Ellen and John lived in Southern California and helped out in the ways they could, given the distance.

The experience of visiting him in the nursing home left us questioning how the infirm and elders are cared for in our society. Although the facility where our brother lived had a good reputation, we were appalled by the turnover of personnel. We would no sooner get Steve's caregivers up-to-speed on his needs when they would leave for other jobs. Certainly, this revolving-door situation left him and other patients with inconsistent care and confusion. We thought there must be better, more compassionate ways of doing this.

The four of us had a tough time with Steve's declining health. We literally did not know what we were in for. His bleeds moved faster than our decision-making about housing options and such. But we got through it. And we learned from it. We learned that even the best nursing home is a bad place to be. Maybe the assisted-living facilities are okay, but they mean separation from loved ones and the beginning of isolation. Those of you who have had similar experiences with family members know this. One of our purposes here is to keep you out of such places, to give you options, to give you more dignity at the end of your life.

CHANGES TO THE THIRD EDITION

The remainder of the book is organized in a similar way as the earlier editions had been. But, here in the third edition of *Under One Roof* (previously titled *All in the Family*), we have updated all the statistics as additional data have become available. We have also been able to add new stories about both successful and unsuccessful experiments in multigenerational living as reported in the media and online commentaries. We also introduce material on the latest thinking about creative processes that can be applied in family meetings. The emphasis in all this new material is on the inventiveness of families as they adjust to circumstances in the third decade of the twenty-first century. Indeed, the complex mix of cultural and legal constraints; family resources including both housing and finances; the numbers, ages, and health of extended family members and geographic limitations, personality clashes, and differences in cross-generational values all makes family design processes daunting—while at the same time provides exciting opportunities for invention.

In this new edition we also add material on the evolution of the American health care system that involves more care being delivered at home, by both medical professionals and family members. And we now close the book with a chapter on palliative and hospice care and death in the family, and the importance of family bereavement and the celebration of life.

Finally, you may have already noticed we do not use the term *elderly*. Rather we refer to Americans aged sixty-five and older as *elders*. Perhaps the distinction seems petty. But the adjective *elderly* evokes an image of infirmity and an associated pity. Alternatively, *elder* suggests wisdom and deserved respect. And, as you might guess, this is John's idea; after all, he is the elder author among us.

PART ONE

SEEING YOUR FUTURE

DODGING THE NURSING HOME

Age is not a particularly interesting subject. Anyone can get old.
All you have to do is live long enough.

—Groucho Marx

T his is a book about families—in particular, families that are taking inventive approaches to coping with the stresses of our changing society as the United States enters the 2020s after a global pandemic. Our focus in this introductory chapter is on how families manage the deteriorating health of a member. Some families handle things well and some don't. Of course, one still-popular option is placing our infirm elders in assisted-living facilities.

We appreciate that some of you have had the good fortune to never have visited a nursing home. We want to change that. Before you read another page in this book, we have a little homework assignment for you—call up the nicest nursing home in your area and ask for a tour. The easiest way to find one is to go to Medicare.gov, input your zip code, and hit Search. You can also narrow your search on the website by price and needs if you like. Contact information is listed as well as consumer evaluations. But nothing will be as informative as your own visit. When you get there, take a look at both the assisted-living apartments and the medical care facilities. Be sure to ask to see their state-produced quality report, called either a Form 2567 (from the U.S. Health Care

Financing Administration) or the state inspection survey. We believe that after that tour, you will be more interested in the ideas in this book. So, seriously, close the book and make the call now.

Close the book and call!

THE CURRENT STATE OF NURSING HOMES

There's a lot to read these days about nursing homes. You can find more than 2,000 books on this topic if you punch in "nursing homes" at Amazon.com. Assuming you did your homework as assigned above, you now know more than most of the books can teach you. In particular, you know what things are like at nursing homes in your specific neighborhood. Since your visit was not unannounced, we'll guess you didn't run into any of the top ten common problems in nursing homes listed by *Consumer Reports* (see exhibit 1.1).

Exhibit 1.1. Common Problems Found in Nursing Homes

The following list covers state surveyors' required conditions for nursing homes:

1. The facility must store, prepare, distribute, and serve food under sanitary conditions.

2. The facility must ensure that (a) a resident who enters the facility without pressure sores does not develop pressure sores unless the individual's clinical condition demonstrates that they were unavoidable; and (b) a resident having pressure sores receives necessary treatment and services to promote healing, prevent infections, and prevent new sores from developing.

3. The facility must ensure that it is free of medication error rates of 5 percent or greater.

4. The facility must not use verbal, mental, sexual, or physical abuse, corporal punishment, or involuntary seclusion.

5. The facility must provide each resident with sufficient fluid intake to maintain proper hydration and health.

6. The facility must establish and maintain an infection control program designed to provide a safe, sanitary, and comfortable environment, and to help prevent the development and transmission of disease and infection.

7. The facility must ensure that each resident receives adequate supervision and assistance devices to prevent accidents.

8. The facility must promote care for residents in a manner and in an environment that maintains or enhances each resident's dignity and respect in full recognition of his or her individuality.

---

continued

9. Each resident must receive, and the facility must provide, the necessary care and services to attain or maintain the highest practicable
physical, mental, and psychosocial well-being, in accordance with
the comprehensive assessment and plan of case.

10. The facility must provide for an ongoing program of activities
designed to meet, in accordance with the comprehensive assessment, the interests and the physical, mental, and psychosocial
well-being of each resident.[3]

Source: State Operations Manual Provider Certification,
U.S. Health Care Financing Administration.

This is a scary list indeed.[4] But it's not our job to criticize elder care facilities—plenty already do that. Instead, our job here is, first, to keep you out of
such places and second, to help you better enjoy growing older in the close
vicinity of your family. So please read on.

WHY THIS BOOK IS FOR YOU

We expect the typical reader of this book to be a member of the postwar baby-
boom generation, aged sixty to seventy-five or so. People already into their
sixties and seventies will find immediate uses for this book as well. Or perhaps you're one of their grown children? We're going to address our comments
mostly to the older folks facing retirement during the next decade. But, for you
sons and daughters of baby boomers, there's much here, too.

John's cousin Lee, born in Nebraska in 1940, was always fond of describing all
the trouble baby boomers have caused America over the years. He should know—
his younger brother was born in 1946. According to Lee, first it was bikes. Come
Christmas 1951 and there was a big bicycle shortage in the country. Then it was
classrooms and teachers, including not enough seats in colleges around the country beginning in 1963. Come 1965 and there weren't enough entry-level jobs to
go around. About 1972, as the first baby boomers started families, there weren't
enough houses. Baby boomers thinking about retirement drove the late-1990s
stock market run-up—there was a shortage of good investments. Economists
were completely blindsided by the 2008–2009 Great Recession because they

ignored these demographic demons. For demographers the prediction was easy—indeed, John wrote about these issues in 1997 and 2011 (see the appendix). And, of course, now there is a shortage of retirement and pension funds, and health care facilities and personnel. Undoubtedly, the most frightening recent headline we have seen on the topic comes from the *Washington Post*: "Seniors Are Flooding Homeless Shelters that Can't Care for Them."[5]

Among the best representations for this problem is a comparison of the number of births in the United States over three periods:

1931–1945: 40 million births,

1946–1960: 58 million births, and

1961–1975: 55 million births.

Even better is to compare the population pyramids (a representation of the age distribution of the United States in any one year) in figure 1.1—first 1960, then projected into 2030:

For the fun of it, find your age cohort in the two pyramids. Also, notice the near doubling of the U.S. population between 1960 and 2030—that is, in about one lifetime.

The bill creating Medicare in the United States was passed in 1965. Circa 1960, when the discussions about it began, the population in the country represented a pyramid. That is, greater numbers of younger Americans would be able to support the retirement and health care of their elders, no problem. Decades earlier in 1935, when the Social Security program was created, the

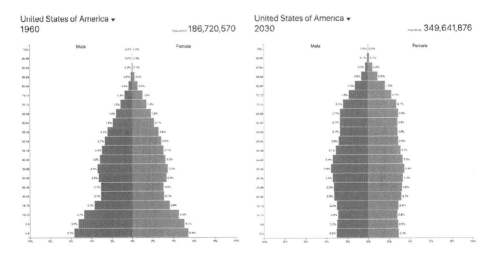

distribution of the population also reflected a pyramid. These approaches to supporting elder Americans no longer make sense, neither now nor certainly not by the end of 2020s. For even more fun with population pyramids, you can see the demographics of the baby boomers causing the current problems in the slow motion of an animated presentation for the years 1950–2060: visit the Pew Research Center's age pyramid page (https://www.pewresearch.org/ age-pyramid/). Few saw this demographic disaster coming—John was one of them. You can see his article on the topic written in 1997 in the appendix.

Room for Thought 1.1.
The Impact of Demographic Shifts

. . . declines in fertility are already advanced in most of the world. Over 80% of humanity lives in countries where the fertility rate is either below three and falling, or already two or less. This is thanks not to government limits but to modernization and individuals' desire for small families.[6]

Authors' Note: We in the U.S. are about twenty years *ahead* of the Chinese on this demographic disaster! And, the Japanese have been about ten years ahead of us.

Cousin Lee was right: America has never done a good job of handling those 58 million kids and the incredible demand of their numbers. And now our retirement system, designed for the 1930–1945 cohort, faces the boomer onslaught. Indeed, you can already see some of the key systems beginning to fail. During the Great Recession, many baby boomers' pension funds, retirement accounts, and housing values deflated. Consequently, boomers en masse kept their jobs longer, thus adding to the country's unemployment problem as younger workers were, in effect, locked out. Some theorize that Social Security and Medicare will dissolve circa 2030; the private pension funds were beginning to creak even before the disaster of 2008–2009.

If you think the nursing home you visited today is a place you want to stay out of, wait until you see the 2030s version. Who will build enough of them? Who will staff them? Who will pay for them? And, with the new medical technologies, we'll all live longer. Rather than dying from diseases, baby boomers will just wear down and wither away. The demographics make the future easy to see, and that future is far different from the "retirement party" boomers' parents experienced.

Getting ready for this future is what the rest of this book is about. We predicted and are seeing that the baby boomers' retirement will be accommodated by a fundamental change in American culture. Three-generation households will not be seen as a kind of subsidy for our "irresponsible" kids. Rather, three generations living together again, as they have done in many countries (except the United States and Northern Europe in the last sixty years) throughout history, will be the norm. Investing in our kids will be seen as a new kind of pension fund—one that helps everyone. And the close relationship that has held societies together throughout history, that between grandparents and grandchildren, will be renewed.

Baby boomers' parents could afford the independence of living separately. *I will not be a burden to my kids* has been their mantra. The baby-boom generation will not be able to afford the apparent "luxury" of such independent living. And perhaps it's really not a luxury at all. As we adapt to the new cultural realities, especially in the post-COVID age, perhaps we'll actually be happier with our rediscovered freedom to live together again in inventive family living arrangements.

In the following pages, we describe what many inventive Americans with foresight are already doing to bring their families back together again. The bricks of our story are the words of the more than one hundred Americans we interviewed who are now building multigenerational households. To protect their privacy, we have disguised the names and locations of the folks we interviewed. But we have remained faithful to the content and context of their comments. These Americans are from all over the country: east, west, north, and south. They are Black and White, wealthy and not. They speak English, Spanish, or Chinese as their first language. They work as manicurists and writers, realtors and finance professors. The youngest is nine years old, while the oldest is ninety-seven. And in this third edition of our book, we also add other new ideas, posted on internet commentary sites, in response to a variety of media reports on multigenerational living.

The people we've talked to have given sage advice:

Helen (a Realtor in her 60s): When I work with people that are in their late 60s and early 70s, I try to help them see that they are going to be happier if they can move to their final home while in that age bracket . . . They are not selling their house when they are under pressure for medical reasons or when they are not making good decisions. They don't have to make quick choices about the things that they have loved for so many years, valuable and sentimental things. Also, it helps because folks are more adaptable moving into a new situation and developing new friendships when they are in their early 70s. The longer you wait after 75, the harder it gets. I have seen people in their 80s; they just can't do it . . . That is why I have explored all these options for myself, so I can make my own choices.

And they bring tears to our eyes:

Sarah (a seventeen-year-old, talks about having Granddad across the way): I took a class sophomore year about American history. I fell in love with it. I remember in my junior year, I was studying fascism and communism for an exam, and Granddad helped me. He launched into a twenty-minute explanation of world history, just clarified a bunch of things, and it was one of those [times] . . . you know, I'll remember in twenty years. When I'm getting married, I'll have a funny story to tell about how my grandpa was helping me out with a test when I was 16 . . . It's like having your encyclopedia right across the road, across the grass.

Sarah added in her college application essay, "It is listening to your grandfather quote the page you just read in *Macbeth* last night word-for-word or that afternoon that you spent playing double solitaire with your grandmother as you watch a TCM movie. It is through such life experiences that I begin to realize that because of my past, I am ready for whatever the future has to bring."

The mortar of our story is our observations about, and analyses of, this growing trend in America. Three generations living together is on the increase, according to all sources, including the most recent U.S. Census Bureau data. Our goal is to help push this healthy trend along and to help ease the transition from a culture of independent retirement to one of interdependence. We are convinced the latter will be better for all.

AN UNPRECEDENTED DECADE OF CHANGE FOR AMERICAN FAMILIES

Happiness is having a large, loving, caring,
close-knit family in another city.
—George Burns

The advantage of growing up with siblings
is that you become very good at fractions.
—Robert Brault

O n this topic humor is important for a couple of reasons. First, a little levity will help us all get through the rather serious adjustments we'll be making to our family lives during the next decade. Second, we know that humor is an important tool for stimulating creative thinking. So, while we very much appreciate the Burns and Brault quips above, we must say that the folks we interviewed for our book hold very different views than theirs. Here, we report the stories of scores of American families that have invented ways to live together that serve the fast-changing needs and constraints of our twenty-first century society. Their stories are about locating close by one another to work together creatively and cooperatively, rather than just dividing things up.

The media began to take notice about ten years ago.[7] The burgeoning elder population, with their inevitable infirmities and failing finances and pension systems; the care of children in households where both parents work full-time; and the volatility of employment and housing markets are the most obvious challenges facing Americans today. Increasingly, multigenerational living arrangements are being made where creativity in the design of structures and interaction patterns are reinvigorating extended family relationships. The purpose of our book is to stimulate your own inventiveness as you work through the particular challenges facing your family in these tough times.

Around the year 2006, our vision of the future of multigenerational living was accurate if not blurry. We stated that the American housing bubble started to inflate in 2003, and we correctly called its bursting beginning in 2006 (see page 9 of the first edition). Indeed, John had initially predicted such an economic catastrophe back in 1997. New U.S. Census Bureau data have added much credence to our emphasis on multigenerational housing as a key solution to the demographic and economic problems that have unfolded in the last fifteen years. At the foundation of this edition of *Under One Roof* lay five ideas about how American culture is now changing:

1. The retirement and infirmities of American baby boomers are causing a complete restructuring of government and corporate support for American elders (think Social Security and other pension funds,[8] Medicare, and medical care in general[9]). This will be a ten-year process of adjustment that will be difficult for individuals, families, and institutions. By the way, similar problems are cropping up in other affluent countries such as France and the United Kingdom.[10]

2. Our sixty-year national experiment with nuclear families (the ideal of two parents, two and a half kids, and the white picket fence) is ending. The old and faithful interdependence of extended family relationships is re-emerging as the cultural norm.

3. New housing is being built that is appropriate for mixed-age neighborhoods and multigenerational family proximity. One-third of the present single-family houses can and will accommodate an accessory dwelling unit or the like.

4. The current growth of "boomerang kids," adult children living with their parents amid the present economic travails, will be seen as a kind of spring training for the long, hard season of the baby-boom retirement years. Millions of Americans are now relearning the tricks of balancing proximity and privacy that will be crucial in the next decades.

5. Obstacles to creativity in the design of home structures, as well as societal obstacles to interpersonal independence or local building regulations limiting mixed neighborhoods (which seem to be uniquely American fixations), will fade away during the next decade.

These ideas, which are developed in detail in the remainder of the book, are briefly summarized here by an updated version of an article John wrote for the *Christian Science Monitor*, "Solution to US Debt Woes Isn't Economic. It's Social," appearing July 27, 2011:

> The clock is ticking loudly in Washington over the debt ceiling and long-term funding problems like Medicare and Social Security. Economists have blamed America's current economic malaise on (take your pick): overspending, greed, government regulation, government deregulation, subprime home mortgages, executive incentives, efficient markets theory, the business cycle, the Chinese, the Russians, Donald Trump, and Joe Biden—the list goes on.

But what if the economists have it completely wrong? Suppose (for a minute or ten) that the so-called economic decline is simply a severe symptom of a cultural shift. The longest view of the progress of humankind suggests that governments have always been unfaithful to humans. The current example, our crumbling Social Security system, has really only succeeded in dividing families. In 1940, only 15 percent of women sixty-five and older lived alone.[11] By 1990, that number had risen to over 40 percent. Thankfully, this trend of loneliness is finally reversing in the new century, and particularly so in the last decade. See figure 2.1 for more.

Figure 2.1.
Percentages of Women 65+ Years Old Living Alone
(source: U.S. Census)

Cultural anthropologist Margaret Mead long ago pointed out that the family is the only institution that persistently supports us. What the economists are calling an economic problem is best understood as a cultural reversion to older living patterns. The reason? Our twentieth-century experiment with nuclear families has failed.

That's the problem. *Here's the fix: many Americans are rediscovering the importance of the extended family.*

RETURN TO THE EMPTY NEST

Consider the phenomenon known as "boomerang kids." Estimates vary, but according to the U.S. Census Bureau, almost one-third of all Americans ages eighteen to thirty-four are now living with their parents. That's more than 21 million young adults. See figure 2.2 that shows the recent upswing of this living arrangement. Certainly, *a part* of this change is due to COVID-19.[12] Fifteen years ago, popular culture in the form of newspaper headlines, book titles, movie titles (remember that awful 2006 movie, *Failure to Launch*?), and a *minority* of American parents of twentysomethings complained loudly. But, when you step back and look at the big picture and the moving picture,[13] it's clear that boomerang kids are just another symptom of the greater cultural change affecting American society in the 2020s: that is, the reunification of the extended family.

Grandparents are also moving back in with their children. Three-generation households are on the rise in America, according to the Census Bureau. Based on their analyses of U.S. Census data, the Pew Research Center estimates that 18 percent of the population—59.7 million Americans—lived in multi-generational housing in 2021, up from 28 million in 1980.[14] That number is now more than 6 percent of all American households—see the recent, steady growth displayed in figure 2.3. And certainly the Census number undercounts the prevalence of multigenerational living—not counted are extended families living next door to one another in duplexes or the same apartment buildings. The fundamental point is that people are moving back together again because the societal experiment of the World War II generation hasn't worked. Three generations belong together, and not just for financial reasons.

Fundamentally, humans are psychologically and physiologically designed to, and have evolved to, live this way.[15] We've survived by living in such extended family arrangements. We are happiest in such groups. And we are now quickly learning that other institutions (companies, unions, governments, religious organizations, etc.) ultimately cannot take care of us. Only our families can and will.

Figure 2.2.
Percentages of Eighteen- to
Thirty-Four-Year-Olds Living in Parent's Home
(source: U.S. Census)

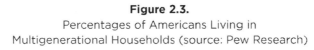

Figure 2.3.
Percentages of Americans Living in
Multigenerational Households (source: Pew Research)

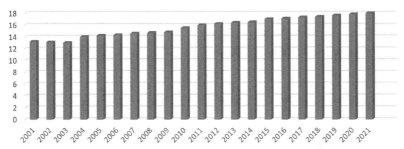

THE HOUSING DEBACLE—REVISITED

The population of American elders is now growing at an accelerating rate. According to Census projections, the elder population will double between now and the year 2040, to more than 80 million. By then, as many as one in five Americans will be sixty-five years old or older. And more than half of them will have at least one disability.

In order to adjust the housing stock of the country to reflect the baby boomers' retirement and the associated growth in multigenerational living arrangements, changes will be required in long-existing, mostly local housing and building codes and associated ordinances. The main battle line in this political fight is over accessory dwelling units (ADUs), popularly called "granny flats"[16] or "tiny homes."[17] Built within or adjacent to larger houses, they can provide living spaces for adult children or grandparents. They offer both proximity and privacy. Public debate and political battles are being fought, won, and lost around the country over making changes in codes that not only allow for, but actually promote, the construction of ADUs in existing neighborhoods and in new developments.

ADUs produce two kinds of complaints. First, physical impacts, such as increased parking and traffic and architectural changes in buildings, are often seen as disruptive to neighborhoods.[18] The second sort relates to social and cultural issues. That is, ADUs deviate from the traditional ways of looking at housing, family, and the neighborhood. They stand for a change in the way the single-family house is used, a departure from the conventional meanings connected to residential zoning categories.

While builders and architects do complain about zoning constraints and such, their own practices are often obstacles to housing appropriate for the new century. They talk more about features that will *sell* to consumers but won't really *serve* them. For example, consider a ritzy Newport Beach, California, neighborhood where folks have been sold $3 million homes with granny flats at the tops of stairs! How's Grandma going to navigate those steep steps?

What America Must Do

Fast-rising life expectancies, the growing costs of elder care, the increasing need for childcare, the frustrating lack of affordable housing, and the new disconnectedness—all are producing unfamiliar challenges for families all around America. Fortunately, our aforementioned twentieth-century dalliance with nuclear families and white-picket-fence suburbia is fast winding down. The "social avalanche" of elder baby boomers will force Americans back to the familiar family form of multigenerational households.

America must spur the comeback of ADUs and the flexibility of mixed neighborhoods with respect to size, value, and use. We must design and demand communities and homes that will accommodate a fast-graying America in innovative ways.

PART 2

THE BENEFITS
OF MULTI-
GENERATIONAL
LIVING

CHAPTER 3

WHY LIVING TOGETHER
AGAIN MAKES SENSE

Never before have so many people lived so far away from the older people
they love. And never before have older people lived to be so old.

—Mary Pipher

The dramatic societal shifts going on in America are pretty easy to discern. The politicians and pundits remind us almost daily. The decades-long rise in life expectancy (before the COVID years), the growing cost of elder care, the increasing need for childcare, the frustrating lack of affordable housing, and the new disconnectedness are all producing unfamiliar challenges for families across America. But, while the problems are easy to see, the solutions are not. The solutions we're advocating here require us to actually look back in time at how families used to live together. And, fortunately, we also have some modern pioneer stories to share about how many American families are now taking more inventive approaches to living arrangements that allow togetherness and privacy at the same time.

A BRIEF HISTORY OF LIVING TOGETHER

We're trying to make this book a multimedia experience for you. We've already sent you on an excursion to your best and nearest nursing home. After that tough trip we owe you a little levity. Now your assignment is to find on Netflix (or another streaming platform) and watch *The Gods Must Be Crazy*. It's appropriate for the whole family, it is hilarious, and actually, it's about the whole family. That is, part of this film shows how competition and cooperation are managed among a large extended family of the San (!Kung or Bushmen) peoples in southern Africa. While the film is a clever comedy, its insights into human behavior and communication are deep.

So, put the book down and watch the film!

Now back to the book. Up until the 1950s in America, and around most of the world up through today, three (sometimes even four) generations live(d) together in multigenerational families. In prehistoric times these family groupings included all the living descendants in either the male or female line. Each family was self-sufficient, with men and women providing the food but with women mostly taking care of household duties, children, and elder parents. The whole family had to cooperate in order to survive. Eventually, around 10,000 years ago when agriculture took hold, families organized themselves into clans, consisting of several extended families, to share certain ceremonies and traditions. Later these groupings evolved into cooperative tribes for protection. Still later, people began depending on local, state, and national governments for protection, and on persons outside the family for food and education.[19]

The Industrial Revolution caused significant changes in family life. In the nineteenth century, people moved from farms to cities where new factories were being built. In the cities, people no longer worked together in extended family units. Men were required to travel to and from their jobs and had less time to spend with their families. New kinds of jobs called for specific skills; this meant that workers frequently moved away from their local communities and kinship groups to live near their places of employment. Multigenerational families began to dissipate in favor of nuclear families consisting of married couples and their children. Women still stayed at home to raise the children. However, with the new mobility, multigenerational households began to decline, along with the expectation that children care for elder parents in their own homes.

Subsequently, assisted-living and skilled-nursing facilities came into existence as new living arrangements to serve the needs of the infirm elders.

Housing evolved into single-family structures to accommodate the new and independent family units. This tradition of single-family dwellings accelerated in the United States after the end of World War II. Since then, America's residential landscape has shifted from city or small-town to suburban living. General prosperity, cheap farmland rendered from new agricultural technologies, easier building techniques, and access to automobiles all combined to initiate the development of suburban tracts of single-family homes for nuclear families in the mid-twentieth century. And still today, Americans value these homes for the space, security, status, and privacy they provide. The single-family suburban home worked for a time, while mothers stayed at home to raise children and life spans were shorter. However, with the advent of new medical technology and extended life expectancy, and with both parents working, the single-family home for nuclear families is no longer meeting the needs of our changing population.

AMERICANS' LIFE EXPECTANCY
HAS WOBBLED IN RECENT YEARS

Americans' life expectancy (at birth) has actually declined during the last five years.[20] It had been the one trend line that almost always went up throughout most of American history. But beginning in 2015 a perfect storm developed of the opioid overdose crisis, increases in homicide and suicide rates, and deaths from Alzheimer's disease. Then the COVID-19 pandemic occurred. All combined to cause an unprecedented decline to a two-year drop in life expectancy from its 2014 peak of seventy-nine years old to 76.4 in 2021.[21] We still do better than the Brazilians (seventy-six) and the Russians (seventy-one). But we are now tied with China (seventy-seven) and falling behind Cuba (seventy-nine), the British (eighty-one), and the Germans (eighty-one). But both the French (eighty-two) and the Japanese (eighty-five) are much longer-lived than average Americans—perhaps it's the wine and fish?

The longevity figures are higher for those Americans who attain the age of sixty-five. In 2022, American men reaching age sixty-five had an average life expectancy of an additional 18.1 years or living to age 83.2, while women could expect 20.7 more years or living to age 85.7. Having found these data, we thought it might be fun (or angst-producing) for you to look up how many years you have left, theoretically, that is. So, we provide table 3.1, the Life Table, for your inspection and interest. These data are a little different from the more common life expectancy numbers reported above because the latter do not take into account your current age and the overall health of your age cohort. So, if you're sixty years old now and you're female, you have about 24.8 years to go, assuming average health and average luck.

TABLE 3.1. LIFE TABLE: HOW MUCH YOU HAVE LEFT (FIND YOUR AGE AND LOOK TO THE RIGHT)

AGE	MALES	FEMALES	AGE	MALES	FEMALES	AGE	MALES	FEMALES
0	76.2	81.3	34	44.2	48.4	68	16.0	18.3
1	75.7	80.7	35	43.3	47.5	69	15.3	17.5
2	74.7	79.7	36	42.4	46.5	70	14.6	16.8
3	73.8	78.7	37	41.5	45.6	71	13.9	16.0
4	72.8	77.8	38	40.6	44.7	72	13.3	15.3
5	71.8	76.8	39	39.7	43.7	73	12.6	14.5
6	70.8	75.8	40	38.8	42.8	74	12.0	13.8
7	69.8	74.8	41	37.8	41.8	75	11.3	13.1
8	68.8	73.8	42	36.9	40.9	76	10.7	12.4
9	67.8	72.9	43	36.0	39.9	77	10.1	11.7
10	66.8	71.8	44	35.2	39.0	78	9.5	11.1
11	65.8	70.1	45	34.3	38.1	79	9.0	10.5
12	64.8	69.8	46	33.4	37.2	80	8.3	9.8
13	63.8	68.8	47	32.5	36.2	81	7.9	9.2
14	62.9	67.8	48	31.6	35.3	82	7.0	8.7
15	61.9	66.8	49	30.8	34.4	83	6.9	8.1
16	60.9	65.9	50	29.9	33.5	84	6.4	7.6
17	59.9	64.9	51	29.0	32.6	85	6.0	7.1
18	59.0	63.8	52	28.2	31.7	86	5.6	6.6
19	58.2	62.8	53	27.3	30.8	87	5.2	6.1
20	57.1	61.8	54	26.5	29.9	88	4.8	5.7
21	56.1	61.0	55	25.7	29.1	89	4.5	5.3
22	55.2	60.0	56	24.9	28.2	90	4.1	4.9
23	54.3	59.0	57	24.2	27.3	91	3.8	4.5
24	53.4	58.1	58	23.3	26.5	92	3.5	4.2
25	52.5	57.1	59	22.5	25.6	93	3.3	3.9
26	51.5	56.1	60	21.8	24.8	94	3.1	3.6
27	50.6	55.1	61	21.0	24.0	95	2.9	3.4
28	49.7	54.2	62	20.3	23.1	96	2.7	3.2
29	48.8	53.2	63	19.5	22.3	97	2.5	3.0
30	47.8	52.3	64	18.8	21.5	98	2.4	2.8
31	46.9	51.3	65	18.1	20.7	99	2.3	2.7
32	46.0	50.3	66	17.4	19.9	100	2.2	2.5
33	45.1	49.4	67	16.7	19.1			

Source: www.socialsecurity.gov, accessed 2022.

The American elder population was growing at a moderate rate for the first two decades of the century. But now, in the 2020s, that rate is accelerating dramatically. In fact, by 2050, there will be more people who are elders (sixty-five years old or over) than young (age fourteen or younger). According to projections from the U.S. Census Bureau, the elder population will double between 2010 and 2040, to close to over 81 million Americans. Perhaps the most noteworthy datum is that 8 million of those people will be over ninety years old in 2040! By then, as many as one in five Americans, or 20 percent of the population, could be elders—see table 3.2. Indeed, focus on the steep growth between 2020–2030, that we are now experiencing, shown in the bar graph in figure 3.3. That steep increase is happening as you read this book, and it best demonstrates the historically unprecedented problems facing Americans in the next ten years. Our current systems of Social Security and Medicare simply cannot handle the baby-boom tsunami affecting us all right now.

TABLE 3.2. ELDERS (65+ YEARS) POPULATION OF THE UNITED STATES (IN MILLIONS)

YEAR	POPULATION	DECADE INCREASE
1960	16.6	—
1970	20.0	3.4
1980	25.6	5.6
1990	31.1	5.5
2000	34.7	3.6
2010	40.2	5.5
2020	54.8	14.6
2030	72.1	17.3
2040	81.2	9.1
2050	88.5	7.3

Source: U.S. Census Bureau data, accessed 2022.

CARING FOR ELDERS

The rapid increase in the number of our elders (sixty-five years and older) combined with decreases in financial support for human and health services

Figure 3.1.
Percentage of Elders (65+) in America
(source: U.S. Census)

is already leading to dilemmas and even disasters for some American families regarding care for the seniors in the clan. Things will only get worse in the coming years. Caring for the oldest old or the super-elders (those eighty-five years old and older) is and will be particularly burdensome. This is the fastest-growing group of elders and the group with the greatest need for assistance.

Of the current 58 million elder Americans, some 50 percent now report some sort of disability.[22] You can see the breakdown of these afflictions in exhibit 3.1. For the oldest old, these percentages can be roughly tripled. At age eighty-five, virtually all of us can expect to have some sort of disability hampering our activities and requiring some level of assistance—for 45 percent of us it will be sensory problems (hearing or vision loss, for example), for 85 percent the problem will be physical, and so on. Such projections lead experts, such as medical ethicist Daniel Callahan, to refer to the fast-approaching "social avalanche" of old age.

Exhibit 3.1.
Most Common Disabilities among American Elders
(65+ years) in Order of Prevalence (Percent Reporting)

Walking/using stairs (40%)
Hearing (31%)
Mental/cognitive (27%)
Vision (22%)

Self-care (9%)
Speaking (8%)

Sources: U.S. Census Bureau, CDC, American Community Living, accessed 2022.

Of the current 58 million elders, some 1.4 million need substantial assistance and are living in nursing homes. But, thankfully, the news on this is not all bad. The most recent studies suggest that during the last two decades, the number of folks living in nursing homes hasn't risen along with the growth in the elder population. The best guess is that about half a million Americans have dodged the dreary places during the last decades. Three factors seem to account for the decline:

1. Today's seniors have taken better care of themselves—less smoking, better diets, and more exercise. These positive steps have at least postponed the kinds of disabilities that require nursing home care.

2. More assisted-living options are open to today's seniors. Home health care has increased thanks to changes in Medicare and Medicaid services, and the variety of assistance to seniors has burgeoned, as well.

3. And, of course, grandparents are moving in with their children and grandchildren. Indeed, the 2020 Census reports that more than 7 million grandparents were living with their grandchildren.

And that leads us to the next topic.

WHO'S TAKING CARE OF THE KIDS?

Many women, the traditional caregivers, are now working. In fact, 68 percent of married mothers with children are employed outside the home.[23] According to a national survey of more than 44,000 working parents conducted by the research organization the Urban Institute, one in five children ages six to twelve years old are regularly left without adult supervision after school and before their parents come home from work. Moreover, "older children are more likely to spend their after-school hours home alone rather than in day care, activities at school, or with a relative or babysitter." The good news is that more than 6 percent of children under the age of eighteen are now living with their grandparents. These demographics not only have implications for who will be available to care for elders but also emphasize the growing need in America for childcare, particularly made worse by COVID-19.[24]

THE LACK OF AFFORDABLE HOUSING

Even before the turn of the millennium, many Americans saw another way to make their real estate more valuable irrespective of the market fluctuations: houses become fundamentally more valuable if they accommodate more residents. That is, a potential source of more affordable housing is to utilize the underused space in single-family-home neighborhoods to create accessory dwelling units (ADUs). These small dwelling units, also known as in-law units, involve no land acquisition costs and minimal new infrastructure. Estimates are that one-third of American homes can accommodate such flexible options. This trend by home builders of high-end developments has been going on since at least 2000.

For the past twenty years, housing advocates have been promoting ADUs because of their potential benefits to individual homeowners and their municipalities. ADUs are believed to offer homeowners a good investment with a healthy rate of return, furnish housing for family members including parents and adult children, improve security in the home, and make better use of existing space.

For communities, ADUs hold many benefits. They are inexpensive to produce and therefore more affordable. They also use existing infrastructure and better fit today's smaller families. And they generate additional property tax revenues for cities. These units have the flexibility to provide both needed rental housing, especially in today's tight housing markets, as well as multigenerational housing.[25]

GETTING RECONNECTED

The hope was that information technology would provide new ways of being together. Certainly, teenagers today in 2024 are using the internet and smartphones to network, text, tweet, and communicate in new ways, disrupting traditional classrooms and providing another new medium for which innovation-lagging adults have to establish rules. Relatedly, John had some years ago been one-half of a U.S. Navy marriage that involved little contact with his family (that is, letters or an occasional call) for months at a time. But nowadays, the internet and Skype allow those serving at sea to participate at home to a significantly greater degree. And who can predict how the next "broadening of the band" will affect societal and familial connectedness?

The problem is that no matter how broad the bandwidth, we still miss the humanness of being together. The hugs and kisses, the warmth of sitting next to someone on a couch, the safeness of sleeping in the same house, the aroma of baking cookies—none of these can be shared electronically. Indeed, some argue that the technological changes, particularly new media, are exacerbating the disconnectedness in American society.[26]

Phyllis Gilly, John's mother-in-law, told the story of how air-conditioning changed neighborhoods in suburban Dallas, Texas. Before air-conditioning, on hot summer days the moms sat outside on front porches, gossiped, and watched the kids playing ball in the street, and so on. But in the 1960s, air-conditioning moved everyone inside. A generation ago, television was the thief of family time. Now computers, the internet, and smartphones make even greater demands on younger people's attention. Indeed, the continuing explosion of media choice is fast dividing twenty-first-century households into one-screen-per-person units.

We Americans suffer these afflictions worse than any others around the world. Author Robert Putnam, in his important book *Bowling Alone*, noticed:

> Compared with the citizens of most other countries, Americans have always lived a nomadic existence. Nearly one in five of us move each year and, having done so, are likely to pick up and move again. As a result, compared to other peoples, Americans have become accustomed to pitching camp quickly and making friends easily. From our frontier and immigrant past we have learned to plunge into new community institutions when we move.[27]

Putnam goes on to explain that the mobility of Americans has actually declined since the 1950s, even if just a little. But, we remain the world champions of mobility and therefore, familial disconnectedness.

A PLEASANT REALITY

So far this chapter has mostly been about unpleasant realities. We've written about depressing developments, from disabilities to disconnectedness to debts and death. We do hope you managed to bring a little levity into the discourse with *The Gods Must Be Crazy*. But, overall, our wake-up call so far has been more dirge than dance. So, we want to end this chapter with a happy story about three generations of Americans living together. We do recognize that living with kids, parents, and grandparents all in one house isn't exactly *Mary Poppins*. But, the approach we advocate in this book not only can work—it is working all across the country!

Our story starts with a two-word question: "A toaster?" Some may say that when a man is involved in gift giving, he may not know how the gift will be interpreted. So when Madeline opened her Christmas present from her son, Jim; his wife, Christine; and their daughter, Katie; the meaning didn't sink in right away. Madeline wondered, "Why was the family buying another toaster?" All four of them had been living together then for three years, and their toaster always worked just fine. Madeline's wrinkled brow betrayed her befuddlement.

Christine noticed first and urged her to open the second part of the package. Then everything became clear. Inside the second part of the gift were the blueprints of Madeline's cottage, to be built on their property in the spring. They had all met with builders and looked at different kinds of apartments to get ideas in the weeks before. And Madeline would need a toaster in her new house across the yard, since it would have a kitchen of its own. Now we'll let the family members tell the rest of the story in their own words, as Sharon interviewed them:

> *Madeline (the grandmother)*: Jim and Christine moved here in July three years ago and I came out a month later. We had long, long conversations before I came out here. I was living

in Florida alone and working. I was then 72 years old. They were coming to a strange place. Christine traveled a lot in her work, Jim some. In California they had had excellent day-care facilities for Katie.

Katie was starting first grade. So they discussed with me the cost of me coming out to live with them, hoping that it would be a win-win situation for everybody. So that Katie would have a constant in her life. And they were busy with work and it would be the same person there when she got home from school every day. It would relieve me from having to work—I had injured my back at that time. So it was a big decision for everybody. The key for me is that *I was invited*. At that time I felt like I was in a position where I could give back something and that I was still able to help. So I did live in the house with them for three years, until I moved into my own house.

Christine (Jim's wife): That was kind of the plan all along. We tried to recover financially from the move from California first. We had talked about building a place for Madeline on the property. But, we didn't want to commit to her, to get her hopes up—in case financially we couldn't. That's why we wanted that acreage so that we would have room to expand.

Jim: When we looked for the house, we looked for a one-story house that had a master suite on one side and bedrooms on the other. That way there would be enough room for it to be comfortable for people. You know, in case someone had to move in with us, like my mother or my dad or her parents, we wanted to provide a facility without having to go up and down stairs. Also, we knew at some point we were going to have to either provide more financial help for my mom or bring her to live with us. It worked for her to come live with us and help with Katie. We were already paying the house payment and utilities, so it wasn't a big issue compared to getting extra help for us from someone else. It allows Christine and me both to work and keep our lifestyle.

Christine: We talked to a lot of people about the idea ahead of time. I think everybody thought we were nuts. Nobody supported us in our decision.

Madeline: I didn't, either. Well, you can't really live together in a house, you know, especially three generations.

Christine: I want to say we do better in separate houses. But, I think regardless of the input either Jim or I got, we still felt it would be a good win-win situation. I mean I don't know if that would work for every family. Not every daughter-in-law and mother-in-law could do it.

Sharon: Had you heard of others—your parents—participating in similar living arrangements?

Madeline: My grandmother lived with us—same house, the last couple of years before she died. Then later on my grandfather lived with us for a couple of years. They both lived a long time. My grandfather was 93 when he died. My grandmother was a very important part of my life.

Christine: We have ground rules. We have two. We talked about one—Madeline was a smoker and both Katie and I are both very allergic to smoke. So that was my biggest issue. She went outside to smoke. That was fine with her. That was a make-or-break deal for me. The other ground rule was that when Jim's dad visited, we would have to do something different.

Jim: My mom and dad are divorced. So when my dad would come to visit, my mom would leave so we didn't have them both in the same household.

Madeline: I've been divorced for several years now. But, my former husband has a live-in companion. When I was living in the house with the kids, if he and his companion came for a visit, I left. I either went down to San Diego to visit my son or back to Florida to visit my relatives. He and I had discussed that before I moved in with the kids. That's how we worked things out.

Christine: It sounds like a piddling thing, but we did not want to cut Jim's dad out of our life and make this uncomfortable for anyone. I am somebody who tries to anticipate conflicts and get them resolved before things happen.

Madeline: It never was a conflict.

Sharon: Anything else? For example, do you have a call-first rule? If you want to come see the family, or you want to go see her, do you call her first? Or do you just go and knock on the door?

Christine: Oh, now that she is in her own house, I always call first—maybe 99.9 percent of the time. We never talked about it; it just sort of happened.

Jim: With all the moving, we did have to figure out what furniture to keep. When Mom came we had to figure where to put it and where to keep it.

Madeline: Their house is large enough that when I moved in with them, I had my bedroom, bath, and a sitting room. So you know I was able to bring with me the important pieces and be surrounded with my things. I'm not really big about being attached to things. But, certain things, yes. I had my old things and that worked out.

Jim: Also, she was allowed to pick out all the colors and all the carpet for the new cottage we built. The only things that we picked were the cabinets that would stay in the cottage.

Christine: We picked the permanent fixtures that will be there forever, because eventually that will probably be our office. And then anything else, such as paint, wallpaper, or flooring, Madeline picked all that out.

Madeline: It is 800 square feet. The building, the design of it, I like every single bit of it.

Christine: It has one bedroom, a living room, a kitchen, a bath, a lovely roof, and a very large closet off the bedroom which is almost big enough to fit a bed. It also has a covered patio. The cottage is absolutely lovely.

Sharon: How do you handle expenses such as taxes, utilities, cell phone, that kind of thing?

Jim: The things we pay for are the utilities because they are tied into our account and the water is off our main meter. And we pay the mortgage, insurance, and property taxes.

Madeline: Yes, they do. I pay for my cell phone bill.

Sharon: What do you like about your housing situation?

Madeline: Well, I finally have my privacy. Before coming here, I had lived alone for so many years and gotten used to that. I don't think we ever had any issues while I lived with them. But when they had guests over, I was always concerned about how visible I should be. I didn't want to act like I was ignoring their guests, especially if it's people that I knew. But on the other hand, I didn't want to be in the middle of their conversations. So this way I think we each have been able to enjoy our guests more. I also enjoy the fact that they are so close. Katie can run back and forth across the yard, come over and visit me, and tell me what happened that day at school. The dog—we also share the dog.

Jim: The dog stays between both houses. So she can watch it too.

Madeline: The dog spends the weekends with me when they're away. I take care of the dog and the dog takes care of me. It's the best of both worlds. I mean they are right there if I need anything, should I need them.

In February I started walking into the walls, so I went to the doctor and he said I had an ear infection. Then they started testing me and figured out that it was a brain tumor. I had surgery last April and the tumor was benign. But, I stayed with them for six weeks before moving back into my own house.

Sharon: Is there anything that you dislike about your current housing arrangement?

Christine: I don't think so. I think what we have now is perfect.

Jim: Actually, it has worked out very well for all of us. It took a lot of planning and thinking about what we were going to do. At one point, we went out and looked for a small single-family home to buy for my mom. We looked everywhere and the closest thing we could find in our price range was probably six or seven miles away. We thought that's not convenient, if our daughter is coming home and neither one of us is here. We looked at apartments, but apartments were too expensive. We were trying to find a way to give her private space and keep her close enough. The cottage in back ended up being the most affordable.

The best solution for us was to build on the property, and it was much cheaper than any of the other options. A rented apartment would have just been throwing money away. Whereas, with the improvement to our property, the appraisal value is now double what we paid for the house three years ago. It made the most sense financially and she doesn't have to drive to come see us. She can walk across the yard. It all worked out for the best. We've given her her own space and privacy. We enjoy our privacy and still have a family between us.

Christine: It is important to me for Katie to have easy access to Madeline because she is the only grandparent that lives anywhere close. I want their relationship to grow and develop. The mail sits on our counter until Katie comes home from school every day. I have Katie take it out to Madeline, so that they can visit with each other, even if it is only a two-minute exchange. Madeline does a lot of cooking. She can tell her stories that I don't know. Our perspective is that it has been great to give Katie that other generation's sense of family. I think looking down the road twenty years, eventually Madeline's health won't be as good. It will be a lot easier to have her just out back than to drive ten miles up the road to take out the trash or bring her dinner. It is perfect.

Sharon: Would you recommend your living arrangement to others? Why or why not?

Jim: In these poor economic times, with the cost of housing, I honestly see more and more of it happening. I've had other people at work ask me about the property. Other people in town have said the same thing: "Can I come take a look and see how you did it?" We've been really open to anyone who has thought about doing this. We share what we went through and what we thought about to try to make it easier for them. Then, maybe they don't have to go through the struggles or make a mistake, financially or emotionally. I think the key thing to this is you give the women in the family some privacy. There can be two or three days that we might not see her. We don't see each other every day, but we are only 75 feet apart.

Madeline: I am a very fortunate person; I have a beautiful home. I don't know if that would work in every family.

Christine: I think one important thing is that Madeline was able to move out here and get acclimated to the area while she was still able to drive and have the opportunity to meet people and get involved in church. I think it's better to relocate before someone is disabled and can't get out. Do it before it becomes a necessity. If you can swing doing the granny flat or cottage, I think that is a better alternative than a plain house miles away.

Jim: The thing for us is that we already had the property, so it is not like we were going out and buying a second piece of property. We were just doing home improvements. So you know 30 or 40 percent of the cost of buying a house is the land and the rest of it is the building. If you can eliminate that, it becomes a more viable option.

Christine: I don't look at it so much from the cost perspective. I know that Madeline gave up a lot when she moved here with us. When I took her to the grocery store for the first time to stock her kitchen, she bought things that she had never bought in three years. Yes, she did all the grocery shopping in our house. We'd leave her the money, and she'd go do it. I just assumed she was buying what she would like for herself, too. I think having two kitchens and two refrigerators allows you more freedom to buy what you want. Madeline is so considerate with not wanting to impose anything on anyone. I think she gave up a lot of herself that we didn't even realize, until she was out on her own.

CONCLUSIONS

So, Madeline has dodged the nursing home. You or your parents can, too. Indeed, as we have crisscrossed the country we have found other pleasant realities about how families are moving in together again. Certainly aspects of Madeline, Christine, and Jim's story are unique. For example, an acre of land in their Oregon town is much more affordable than in suburban areas in California or Connecticut. But, we have consistently found folks that have similarly seen the substantial advantages, both financial and psychological, of living together again in more flexible housing arrangements. And, there are important lessons embedded in their comments about how things work. For example, Katie taking the mail to her grandmother every day accomplishes a number of good things for the family.

In the chapters to follow, we describe in some detail how others are adapting to their own special circumstances and how inventive ideas make things work better for all. We hope you'll find your own family somewhere in these pages. Our goal is to help you see new ways to best manage the financial, health care, and childcare challenges that face us all in the next decades.

Finally, we must say that we are so happy to include Sharon's voice in our book. Her kind, valuable interviews reported throughout the pages provide an essential aspect of the research supporting our recommendations herein.

STORIES ABOUT CAREGIVING BENEFITS FOR THE YOUNG AND OLD

Only a life lived for others is a life worthwhile.
—Albert Einstein

With extended families so geographically spread out, and with so many situations where both parents work, who is raising the children and caring for the elders? Today, child and elder care are frequently neglected. One way to meet both needs is for families to return to pre–World War II extended families living in close proximity to one another. Grandparents could help raise their grandchildren, for example; then later in life, they would be nearby to receive help with their own care, if needed.

GRANDPARENTS HELP OUT

One Southern California woman has done just that. Susan is divorced and lives in a small residential community. She currently teaches part-time at a university. Several years ago, she came up with an inventive way to age-in-place with a multigenerational living arrangement that utilizes a detached cottage on the same property as her house. Initially, she allowed her daughter and son-in-law to live in the unit while they both worked on their graduate degrees. After they earned their degrees, they found local housing to be prohibitively expensive. So Susan continued to allow them the use of the cottage while they established their careers. A few years later they started their family. At that point, Susan decided she didn't need to live in the big house anymore. It was more space than she needed, and she was tired of taking care of it. So she offered the house to her daughter, son-in-law, and grandchild.

Susan subsequently had the cottage remodeled, adding a sunroom, and moved in there herself. She says there is adequate space for her in the smaller place. She is pleased to keep her garden and doesn't have to deal with maintaining the larger house. Her daughter and son-in-law do that. She helps them by babysitting the (now three) grandchildren one and a half days per week. Here's what she said about that childcare arrangement:

> *Susan*: My daughter and I kind of made this deal. I taught on Monday and Wednesday and Friday mornings. So she ended up with a part-time job on Tuesday and Thursday and Friday afternoon. My daughter asked if I could take care of the children on the days that she works. That was the deal we made before the eldest boy was born.
>
> *Sharon*: You babysit, then, two and a half days a week?
>
> *Susan*: No, we ended up deciding that I should have a day off on Thursday. It turns out that when my neighbor next door died, her son and his wife moved into her house, and now they run a playschool there. On Thursday morning, I simply walk the twins over at 8:30. They are not picked up again until 4:30. I play golf and do other things on that day.
>
> *Sharon*: So you're still babysitting one and a half days a week?
>
> *Susan*: Yes. It's wonderful being able to do that. Also, if I had to drive somewhere else to take care of the children, that would be quite a hardship. I have a friend who has to drive over an hour to babysit her grandson. She doesn't like to come back here the same day because the traffic is terrible. So to help out, it means at least one overnight stay for her, in a place that's not her own.

Sharon: If you want to take a vacation, how do you manage childcare for the grandchildren?

Susan: Well, I just let my daughter know in advance and she works it out. Sometimes she just takes off the days that she would usually be working. The oldest is now in school until 2:30. What she's done more recently, now that the twins are older, is send them to preschool on Tuesdays and Thursdays. By the way, the preschool will pick them up. I'd never even heard of that before. Apparently, it's become more common because so many mothers are working. That's an enormous convenience for everyone.

Certainly, Susan's grandchildren have the benefit of daily interaction with their grandmother, and of course, the parents have a built-in babysitter. Later in life, she will be in close proximity to receive help with her own care, should she need it. In fact, she already has. Here are her comments about her recent hip surgery:

Susan: One other thing I thought of as a benefit to the housing arrangement is them taking care of me when I'm hospitalized. Of course, just having had hip replacement surgery, I am very aware of that. I just got out of the hospital five weeks ago. I needed a lot of care, and they saw to it that I got to and from the hospital. That would have been very hard to do if I lived alone. In fact, the hospital would not have let me come home if there had not been someone there to help me out. Because they live right here with me, they didn't have to drive a long way or fly out from somewhere to help me out.

Close proximity also allowed John's sister, Mary Ellen, to help out with her grandchildren. A number of years ago Mary Ellen moved to Texas to a small house just blocks away from her daughter, son-in-law, and two granddaughters. Because she lived nearby, she was able to help out in a number of ways. Mary

Ellen is single, an artist, and has a flexible work schedule. Not only did she frequently pick them up after school, but she also assisted them with homework. She told us about a science project that she worked on with her granddaughter, Danielle (then eleven years old):

> *Mary Ellen*: Danielle's parents were out of town, and I was babysitting. The project involved comparing the evaporation rates of both clear and colored water over a seventy-two-hour period. The assignment was to determine if one would evaporate faster than the other. Initially, we labeled six glass jars that were the same size and filled three with clear water and the other three with colored water. We placed one pair outdoors, one pair in the kitchen, and one pair in the bathroom. Then, every twelve hours we measured with a ruler how much the liquids had evaporated. I helped Danielle design charts and graphs for the project. We determined that, in fact, the evaporation rates are the same for both clear and colored water. She got an A on the project!

Mary Ellen often used the computer to go online with the girls to assist them with their homework. Also, she helped Michelle (six years old) with spelling and told us that she also taught her how to play gin rummy and dominoes:

> *Mary Ellen*: I think both dominoes and gin rummy were great games for helping Michelle learn her numbers, especially since I allowed her to keep score for both of us. She is so good with numbers. My only frustration is that she consistently beat me!

Surely, Mary Ellen could feel better when she put her great artistic talent to work with them. She enjoyed giving art lessons to Danielle, Michelle, and their friends. They did a number of T-shirt projects together to commemorate various holidays. In turn, Mary Ellen talked about how Danielle helped her in her professional life:

Mary Ellen: When I have a painting that needs to be framed, I
often take Danielle with me to the frame shop. In teaching her
how to do framing, she actually helps me pick and choose the
large frames for my paintings. Now, we're talking about hundreds of dollars' worth of stuff. She is very good at making the
right selections. Where else could she learn about these materials? Certainly public schools don't do this, especially with all
of the cutbacks in the arts programs. Yesterday, I had to go to
the framers by myself since Danielle was away at camp. I really
missed her good advice.

Speaking of artwork, we all love Mary Ellen's paintings of our brother Steve's
pet rabbits. Several years ago, she saw a family photo of Steve as a boy with his
rabbits in a box. It inspired her to use it as a theme for a painting (see figure
4.1). We also like the painting because it captures the theme of our book. You
can see the three generations of rabbits living together with both the proximity
and privacy that we recommend!

Figure 4.1.

Additionally, Mary Ellen babysat the girls when their parents were away on business trips or vacations by themselves. She also watched their dog for them if they all were away. One of her favorite activities with the girls was teaching them how to prepare food. For example, she taught Danielle how to make her own tuna sandwich with pickles and mayonnaise. She also has introduced the electric mixer to them, while making walnut pancakes. Her daughter has said to her, "Mom, you're out there building memories with the girls." Indeed, she is.

On the flip side, Mary Ellen also received help from them recently when she suffered a back injury. Her daughter helped her with grocery shopping, cooked meals for her, and drove her to appointments with the doctor and physical therapist. In turn, her granddaughter Danielle helped decorate her Christmas tree and vacuumed her house before Mary Ellen's bunco game night with her friends. It turned out that one of the adults wasn't able to make it, and Danielle not only filled in as a substitute player, but she also won!

Do Susan and Mary Ellen's types of intergenerational living arrangements portend a trend for the future? Indeed, these women may be ahead of their time and may even be signaling a shift in the way some families are housed in the future.

Not only did we ask grandmothers about ways they help out with babysitting their grandchildren, but we also asked a young couple about their childcare arrangements with the woman's parents. Carol and Greg live on one side of a duplex with their one-year-old son, and Carol's parents live on the other side. The duplex is in a residential community in Northern California. Both Carol and Greg work full-time, she as an administrator for a university and he as a supply manager for a computer firm. Coincidentally, they were both raised during parts of their childhood in the same households with their respective grandparents. Carol and Greg regard these experiences as having been very positive for them and are delighted to be repeating the life cycle pattern with their child. Here's what they had to say about ways Carol's parents help with their one-year-old son:

> *Sharon*: Do your parents help you with babysitting?
> *Carol*: Yes. They actually help us most of the time. My dad watches our son, Ryan, in the morning. My mom works half

a day. So after she comes home at noon, she looks after him in the afternoon. We do have a sitter one day a week to give them a day off.

Sharon: What happens if they want to travel or go on a little weekend trip?

Greg: We are usually the ones going on a weekend trip. They don't go out that much and don't seem to mind babysitting for us when we want to go out ourselves.

Sharon: How fortunate for you. What else do you like about your living arrangement?

Carol: Overall, it's just nice having them here. I think for me, it's a sense of security. There's always somebody here when we've had emergencies. For instance, when one of the cats scratched my face at about 10:00 one night, I had to go to the hospital and get five stitches. Ryan was asleep and only 6 months old at the time. It was just so nice that we could run next door for help and just let our baby sleep.

Certainly, they help us out with Ryan every day, and we are incredibly lucky to have that. I think he's incredibly lucky to have that, too. He has such a good relationship with all four of us. It is a wonderful situation. Like I've told you, it started out as kind of an economic necessity for us to live here, but now it's something that we're planning to continue in the future. We want to buy a bigger place where we can continue to live together, because it's nice. It works, and I think we all enjoy it.

Greg: In fact, the benefits for Ryan developmentally are fantastic because he does have more people. There is no such thing as too much love, and he does have it all day long. He has someone around him who is completely devoted to him. After a few hours, he has somebody new to look after him, someone who has energy. Because you can get exhausted being with a small child, after a while you can pass him off to the next person. His grandparents are always excited to see him. They're ready to read him five books and take him to the park or do something else with him.

Sharon: So he gets lots of positive energy rather than a tired parent.

Carol: I don't know how single parents do it.

Sharon: Anything else you'd like to add?

Greg: Yes. Generally speaking, I think that the way Americans are so geographically dispersed is not healthy for relationships among family members. I think our own housing arrangement is a good way to bridge a lot of that, assuming that the parties can actually get along and make it succeed. Traditionally, people have lived in multigenerational households, and it has worked with a tremendous amount of support inherent in that. Nowadays, people have lost out by moving so far apart from each other.

Carol: I agree. I think it's just healthier for society overall to live like we do. Certainly, it's nice for us now raising a child. I think that twenty, thirty, or forty years from now, we'll help my parents to maintain their independence and continue to live in their home. We want them to have the life that they want to live, before they have to go into a nursing home, if they ever have to. So many people end up in that kind of a situation just because they don't have a support network to help them. I think that's wrong. I really think that families should be taking care of each other and helping each other out.

Down the line, Ryan could have a place where he could come back. He could potentially have my parents' home after they pass on. It just makes sense to me. It seems healthier and more natural, rather than just everybody doing their own thing. I think it stems from American overconsumption. It's like everybody has to have a house with a spare bedroom, a living room separate from the family room, and all of this extra stuff that you don't even use. And everybody has to have their own separate house. I think it just keeps people farther apart from each other, and families farther apart. I don't think that's a good thing.

SIBLINGS HELP OUT

Not only are grandparents helping out by babysitting their grandchildren, but more adult siblings are starting to help each other with childcare. In one instance two sisters and a brother, all married with children, decided to relocate together in Denver. They live in separate homes within blocks of each other and constantly look after each other's children. Their mother called her adult son one day to see how he was doing. He said, "I'm sorry, Mom, I can't talk right now." He was babysitting for both of his sisters while they went skiing together that day.

In another case, two sisters who now live in the Chicago suburbs had debated whether to stay at home with their children or continue to work. Jean Korelitz describes how they solved their dilemma together in an article she wrote for *Real Simple* magazine, "All in the Family." Initially the sisters and their spouses lived half a mile apart in downtown Chicago and shared a nanny for their children while they both worked. Subsequently, one of them moved to the suburbs and the other followed, buying the house across the street. One of the sisters wanted to stay home with her children, while the other wanted to continue working outside the home at a job she loved.

The sisters came up with an arrangement where one works and pays the other enough to be able to stay home and babysit all their children. Initially, the spouses expressed concerns about the two families retaining their separate identities. However, they talked things over and agreed, "This isn't about you or me. This is about what's good for our families." One of the sisters said, "And it's good for our kids to grow up across the street from each other." The other sister commented, "I don't think I would still be working if I didn't know my kids were loved all day. All of our lives are better because of what we have."[28]

A sister and brother living in Los Angeles would certainly agree about the proximity benefit. Kathleen, an architect, and her husband bought a home for themselves and their two small children. Soon after, her brother and his wife bought the house next door. They also have two small children. Kathleen and her brother both married French-speaking spouses and now share a French-speaking nanny for childcare, since all four parents work. Kathleen describes their arrangement:

> *Sharon*: Why did your brother and his family decide to live next door to you?
>
> *Kathleen*: After my younger brother had his second child, he and his wife started looking for a house to buy in our area. It just so happened that the house right next door to us came up for sale a year ago, and they bought it. My dad and I helped them remodel it. Now I'm working on the gardens. I do both landscape design and architecture.
>
> *Sharon*: Aren't they lucky to have your help!
>
> *Kathleen*: Yes, and everybody who hears this story thinks that we're nuts. They ask, "What's it like living so close to your brother? Doesn't it get kind of weird?" Well, we just love it. His older daughter and my younger son are eleven months apart and have been like brother and sister. They've been together every single day. Generally, the way we keep our sanity is just always helping each other out. We're always picking up someone's children or helping run errands or babysitting. My sister-in-law also works, and my husband and brother are at the same firm. If she has to work longer hours or go out of town for work or even go to the market, she lets me know. Both of us have schedules that are somewhat flexible, so we could take over for the other person.
>
> Also, we share the same nanny, who has an apartment very near where we live. She started working for us after my sister-in-law decided to go back to work after her second child was born. We were now living next door to each other, and I just said to her, "Listen, we should go and find somebody that we both really like, who is French-speaking and can help my mother." The nanny works for me two days a week, and, on those two days, the nieces are with my mother. She works for

my sister-in-law two days a week, and on those days my boys go with my mom. Then, one day a week, the nanny will have all four kids. Our kids are all at the same school, so it works out really well. It helps my mom a lot, too, because it allows her to have her own life.

Sharon: How do you pay for the nanny?

Kathleen: We each pay the nanny on an hourly basis. It probably would be more cost-effective if we put her on a salary. My sister-in-law ends up having to pay more because the three days a week that the nanny is with her girls, the youngest is not in school yet, so she has to pay her during those hours.

Sharon: Then your kids are in school part of the time, too?

Kathleen: Yes. For us the nanny comes from 3:00 in the afternoon until 6:00 p.m. For my sister-in-law, it's really like from 7:30 or 8:00 in the morning until 6:00 in the evening. That can vary depending on her schedule because her schedule can be kind of erratic.

Sharon: So, if she's babysitting all the kids at once, do you pay the hours that your kids are with her, and then your sister-in-law pays the hours that her kids are with her?

Kathleen: Exactly.

Sharon: Since they're right next door, do you have ground rules for making contact?

Kathleen: You know, it's funny because we don't really have anything explicit. I think both my sister-in-law and I are respectful of each other. So we'll always call or yell over the fence when the children come over to play. We're actually going to knock down a little section of block wall in the rear of both of our properties and put in a gate so the children can pass back and forth without having to go out front.

Sharon: Do you have any friends doing what you're doing?

Kathleen: Nobody. Most people look at me sorta like, "There's got to be a catch to all of this. Like, it's not got to be that great." It just works out so well for us. I mean, I take my niece to school every day because she's in school with my son. We're just starting up this new thing now where we switch weeks babysitting so that each of us can go out.

Sharon: So you get like a "date night"?

Kathleen: Exactly. I'm watching her kids one night, and then the next week she'll watch our kids.

Sharon: If you were telling someone what you liked about your housing situation, what would you say?

Kathleen: I like the convenience of having family so close. I also like the fact that my children really will know their aunts, uncles, and cousins. Also, I have two nieces that are just like daughters, who I see every single day. It really helps that we have similar backgrounds and speak both English and French.

Sharon: Sounds like you would recommend your living arrangement to others?

Kathleen: Oh, definitely. But only if people get along. I've got a very loving relationship with my brother, so I really like having him around. The fact that he is living next door to me is wonderful. My brother is also the godfather of my children. All the families get along. For us, while growing up, we were really close to both sets of grandparents, and my mother's brother, and my cousins. I really like the fact that my children have a real sense of who their family is.

ADULT CHILDREN HELP OUT

From accounts about grandparents and siblings taking care of children, we now go to stories about adult children providing care for their close-by parents and grandparents. The folks we interviewed reported mostly positive experiences. However, caring for elder parents can cause stress on families and their children, and sometimes it can be unbearable. The books and articles on the travails abound. Two recent headlines from the *Wall Street Journal* summarize the issues: "When Caring for Aging Relatives Stirs Emotions You Wish You Didn't Have" and "A Painful Source of Marital Strife: When an

Elder Parent Moves In." While we recognize these potentially unpleasant aspects of helping out elder parents, this is generally not what we heard from the folks we talked to.

A case comes to mind where a married couple owns some acreage in California, near Napa Valley. Jane writes children's books and Bob operates a family winemaking business on the property. They also have a family compound there. Both sets of parents have had separate houses on their property for the past thirty years. Today, Jane's and Bob's mothers are both widowed. Jane's mother is an active ninety-seven-year-old who still drives and lives alone in her small house nearby. Bob's mother is eighty-three, has developed Alzheimer's disease, and now lives with them. They talk about what it's like to have both of their mothers in such close proximity:

> *Sharon*: What prompted you to build houses for both sets of parents here?
>
> *Jane*: We moved here a few years ago. A year later my mother and stepfather moved up. We looked for a house for them with the idea of finding one nearby but not too close. We thought we would like to be more independent. We looked in other cities that were within a half-hour drive from us. Then we decided that it would be better just to build the house here on our property. There is a road right below our house, and there was a plot of land there that was perfect. We built the house for them with their input. It has one level with a garage underneath. It is built on a hill, so it has a basement and a garage inside. Her house is on top with a wide deck and looks out toward the trees.
>
> As the years have gone by, we've realized that this really has been the best situation. When we were gone on vacation, my mother would keep an eye on the house and look after our animals. We've always had dogs. When we were away, they could go down to my mother's house and stay there. It was good for her because she felt safer having a dog there, rather than being alone in the house.

Sharon: Did she also help out with the children?

Jane: Oh, yes. John was in the third grade, Kristin in the sixth, and Megan in the seventh when we moved up here. So she was able to watch them. At that time, we were taking our children with us on vacation. But, if we were gone without them, the children could stay with their grandparents. If we were gone, they could pick them up from school. So there were a lot of advantages. The children had a close bonding with both sets of grandparents.

When Bob's parents retired, they came up here to live. We had a small house on the far corner of our property that we were able to tear down. They ended up purchasing a mobile home and had a garage and deck added to it. It has three bedrooms, a kitchen, a dining room, and two bathrooms. Then, after about ten years, his father died of lung cancer. After he died, Bob's mother became very depressed. She just didn't do much and had health problems. She started sitting in her chair and smoking, and that was it. Eventually, with her lack of mobility, she just couldn't walk very far and now needs a wheelchair to go anyplace.

We would have somebody come and stay with her. One time her grandson and his wife and their two little girls came to live with her. But she would not give up smoking. Since they did not want to live in a smoky environment, they moved out. At that time, we did not realize that she was in the beginning stages of Alzheimer's.

Sharon: Bob, what prompted you to move your mother to your house?

Bob: She was really getting to the point where she couldn't live alone, mainly because of her medication. We moved her in here with us and added on to our house. We ended up putting her in our bedroom downstairs and built a new bedroom for ourselves upstairs. At first, she was not happy with the move, but now she seems to accept it.

Jane: After a short time, she became more interested in things. We have a business down below. It's a winery, and our son is now manager of it. Our other son also works there. So we have the two of them going in and out of our house all the time. They talk to her, and so does our bookkeeper, who works downstairs. Occasionally, our bookkeeper's sister comes to stay with Bob's mother while we are gone. They both smoke, like to talk, and get along very well.

Sharon: Any problems with her living here with you?

Bob: She still smokes and is not going to stop now. We put a giant fan right over her chair in the kitchen corner, so it can suck the smoke out of here. She knows this is the only place in our house she can smoke, and she cooperates with us on that one.

Sharon: How do you manage taking care of her in your home?

Bob: You have to have a wife like Jane. I don't know if I could handle it, if she could not. I don't do as much of the caregiving as she does. It is easy for me to be busy with other things in my life, even though Jane is very busy herself. I do get all of my mother's pills ready every Sunday and take her places. What I have found is that this works, as long as the husband and wife work together to make it work.

Sharon: So it is really a personality and disposition type of issue, too. The kind of people that are both giving and willing to help out are the ones to do it.

Bob: Jane is an angel, too. She likes most people. Also, Jane takes care of her own mother. I don't think about it a lot of the time, but she is the one that does. It is rough on her, I think. She doesn't show it, but her mother is pretty demanding. Jane is always there. We get concerned about how her mother is going to hold up in the future. One time, when she had a health problem, Jane went down and stayed with her at her place because we didn't know what we'd do with her here. We may be faced with full-time caring for both our mothers.

Sharon (to Jane): How do you handle communication issues with your mother-in-law?

Jane: We try to make her life comfortable and enjoyable. With Alzheimer's, she forgets things. For instance, she always pulls the ice tray out of the refrigerator and never remembers to put it back. For me to tell her every day to put the ice tray away is not going to make anything any different, so we laugh about it. I just avoid getting into confrontations with her. I find that as long as we maintain a fairly happy relationship, I can get her to get dressed every day and I can get her to take a shower every third day.

Also, she likes drinking Dr. Pepper. She doesn't get hungry, but she will go to the refrigerator to get a Dr. Pepper. I'll say, "Paula, you can't have a Dr. Pepper until you have something to eat." She will usually say, "Why?" Then I will say, "Because you need to take your pills." So she will go ahead and have her breakfast and pills, and then ask, "Can I have a Dr. Pepper now?" When it first happened, I remember looking at her and starting to laugh. I said, "Do you mean to tell me that, if I told you no, that you wouldn't have it now?" She looked at me and said, "No, I would have it." She is a very good-natured person. There just has to be laughter there.

Sharon: So you are using Dr. Pepper as a negotiating tool to get her to cooperate. What you are using is humor and a positive lifestyle to keep the peace.

Jane: Instead of telling her what to do, I have learned to ask her, "When would you like to take your shower? Now, or at a different time?" Then, she will look at the clock and say a time. If it's a good time, then I will agree with it. If it's not such a good time, then I will come up with a compromise time. We're kind of bartering to do it. But that is the most difficult issue because she does not like to take a shower.

Sharon: Also, by posing questions like that, you're allowing her to have control of her life. It's a clever way of doing it.

Jane: There is a conflict, though, in having both my mother and mother-in-law to deal with. Now, because my mother-in-law is in the house, I am not spending as much time with my mother. So, my mother gets her feelings hurt. It's easier to be with my mother-in-law because she's not very demanding. For example, I do the things I have to do in order for her to go to the doctor. I need to get her into the shower, make sure her clothes are clean, and curl her hair with the curling iron. With my mother I do not have to do all that. Instead, my mother needs me to spend time with her. I work this out by sometimes going over to her place or talking to her on the phone, practically every day. If I am home, I might go down before dinner and play cards with her for a while. It doesn't have to be long, but it has to be some kind of contact.

Sharon: What do you like about your housing situation?

Jane: It's so nice to have them right here. It's so much better than having to drive half an hour to go and pick them up. You know how they are doing. You know how they are eating and caring for themselves. With my mother-in-law and her medications, there is no way that she could live by herself. I know that some of my friends have caretakers who stay with their parents, and that works out very well for them.

Sharon: What do you dislike about living so near your mothers?

Jane: If we're going to be gone for a time, we have to make arrangements for someone to look after Bob's mother. His brother lives less than an hour away. When we are going to be gone on the weekend, he will have my mother-in-law come over and stay with them. He is really very good about that. We can leave for a few hours to go shopping or out to dinner, and she is fine. But, if we are going to be gone overnight, we can't leave her by herself. That is when Bob's brother comes over, unless my son and his wife come and stay in our house.

We want to interrupt the dialogue here for a moment just to emphasize a key point. A major difficulty folks have often mentioned in our interviews is the problem of finding help for disabled parents when they are traveling either for business or a vacation. Hopefully, siblings, other relatives, or friends can help out in the way Bob's brother does with his mother:

Sharon: So you have an advantage being in close proximity to both of your mothers. Do you recommend your living arrangement to others? Why or why not?

Jane: I would because I think it is just important to keep the family together. You know, we are used to doing this. Why would you not do it? Now sometimes parents themselves don't want to live with their adult children. My grandmother was 99 when she died, and she didn't move in with my mother until about three years before she died. She was perfectly capable of taking care of herself. With my own mother now, she does not want to move in with any of the younger ones. She likes her independence. I think it is a matter of what has to be done health-wise for the parent.

I belong to a bridge group and some of the members are my mother's friends. Some of them are at the point where they are either moving in with their daughter or son or going into an apartment. Most of them are going into senior apartment complexes by choice. They do not want to move in with the family. I have another friend whose mother asked if she could move in with her family, and my friend said absolutely not. She said the relationship was so strained, and she knew it would not be a good thing. Actually, her mother only lives a few blocks away. They hired a caregiver to come in and stay with her.

Sharon: So what would you change if you could change anything at this time?

Bob: Well, you accept what is your debt. I don't think I would try to change it. You know, they took care of us. It is kind of our turn. Every Christmas I'm part of a group that delivers Christmas trees to convalescent homes. I wouldn't wish a convalescent home on anybody. I keep thinking of the times where my mother will need a lot more help than we can provide. Then what will happen? So we are trying to avoid that.

Bob and Jane certainly are doing an admirable job of helping out their elder mothers. Along with everything else they do for them, Jane mentioned they also include their mothers at neighborhood gatherings and sometimes take them to Rotary Club meetings. Certainly, a key aspect of elder care is providing social activities.

A woman we interviewed in South Carolina built an apartment attached to her house for her mother to live in. Joan had this to say about how she keeps her mother socially active:

> *Joan*: It's so important in this type of living arrangement that whoever is living with you doesn't feel like it's only the family they are interacting with. They need to have other outlets. My mother fortunately has some very close friends. We make sure that they get together at least once during the week, and then again on the weekend. They will just gather at one of their houses, have coffee and dessert, and talk. My mother now goes to a senior center in the afternoons and it's something she looks forward to. She has a place to go where there are other people who enjoy seeing her and appreciate her, other than her family.

GRANDCHILDREN HELP OUT

Usually, it's the adult children who provide help to their parents, if needed. However, if you think those in today's so-called sandwich generation have a lot of stress, consider the possibility of the children of baby boomers taking care of not only their own children and their parents but their oldest old grandparents as well. We still like the story about such a scenario, told by Ellen Graham (no relation) for the *Wall Street Journal*, "Two Generations: One Nursing Home." A man with teenagers is responsible not only for coordinating his sixty-six-year-old disabled mother's stay at a nursing home but also that of his eighty-six-year-old grandmother, as well.[29] In fact, according to a recent study, "8 percent of informal caregivers for elders are adult grandchildren—a number many experts believe is bound to grow."[30]

Another woman who lives in Connecticut with her husband and three small children bought the house next door for her grandmother. Dana, the granddaughter, is currently a full-time mother and community volunteer. She had been raised by her grandmother after her own mother died when she was three. She talks about both the benefits and hardships she has experienced having her grandmother so close:

> *Dana*: Before my grandmother moved next door to us, she had been living with my aunt for many years. But my aunt worked full-time, so my grandmother was home alone from 6:00 a.m. until 7:00 p.m. every night. My aunt did everything she possibly could to entertain, spend time with, and provide comfort to my grandmother. However, you can't leave somebody when they are a senior citizen at home alone every day. Emotionally, she just couldn't handle it.
>
> When we moved out here from New York City, my grandmother was only one town away. So every other week, I would go and get her and she would spend the week with us. Unfortunately, it would take me two days to get her out of her emotional funk. By the time I got her cheered up and comfortable being around other people, it was almost time to take her home. It was also hard because she was living in my house all day long. Today, she is 87 years old. Then, she was younger, but I think anyone in their mid-80s would have trouble adjusting to living with a young family full-time. It was very difficult for all of us.
>
> Fortunately, we were able to buy the house next door for her. I wanted my grandmother here. I did not want her to

live in the depression she was living in anymore. I couldn't physically do the every-other-week thing on top of having two babies and having her in my house twenty-four hours a day, along with a husband who travels. It's hard. She's not even my mother, she's my grandmother. I appreciate the financial level that we have. I'm lucky we can give her a place of her own.

Sharon: Even though she is your grandmother, she is like your mother?

Dana: Yes. My grandmother has four children, including my father, who lives in Maine; my Aunt Peggy, who lives in Oregon; my uncle Don, who lives in California; and my aunt Jean, who currently has moved nearby. She is the one my grandmother lived with who works full-time. They all were doing everything that they could to comfort this woman and make her part of the family, but they all worked full-time. It would have been so hard for them to have her live with them.

Sharon: What do you like about your housing situation?

Dana: I like that she's not here twenty-four hours a day. I have my own space, so I do have the luxury to breathe. However, she is here for breakfast, lunch, and dinner every day. I think it's important that she eats with us because I think for a senior citizen the loneliest time of the day is mealtime, especially dinner.

Sharon: Does your grandmother have any medical issues?

Dana: Yes. The hardest thing that we are dealing with now is her arthritis. Otherwise, she is as healthy as a horse. Arthritis is relatively new to her, and she doesn't know how to deal with the pain. Therefore, her daily demeanor is negative. She doesn't have a life that's very fulfilling. Certainly, I can do things for her, but I think it is very important for her mental health that she do things for herself. She won't unless I force her. I make her go to the senior center. I push her to go out to lunch with her friends, particularly the one across the street who still drives.

Sharon: How do you deal with her negativity?

Dana: I ignore it most of the time. I'll say to her, "Grandma, how are you today?" She'll typically respond, "Oh, it hurts." I'll ask, "What hurts?" She'll reply, "My arthritis hurts." I'll ask, "Did you take your Tylenol?" She'll say, "Yes, I took it." Then, I'll change the subject with a comment like, "So how about those Red Sox!" So I do ignore it.

Sharon: You are very gracious with a difficult person.

Dana: She is difficult, but she's not difficult all the time. She is very grateful for where she lives. She does know that life could be worse. I deliver Meals on Wheels with her once a month because I want her to see how life could be worse for her. When she returns home, she'll call and say, "I know how lucky I am."

Sharon: So it's an activity for her, and she gets to do volunteer work. Would you recommend your living arrangement to others?

Dana: Absolutely. Once again, it's an ideal way to live. To have that type of multigenerational living arrangement that close to you, and yet still have a little distance, is the perfect world. I love having my children grow up with her. Despite her difficult personality, they still have a feeling of responsibility toward their family. And I also think it's going to build their character one day. Not necessarily right now. Jimmy is 8 and Blaire is 6. But Sam is 2 and he loves her. He runs back and forth. She loves him. They play ball. They watch baseball. When I need my kids out of the house to get something ready, I send them to Grandma's.

Sharon: So she does help you, then?

Dana: As much as she can. I usually have to send Jimmy, too, but she tries. She is most helpful with babysitting, while I'm at my night meetings. After I put my children to bed, I'll leave her in the house with them, along with my cell phone number, and go to my meetings. She can watch television. If anybody gets up or wakes up or if there is a problem, she'll call me immediately. We live in a very small town, so it's very easy for me to get home.

Also, she helps me with my volunteer work. I have her stuffing envelopes. I want her to feel useful. I want her to feel ownership. I want her to feel part of this world. I try and give her chores, almost like I give my children chores, because I want her to feel a part of this family.

Sharon: What are her chores?

Dana: She is responsible for emptying the dishwasher every day. It's a simple chore, but it's her chore. It's her contribution to our family. It takes me three seconds to empty the dishwasher and it takes her forty-five minutes. But that's not the point. The point is that's her contribution to the family. It also takes away some of her feeling so guilty about accepting so much financial help.

Sharon: She feels like she is working for her room and board.

Dana: Yes. Every time she babysits she feels like she is working for her room and board because she always says to me, "Well, it kind of helps take care of the heating bill." I say, "It absolutely does."

Sharon: Anything else you'd like to add?

Dana: I try not to talk too much about my grandmother with my girlfriends. It's a very difficult situation, and no one wants to be around somebody who is always talking negatively. But the one stock phrase I always use with them is "No matter what I do in my life, this is my guaranteed ticket to heaven." I could do anything else in the world wrong, but, because I've taken such good care of this woman, she is my guaranteed entry into heaven. I live by that. I'm glad I'm doing it, have no regrets, and would do it all over again.

CONCLUSIONS

In most cases, people profess to be happy with their caregiving arrangements. Certainly, there are hardships involved, but also we've heard many stories about benefits. Both Susan and Mary Ellen are examples of grandparents who are both helping out and in turn receiving help when they need it. Carol and Greg talked about how wonderful their lives are to have her parents help them care for their one-year-old. Kathleen told about how convenient it is to have her brother and his family living next door to exchange babysitting. Both Jane and Bob are pleased to have their elder mothers nearby to look after. Joan shared how and why she keeps her mother socially active. Dana talked about benefits going both ways as she cares for her grandmother. Coming up in our next chapter are stories about the benefits of "grand" relationships. There you see why "intergenerational activities with household members" is the most often mentioned factor making multigenerational households work well, according to a study from Generations United, an advocacy organization.[31]

CHAPTER 5

STORIES ABOUT
GRAND RELATIONSHIPS

*The closest friends I have made all through life have been people who
also grew up close to a loved and loving grandmother.*
—Margaret Mead

MEMORIES OF OUR OWN GRANDPARENTS

Emily K. Graham: I consider myself lucky to have known my grandparents. Unfortunately, my maternal grandmother died before I was three, so I don't have memories of her. That has always been sad. However, my maternal grandfather remarried, and we embraced his wife as our own grandmother, and she was in my life longer than any of my blood grandparents. I shared great talks and dinners weekly while I was in college and I lived nearby. My grandfather was a great man; he gathered the entire family for many summers in Hawaii and I got to know my cousins, aunts, and uncles because of that. He also shared his love of skiing with us, too. We had a great time and those memories will be cherished forever. He also was a great cheerleader for me and encouraged me to write.

My paternal grandparents are sharp in my memory as well, although they died when I was around eleven years old. My memories with them involved trips to the cabin where all my cousins on that side of the family would play pool in their basement, golf, fish, and go to the swimming pool. We share great times with the whole family because of them. I especially remember taking drives with my grandfather in his big tan Lincoln. My sister and I would sit in the back seat, he'd buy us a big bag of Peanut M&M's, and we'd go cruising around with him. I distinctly remember his whistle. I remember eating Kentucky Fried Chicken, and my grandmother shared her love of apple pie. I know I reference food here, but that is part of what creates connection, and every time I see Kentucky Fried Chicken, I think of her.

I am grateful for all those memories on both sides, and they really connected me with the extended family members I stay in touch with today.

Angel L. Vargas: "Grandparents" also meant Grandma and Grandpa but not far away—literally a block away. Our family was very close: over the stretch of three blocks my family, my sister, and my grandparents all lived. I saw Grandma and Grandpa every weekend and sometimes during the week. It was truly a great time for me, as I always honored my grandparents as elders who deserved respect. They often babysat me as I grew up, and I remember my grandfather's throat-clearing when we were watching the Chicago Cubs baseball games on the TV set. I'll never forget as a kid when my parents took me to drop off my grandfather at the steel mill during his last few months before retirement. What a work ethic—I was so inspired by it. Looking back, I wish I asked my grandfather more about his life, but I was just a young teen when he passed away. My grandmother lived on nine years longer and was just an amazing woman. She de facto adopted my sister's newest son and babysat him every single day. It was wonderful to watch my grandmother establish such purpose in her great-grandson, my nephew. I miss them very much and hope to be an amazing grandparent one day!

John L. Graham: "Grandparents" meant Grandma and Grandpa, who lived far away in Nebraska, and Grannie (my mother, an orphan who grew up in her aunt's house), who lived a few towns away from me in California. I have wonderful memories of Grandma reading to us kids and baking bread, as well as Grandpa taking us fishing and working in his garden; we can still smell the sweet peas growing there. As for Grannie, she was all smiles when she saw us and always wanted to hear about what we were doing. Not only was she an avid listener, but we also remember her gardening, sewing, and raising birds and dogs. Moreover, while babysitting, she introduced us to dancing, music, and hot-fudge sundaes. Although our grandparents were positive influences in our lives, surely they would have made even more of an impact had they lived in closer proximity to us.

DEFINITION OF *GRANDPARENT*

Looking at the word *grandparent*, we wondered how the word came into the English language. Our thesaurus has several synonyms for *grand*, including *great*, *exalted*, *illustrious*, *magnificent*, and *important*. Equivalent words for *parent* include *source*, *ancestor*, *forefather*, and, of course, *father* and *mother*. Perhaps the *grand* part of the word *grandparent* evolved because, by the time you get to be a grandparent, you know the job. Because of the experience you've had raising your own children, you truly are in a position to be a "grand" parent the second time around.

Neale Walsch, in his book series *Conversations with God*, would certainly agree. He says that the mother and father are the wrong people to raise children:

> It's a miracle that so many of them do as good a job as they do. No one is more ill-equipped to raise children than young parents. And no one knows this, by the way, better than young parents. Most parents come to the job of parenting with very little life experience. They're hardly finished being parented themselves. They're still looking for answers, still searching for clues.[32]

That could be why multigenerational households in the United States have been so successful in the past and are now making a comeback.

ROLE OF GRANDPARENTS

"What are grandparents for? And what do they mean?" These two questions were asked by a five-year-old grandchild in a conversation with her grandmother, Sharon. The child's queries raise the subject of grandparents' changing roles in today's family structure. With the unprecedented increase in life expectancy of most of the last century, more people are becoming grandparents and, increasingly, great-grandparents. Women now have the chance of being grandparents for 50 percent of their lives. And, more than 75 percent of grandchildren can expect to have at least one grandparent alive when they are thirty years old. Certainly, the prevalence of grandparents who have adult grandchildren is historically unique.[33]

The meanings and roles of being a grandparent are directly influenced by a number of social factors, including geographic proximity, divorce, reconfigured families, and employed, middle-aged grandmothers. Today, grandparents range in age from their late thirties to over the age of one hundred, with grandchildren ranging from newborns to retirees. Consequently, there are multiple roles and meanings for grandparents, depending on the bonds established in these multigenerational and continually changing relationships. Initially, the bonds between grandparents and grandchildren are fostered by the parents. But over time, direct and voluntary interaction occurs.

Typically, all sides gain from the relationships: Parents of young children may receive help with childcare from grandparents. The grandchildren obtain the gifts of time, unconditional love, and attention from their grandparents. In turn, grandparents get emotional satisfaction from frequent interaction with their grandchildren and from the responsibilities in helping them. Their role also "serves as a symbol of continuity and stability in family rituals and values."[34] Moreover, grandparents can give grandchildren an appreciation of the past and a sense of history with their stories. Surely, this type of interaction could be more easily facilitated if grandparents lived nearby or with their adult children and grandchildren.

A young father who lives with his wife and two children next door to his mother-in-law in Connecticut would agree with the benefits of proximity. When asked what he liked about his living arrangement, Jeff said, "The best part about it is that my children get a chance to be with their grandmother a lot. They get a sense of 'it's not all about them, and it's not all about the moment.' I think our society right now is a sound-bite world. With a grandmother here, they get an idea that there's a lot of other people out there and a lot of people that lived before them."

GRANDCHILDREN SEE BENEFITS

We found evidence of mutuality across all the interviews we did with grandchildren. In one instance, a nine-year-old talked about how fortunate she is to have her grandmother living in a cottage in the backyard. They live in a small town in Georgia, and both her parents travel for work. Julie said, "If my mom is going away, and my dad is going away the same day, then I'll spend the night at my grandma's. That way, I don't have to deal with a babysitter." When asked if she saw anything else as a benefit to being near Grandma, she replied, "Since she's so close, we don't have to wait until a vacation to see her." Certainly, Julie's comments argue in favor of proximity.

In another case, a nine-year-old grandson talked about the benefits he receives from both of his grandparents living in a cottage in the backyard. Peter lives in a residential community in Northern California, where his mother is a homemaker and his father is a general contractor. When asked to give examples of what he did with his grandparents, he responded, "After school I go over there and they help me do homework. I have snacks and stuff. We also watch TV and play card games." In addition, he said they worked in the household garden together, growing "flowers, carrots, pumpkins, and squash." Of course, as a result of this interaction, the chances are good that Peter will have his own garden when he grows up.

Further testimony that grandchildren see benefits came from an interview with three teenage sisters. It was their father who approached his in-laws about the idea of buying a place together. In his case, his family with three young children needed more space and wanted a swimming pool. In turn, his wife's parents were tired of taking care of their big house. It made perfect sense to all of them to combine financial resources and buy a place together in a small residential town in Northern California. For several years now the maternal grandparents have lived in a guesthouse behind the swimming pool in the backyard. In separate interviews with the grandparents, the parents, and the grandchildren, Sharon learned that the living arrangement has worked beautifully for all of them.

The granddaughters told wonderful stories about how they have profited by living so close to their grandparents. They talked about getting help with homework, learning about values and family history, being driven places, attending sport events, and receiving advice on shopping. In addition, they mentioned the importance of a strong family connection as a deterrent to negative behavior. They also gave accounts of the downside of being nearby. They talked about noise issues, such as having to be quiet in the hot tub at night, being interrupted when doing homework on the computer, and having to introduce a boyfriend to four adults instead of two parents. Here is what they had to say about their "grand" relationships:

> *Sharon*: Have you heard of other people participating in a living arrangement similar to the one you have with your grandparents?
>
> *Kristine (age 15)*: I don't have very many friends who have that situation. When I mention it to them, they go, "Oh, that's so cool that your grandparents live with you." Because their grandparents live far away or in another part of the country.
>
> *Sharon*: What do you like about your housing situation?
>
> *Margaret (age 13)*: It's really cool because if you need something like sugar, you can walk over and get some. But, like, if we have any questions that our parents can't answer, they just tell us to go over and ask Grandpa. So we just go and talk to him.
>
> *Sharon*: Do you have a specific example of a question?
>
> *Catherine (age 17)*: Yes. Grandpa knows a lot about our family history. So with him being a lot older, I want to make sure that we get the real story now. I'll ask him, "How did Great-Uncle Ralph get here?" I have even recorded our conversations. He's a great storyteller. I'm just passionate about learning about our family's history and also American history. I don't know if I would be interested in history if it wasn't for him.
>
> *Sharon*: Anything else you want to add in terms of what you like about your housing situation?
>
> *Margaret*: Besides getting sugar and food from them, I had a situation once when I was doing my homework and needed help with a math problem. I asked my mom if she could look

at it with me. She is not a pro at math like my dad is, but he wasn't home. She said, "Just go ask Grandpa." So I did, and in no time, we had figured it out.

Kristine: Also, what I like about living with them is they help a lot with driving. I'm still fifteen, so I'm not able to drive yet. Sometimes, my sister drives me places, and so does my mom. But at times, if I'm stuck someplace, or if I need to get somewhere and no one can take me, it's really good to be able to walk over and ask them to drive me places.

Catherine: Over the summer we played a lot of water polo across the bay. I had a game at 3:30 one afternoon, and Grandpa and Nani had driven across the bay and surprised me! I didn't know they were coming. They brought their own chairs. I just remember when I was playing and would score, I'd hear, "Way to go, Cathy!" I'd look up, and there Grandpa would be standing with the college shirt he always wears and his glasses. It was like having another set of parents right there, encouraging you at a sports event. It's really special. A lot of people don't even have their parents there, let alone their grandparents.

Sharon: Anything else you want to add? Have you thought about other ways that it's helped you out in your life, having your grandparents around?

Kristine: Nani is a great shopper. She buys us clothes for Christmas. She is a very wise shopper. If I need any advice on sizes or colors, she is always an expert there to help me.

Catherine: Just being older, I know that I've grown up with values that I've gotten from both my church and my family. I feel like as a family we respect older people. I see we are nice kids with great values.

Kristine: It's like the values you learn from the relationship with your grandparents carry into other activities with your friends. Just knowing that helps.

Margaret: I go to my friend's house or we're setting up a play date, but then they say, "I can't, my grandparents are coming." I never think twice about saying, "My grandparents are coming." They are already here, so my friends can come over without feeling like they're butting in on "company."

Kristine: When our grandparents come over for dinner, it's not like having company over, since they're already part of our family. Nani always does the dishes at our house. If she is over here and the dishes are piling up, she'll come into the kitchen, and when she leaves the sink is all clean. I'm sure our mother appreciates that a lot.

Margaret: I think it's a plus for parents, too, because they could never leave the kids home alone once they're in high school. There will never be wild parties thrown or anything like that.

Sharon: Is there anything you dislike about your living arrangement?

Catherine: It was hard sometimes when I would be writing papers or we would be in the family room, and they'd walk in from their domino night. They would interrupt us, wanting to visit. You know, while you're doing homework, you have that surge of energy. Then your grandparents walk in, and it stops.

Kristine: One day, I had a really bad day and I stayed home. Nani asked how my day was going. Truthfully, I was in the mood to just go to my room and not think of anything. But instead, I found myself having to explain my whole day to her. I wasn't in the mood to tell my grandmother what was going on. But I felt like I needed to tell her since she was there and asked me to.

Sharon: What would you change about your living arrangement if you could change anything?

Catherine: I don't think I would change anything. It's so fun. We have such a strong family connection and I think it's definitely because we are living with our grandparents.

Sharon: Would you recommend your living arrangement to your friends?

Margaret: Definitely. I think it helps a lot for the parents, too. If they are going out of town or they are out for the night, then they don't have to hire a babysitter. If there is an emergency, you just run over there. I think if everyone had a grandparent living with them, there would probably be a lot less problems because they could have the extra help.

Catherine: One of my closest friends is Alicia. Her grandma doesn't live with them but will come over every day. She lives in a neighboring city. She is another example of someone with a close relationship to a grandparent. Her parents are married and are close. They have two kids and are just a great, close, functioning family. I would recommend it. Kids would grow up in a more healthy environment.

GRANDPARENTS SEE BENEFITS

Not only do grandchildren benefit from having grandparents so close, but we also encountered instances of grandparents feeling that they learned lessons from their grandchildren. And in our family, Sharon so enjoyed living near her grandchildren and watching them grow and develop. She reported that it was like déjà vu with her two granddaughters, reliving the joys she had raising their mom and aunt:

> When the girls were younger, I spent hours reading aloud to them, just as my grandmother did for me. I'd like to think I played some part in Tori's exceptional love for reading. When I've picked her up from school, she would often read a book on the ten-minute drive home. In fact, her mom told me she prefers reading books to watching movies and television.
>
> On the other hand, they've certainly taught me things. In fact, recently, Tori showed me her science homework assignment, requiring her to make drawings of several forms of sea

life. On the back of each illustration, she listed the creatures' favorite foods and interesting facts. Her drawings reminded me of the small-boat cruise my husband and I took with her and her sister through Alaska's Inside Passage. As we were out kayaking and hiking, one of the many highlights was seeing sunflower starfish. Tori's sea-life drawings brought back these happy memories. I happen to love the ocean and sea life and was amazed at how much I learned from my fourth-grade granddaughter that day!

In turn, I've had fun introducing the girls to my favorite French impressionist artists. A couple of years ago I bought a Monet Memo game, consisting of thirty-six pairs of Claude Monet's paintings printed on two-by-two-inch cards. Similar to the card game Concentration, all cards are placed face down. In each round a player turns two cards face up so that all the other players can see them. If a player uncovers two cards with the same picture, he keeps the pair and goes on uncovering two more cards. If they are not identical, they must be turned over face down to their original position. The player with the most pairs of identical cards wins. Sad to say, try as I might, I've never won! Miranda was only 5 when she beat me the first time—24 to 12! I facetiously yelled at her, "You're not supposed to beat your grandmother!" Needless to say, three years later, it's still the game she wants to play the most when she comes to Gran's.

We've also enjoyed a card game like Go Fish, featuring a number of French impressionist artists. I found it at a local art museum, where I had taken the girls on a tour of a special exhibit of Salviati Venetian glass. One of my favorite grandparent activities has been taking them to art galleries and museums. I get to enjoy the exhibitions and share my love of art history with them, both at the same time. Who knows? As a result of these exposures to art, one of them might become a professional artist or major in art history in college.

Then, when Miranda was only four years old, she asked me several significant questions within a half-hour time period. The first was, "Gran, how did God make everything?" I mentally gasped, thought quickly, and said, "Well, darling, I don't really know how God made everything. I do know that things are made up of tiny atoms." As I started to launch into a description of the structure of atoms, her older sister, Tori, who was 6 at the time, interjected, "Oh, Gran, we're studying about atoms in school right now." I was relieved to be enrolled in a master of liberal arts graduate program at Stanford University where, coincidentally, I was taking a class on material science. How else was I going to keep up with the latest generation of elementary school students!

Now *girls* I understand. I have two daughters and two granddaughters. The last time I remember being around little boys a lot was when I was 12 and my brother Steve was born. I became his second mother, but that was many decades ago.

So, when my grandson John was born, I was in for some grandparenting adjustments. Instead of dolls, I was headed for the world of bugs. Honestly, I hadn't paid much attention to bugs before John. They were just there to be ignored, swatted, or eliminated. However, to be popular with him, I soon learned that it was important to acquire bug-locating skills. When we went to the local park playground, an important part of the outing was for me to locate trails of ants and sow bugs. "Oh, John, look what Gran found!" I would shout. We would examine the ants and try to follow them home. We soon graduated from ants to bumblebees. One time we were watching bees at eye level, only a foot away, as they were pollinating some flowers. I recall saying to him, "Look, John, the bees are having lunch." That was my way of explaining nature to him.

He also got me into bird watching. John loved to chase robins on the grass at the park. One time when we were at a duck pond, he suddenly started to laugh out loud. It seems that while he was watching ducks swimming in the water, they would tip over to eat with their tails sticking up. He thought this was so funny. You know, I found myself laughing, too. In fact, these days, when I see a snake, I don't recoil in fear like I used to. I find myself wanting to watch and examine it. Thanks to being with my grandson, I feel much closer to nature.

In another example of grandkids teaching grandparents, a friend, Diana, told us about an experience with her grandson at a local ceramics store where you paint pottery objects and then have them fired. Begrudgingly, she and her husband went—their darling grandson wanted them to take him there. Surprisingly, they had a good time! In fact, not only were they anxious to see how their creative project turned out, but they have indicated an interest in going back.

Sharon's other grandson Christopher's emerging interests were centered around gardening, vehicles, and tool projects, following the pursuits of his dad and grandfather. Two years ago, his great-grandmother and I had fun working together to create a needlepoint alphabet picture for him. Now he likes to read, too. Sharon felt truly blessed to have such wonderful grandchildren!

Room for Thought 5.1.
Designed for Family Life

And while many observers assume that economy-driven multigenerational living is an emotionally traumatic hardship, that's another myth. The truth? Many grandparents tell us not only that they love having their family back under their roof, they also love being needed again. They say it brings purpose to their days and meaning to their lives. The physical demand of keeping up with the kids makes them feel younger, outdoor play burns off both calories and tension, and helping with homework provides excellent mental stimulation.

There's a lesson here. We humans are built for family life. In a crisis, or after a disaster, it's always family that gets us through. Children must be fed, dressed, and taken to school, so we rally and we do it with a smile. In fact, studies have found that the more we act like everything is okay, the more we actually believe that everything is going to be okay. Family living

continued

forces us to have regular, face-to-face contact, which reduces isolation and wards off depression. The predictable routines of family life reduce stress; the act of nurturing, researchers have found, triggers innate biochemical stress-antidotes.[35]

In another case, Dorrie, a fitness instructor, shares a house with her husband, his daughter, and his daughter's three children. The daughter has a separate apartment downstairs, while they live upstairs. Dorrie spoke to us about the advantages she has experienced from this type of living arrangement:

> *Dorrie*: I think some of the benefits of their living with us is that we've gotten closer to the kids than we would have if they were living someplace else. Not having had children myself— you know Denise is my stepdaughter—I was dropped into being a grandmother. So, for me, it has been certainly more experience with young children than I'd had before. That is advantageous, I do believe, for me. For both of us, I think that having young children around helps keep us young and gives us a different perspective on life. You know, we're at a certain point where we wouldn't reach out to that younger generation otherwise. You just kind of get into your routine. I think that is a real advantage for us and helps keep us current in the world and in a more youthful culture.

Indeed, grandchildren can provide their grandparents with opportunities to be curious about nature, to be excited about life, and to be playful. As Michael Prichard says, "You don't stop laughing because you grow old; you grow old because you stop laughing."

We interviewed Jean, another grandmother, who lives in a house across the street from her daughter, son-in-law, and two grandsons in a small residential community in Northern California. She tells wonderful stories about the interaction between her grandsons and her pet turtle, as well as a special trip to the zoo:

Sharon: Do you have any special activities that you enjoy doing with your grandsons?

Jean: Well, we have a couple of things. I ended up adopting a turtle a few years ago. He came to visit me, and I ended up saving his life because he was trying to cross the street. I didn't know what I was going to do with him, but I went and got some grass and put him in our backyard. Now he is our pet turtle, and the boys just love to come over and see him. We have named him Ernie. Ernie goes into hibernation in August and the boys know we can't find him from August until around Easter time. So they start asking in February, "Is Ernie back?" They like to come over and feed Ernie dandelions, and it's really fun. It's a very unusual thing. Ernie has been with me now for almost three years.

Sharon: Have you bought any books on turtles?

Jean: Yes. This particular turtle is called a redneck slider. The boys and I didn't know what he ate, so we went to the pet store and got some turtle food, which was terribly expensive. Then by mistake one day, one of my little ones gave him a dandelion and we found out that he loves dandelions. Now we don't need to buy the expensive turtle food. Also, right now, outside my kitchen window, I have a bird in a bird's nest. The oldest boy comes over and checks the bird in the nest every day. So I've got nature close by.

Sharon: Do you take trips to the zoo?

Jean: Yes, we do. My fiancé and I took Martin to the zoo a month ago. We told him that we were going to have a mystery trip. I said, "I'll tell you if you want, or we'll keep it a surprise." He decided he wanted a surprise. We headed to San Francisco and he immediately fell asleep. When we got there, I woke him up and said, "Okay, Martin, we are at our mystery location. Where do you think we are?" He had to figure out where we were. There was a construction project nearby. "We've come to see them build a house," he said. I replied, "Not exactly."

So we got out of the car and I said, "Look at the flags." He said, "Why do they have animals on the flags?" Then, all of a sudden, he realized where we were. He was thrilled! We had a wonderful time at the zoo.

Finally, after hearing a lecture extolling the benefits of three-generation households, Bill sent us an email telling about his own experience. He is a retired physician who lives with his wife in Southern California. Here is what he had to say:

> *Bill*: My wife and I enjoyed a few short years of three-generation living in a two-flat house in Chicago. We occupied the first floor. Our daughter and her husband and our two grandchildren lived above us. We sat around the same dinner table every night. Those were the happiest, richest, and most rewarding years of our lives. Today, those two grandchildren are outperforming all their peers. Both are graduates of Harvard. Our grandson earned a master's degree in computer science at Harvard. He then went to Boalt Hall Law School at UC Berkeley and had his pick of law firms. His little sister is in her third year pursuing a doctoral degree in statistics at UC Berkeley. She was a math major at Harvard. Was three-generation living in their early formative years environment enriching? Yes!

A GRANDDAUGHTER LOOKS BACK

We interviewed a landscape architect who currently lives with her husband in a small residential town in Southern California. Elizabeth was asked to recall the benefits of her childhood experience living next door to her maternal grandparents on a family farm in Central California from the 1940s to the 1960s. Her stories demonstrate the lifelong influence grandparents can have, which in her case, determined a career choice:

Sharon: Tell me about your childhood housing situation.

Elizabeth: I was born in a small town in the Salinas Valley in an agricultural community, where my family lived just at the edge of the town on our family farm. It was a complex of houses. My grandparents had lived there since they were married. My mother married my father just at the end of World War II. My maternal grandfather asked my father to go into the farming business with him. That's when they moved to a house already on the property, next to my grandparents' house. Over time it was enlarged and that became our home. So we were right next door to my grandparents' house. There were several other houses on the property, where some of the employees lived and migrant workers would come seasonally. So it was like a compound. I lived there for seventeen years, from the time I was born until I went away to college.

Sharon: How did you benefit from living so close to your grandparents?

Elizabeth: I thought it was wonderful living next door to my grandparents, being able to go back and forth. Their home was like a refuge where I could go to get away from my parents. I could go over anytime, and the door was always open. My grandparents were such good friends to me. My grandfather would see me running out the door in the morning to go to school. If I was running late, he would quickly run out the door to see if I'd like a ride. So he drove me to school almost every morning, even though it was only a few blocks away. My grandmother helped me with all kinds of things. We did a lot of sewing projects together.

Sharon: Did she share your love of landscaping and gardening?

Elizabeth: A little bit. She had a gardener, actually, who lived in another cottage that was out behind her house. He was an old Irishman who came when he was in his 60s. He took care of the chicken coops and grew some vegetables that we didn't grow on the farm. My grandmother loved her geraniums, and we would often sit on her patio together where she planted them. But my grandfather actually loved landscaping and architecture. I was always quite interested in the projects that he was doing, like building little ponds and landscaping different parts of their property. I think watching him while I was growing up influenced my decision to later become a landscape designer.

Sharon: What did you like about your housing situation? You mentioned that you were close to your grandparents. Can you see ways that it helped you out in your life?

Elizabeth: Well, I think my grandparents always gave me a lot of encouragement, along with unconditional love and support. So it was like having two support systems: my parents and my grandparents. It was very stable and nurturing. Also, my mother really had built-in babysitters. I never had a babysitter take care of me while I was growing up because my grandparents were always next door to help out.

A GRANDSON LOOKS BACK

A corporate executive, who currently lives with his wife and two children in a suburb of Atlanta, Georgia, was asked questions about his childhood years. From the 1960s to the 1980s, Ted lived in New York City, in a flat downstairs from his paternal grandmother. His stories tell about the positive interaction he had with his grandmother, including the emotional support she gave him:

> *Sharon*: Tell me about your housing situation as a boy growing up.
>
> *Ted*: Well, we had a set of flats in New York. My family, including my mother, father, brothers, and myself, lived downstairs, and my grandmother lived upstairs. I imagine they would be considered condos today. The upstairs unit had one bedroom, and the downstairs had two bedrooms.

They had separate entrances and backdoors, fully equipped kitchens, bathrooms, dining rooms, and family rooms. It was a freestanding building.

Sharon: Can you give me some examples of how you benefited from living so near your grandmother?

Ted: As a child, I was completely spoiled by my grandmother. I made sure I took advantage of that as much as possible. For example, if my mother said "No," then I could run upstairs and ask my grandmother. Of course, that did cause friction between my grandmother and my mother. That continued until I moved, when I was 17 years old. Also, my grandmother was more affectionate than my mother, so I got more nurturing from my grandmother than I ever did from my mother.

Sharon: Other examples?

Ted: I could use her car whenever I wanted to. Also, we had a black-and-white TV, and then Grandma bought a color TV. So I no longer watched TV with my family; I watched TV with Grandma. If my parents weren't going to our weekend home, I could convince my grandmother to go to the weekend home. That meant I could go to the weekend home with her even if my parents did not want to go. And I enjoyed the different foods she served me, including frogs' legs, rabbit, and sweetbreads. Since she grew up in a small village in France, these were common meals in her house. Of course, nobody cooks those things anymore.

Sharon: Are there other specific ways having your grandmother around helped you out in your life?

Ted: Yeah, it is kind of hard to say because of my parents' situation. Again, she was the nurturing person in the household. If I had a problem, it was easier to talk to her than my folks. She was a good listener. Because she had lived in Europe on her own and was older, she could give you life experience as feedback. When giving advice, she would tell real-life stories to make a point. She would tell stories about family or friends or situations that someone else had experienced. "This is what this person did and that is how it came out. The moral of the story is '. . . and it might end up that way for you.'"

Sharon: What role did your grandmother play for you?

Ted: She was the most secure and stable person in the household. You could always count on her. My parents were alcoholics, so you really couldn't count on them. When I had problems downstairs, I could always go upstairs. Her role was nurturing, secure, loving. She really played the large part of a stand-in mother for me. I loved her as much as I loved my mother and possibly more. Had she not been there through my developmental years, there is no telling what I would have achieved in school or professionally. I think my behavioral makeup would have been different had she not been present in my life.

Sharon: You have certainly achieved a lot in your lifetime, not only with your professional life, but also, here you are in this beautiful home with your lovely wife and two sons. It is apparent that you give your grandmother a lot of credit for the success you are experiencing.

Ted: I have a lot of the security in knowing what good parenting may look like. So I think by her being there, I got to experience what I didn't get through being parented well myself. If you look at families a hundred years ago, they pretty much stayed together because travel was so much harder. Today, that is not the case, and people are spread all over. I think the family does suffer because of that. The children suffer and I think the grandparents suffer. I believe there is a relationship that is missing for many: a nurturing, stable, and secure relationship that should be encouraged. Children should know their grandparents.

CONCLUSIONS

So, in spite of having alcoholic parents, Ted has succeeded in life thanks to the nurturing he received from his grandmother. Elizabeth has developed her career in landscape design, in part due to living next door to her grandfather. Bill credited three-generation living in his grandchildren's early formative years for enriching their environment and leading to their academic and career achievements. Jean told stories about enjoying nature with her grandsons, who live across the street. Sharon gave examples of how she and her friend Diana grew from interacting with our grandchildren. Catherine, Kristine, Margaret, Peter, and Julie all spoke highly of the benefits of their "grand" relationships.

Next, we tell the stories of those involved in tackling the practicalities of living together. We cover when and how to make the decision to live nearby, along with privacy issues. Also, how to find, buy, or build housing is included. If you want to stay in your own house, we tell the stories of those who have remodeled for privacy and accessibility for seniors. *Read on!*

PART THREE

THE
PRACTICALITIES

DECIDING TO LIVE TOGETHER

Life is what happens to you while you're busy making other plans.
—John Lennon

Sharon's granddaughter, Tori, once told her, "Gran, I love you . . . and, I like you, too!" Sharon always regarded her statement of affection as one of the highlights of her life. *Love* is one thing, but *like* is quite another. For many, *love* can also mean *like*. For others, to love a family member can be considered an obligation that doesn't necessarily mean that the person is also liked. In fact, one of the major factors in deciding to live together is whether or not family members like each other. After all, if you like someone, chances are better that you'll get along, if you should decide to live together.

On the other hand, for some grandparents, living adjacent is not a viable option because they don't want daily interaction with their grandchildren, or to be on call to babysit whenever needed by the parents. Some people simply don't feel comfortable being around crying babies or physically cannot lift them. They prefer not to deal with noisy, active children who might trip them, or with teenagers who play loud music. Nor do they desire to be in close proximity to a son- or daughter-in-law with whom they don't necessarily get along. Ultimately, these people want to preserve their ability to make choices, preferring to retain their privacy and independence by living apart.

Often, making the decision to live together is not easy, but it is most assuredly a crucial decision influencing human happiness. This chapter is about when and how to make such decisions. The following true story illustrates the need to plan ahead.

The ugly headline read, "Car Plows through Market, Killing Nine." An eighty-six-year-old man drove his Buick through a crowded farmers market in Santa Monica, California, injuring fifty-four men, women, and children and killing nine, including a three-year-old girl. The driver, unhurt, reported that his foot may have hit the accelerator instead of the brake. A bystander said of the driver, "He looked very confused when he stepped out of the car. He definitely shouldn't have been behind the wheel. He was definitely not quite with it." The police reported after his arrest that the man had no alcohol or psychiatric medications in his system.[36]

WHEN TO START TALKING ABOUT CHANGES

The toughest part of making decisions about living arrangements for elders is *when* to start talking about it. For most families it seems such decisions are forced by incidents like the Santa Monica farmers market crash, or perhaps health problems of some sort. Clearly the driver should have been in a living situation that allowed him the freedom *not* to have to get behind the wheel of a car.

Now, we appreciate that age itself doesn't define one's driving abilities. Some ninety-year-olds are fully capable of driving safely. And, of course, some twenty-year-olds shouldn't ever be behind the wheel of two tons of steel. Our point is simply that you and your family should not wait until some sort of disaster strikes to begin talking about alternative living arrangements. Indeed, if you're lucky, your family has already begun the planning.

One story illustrates well the advantages of foresight and action. Bob, a small-business owner in Northern California, talked about his mother-in-law:

"She was really getting to the point where she couldn't live alone, mainly because of her medication. If she didn't take her medication, there were problems. We finally said, 'Look, you can't live alone,' and moved her in with us. Initially, she wasn't real happy with it, but now she has adjusted to living with us. We're not worried about her taking her medicine anymore," Bob said.

Based on our studies of the matter for this book, the discussions should begin when the older parent hits age seventy. We suggest waiting until about a month after the actual birthday. At seventy-five, when most people have about ten years to go (see exhibit 3.1 in chapter 3), older people need to be in a place and situation that can accommodate disabilities that are beginning to become problematic. And, starting the talking, research, and experimenting when that loved one is around seventy years old gives everyone time to comfortably consider all the options and implications.

Charlene, a Realtor living in Washington, describes the problem of waiting too long:

"I've been working with my mother-in-law who, because of a medical crisis, is now in a facility. Her daughter and son, and my husband, helped her with the move. She is now missing several of her things. She did not directly supervise the dispersal of her things. Today, we had to shop for summer clothes because she didn't think to save any. Where is her swan pin? Where is another necklace? It's hard to dispose of a lifetime of things. Imagine yourself having to break up your house and get rid of things you've had all your life. Wouldn't it be nicer to go through things when you're feeling okay, instead of being groggy on meds? Do it while you're young. Be where you want to be before you're seventy."

These interview snippets may seem bleak, but we leave you with some hope. The AARP provides a wealth of information on the topics we cover in this book. In exhibit 6.1, you will find AARP's very useful checklist about signs indicating it's time to start the dialogue with your loved one. While it is possible for families to complete assessments on their own using standard checklists, there also are experienced professionals who can help. While checklists and professionals will vary somewhat, here are some basic areas you and your older family members may want to focus on:

Exhibit 6.1. The AARP Answers the Question:
"How Do I Help Them Know If They Need Help?"

Physical Health. Have they been diagnosed with any chronic diseases, such as diabetes, high blood pressure, arthritis, or emphysema? Or other diseases, such as bowel or bladder problems, heart disease, stroke, or can-cer? Do they have vision or hearing problems, excessive weight loss or gain, or difficulty walking? Make a list of health professionals they cur-rently see. Add any recent hospitalizations.

Mental Health. Have they been diagnosed with any psychiatric disorders, such as depression, anxiety, or psychosis? Have they been diagnosed with Alzheimer's or another form of dementia? Are they showing signs of confusion, disorientation, or isolation? What about mood swings or forget-fulness? Sadness or loneliness?

Medication Use. What medications are they currently taking? What is the dosage? How often? Include over-the-counter medications. Are they tak-ing their medication as directed?

Daily Living Skills. Are they able to dress, bathe, get up from a chair, use a toilet, climb stairs, use the phone? Do they know how to get help in an emergency? Can they shop, prepare meals, do housework and yard work? Can they safely drive?

Home and Community Safety. How safe is their neighborhood? Does their home have smoke alarms, and can they hear them adequately? Can they avoid phone and door-to-door fraud? Can they maintain their house?

Support Systems. Do your older loved ones have frequent visitors or see friends? Do they go to a senior center or get out of the house for other social reasons? Do family members live close by? Do they keep handy the names, addresses, and cell phone numbers of key friends and family mem-bers who they can call in an emergency?

Appearance and Hygiene. How is their overall appearance? Hair clean? Teeth brushed? Shaved? Do they dress appropriately in clean clothes?

Finances. Can they live on their current income? Can they meet future needs with their current income? Are there any legal documents, such as trusts, living wills, and/or durable power of attorney? Do they pay bills on time and make informed financial decisions?

Interests/Lifestyles. Do they engage in their favorite hobbies, read books, watch their favorite TV shows, exercise, play a musical instrument, go to church, keep up with their friends? Are they still engaged in the activities they have always enjoyed?

Source: www.aarp.org, 2004

There are good assessment tools and professional consultants who can help you and your older loved ones decide when assistance is needed. Some hospitals and clinics offer geriatric assessment centers. City or county agencies on aging may provide this service. There are also independent geriatric care managers (also called case managers).

HOW TO START TALKING

If you're older than one month over seventy, then your job is pretty easy. You've already read this far in the book, so some of what we are saying must be making some sense to you. So, all you have to do at this point is begin talking to your kids or your kin about your plans for the next couple of decades. Your conversation might start out something like this:

"This book I'm reading tells me that I've got about fifteen more years to go before I kick off. It also says my brain or body will begin to fall apart pretty soon.[37] So, here's my (our) plan for the next couple of decades. Please tell me what you think."

Even if you have it all figured out so that your kids don't have to participate or help, just telling them about your plan will accomplish three good things. First, they won't worry about you. Second, they can plan accordingly. And third, they may actually have some ideas about ways to make things even better for you—and for everyone.

Alternatively, if it's your parent that's hitting seventy and a month, then the task is tougher. This is particularly so if you were raised in an autocratic family with Mom or Dad giving orders as the bosses. Even if you come from a more democratic family where everyone is heard, you still cannot tell your parents what they should do. So how to start? Here's how some folks got the conversational ball rolling. Sometimes it's easy:

> *Alice (a ninety-seven-year-old widowed doll maker from Northern California)*: Actually, my son Bob came over and said that I should come to live with them. He used to come to San Jose and visit me and it was a long way to bring the children. So he said, "Don't you think you could sell your house and buy a place near us?" Right away, I said, "Fine." I was lonely there without them. Even though I had lots of friends and belonged to clubs, it's not the same. I'd rather live here.

For some it just seems to dawn on them. At least that's how Janet and Craig described their decision to buy a home together with Janet's parents, Nancy and Rick, in Northern California. Nancy and Rick were both in their midseventies and retired:

> *Craig (mid-40s international finance executive)*: We've been living here since '96. It actually happened when my in-laws, Nancy and Rick, were looking to downsize from the home they had lived in for decades. At first, we were actually trying to get Janet's brother and sister-in-law, who were planning to move into a bigger house, to combine with them. They weren't interested at the time, so we said, "Why don't we do it." We can get a lot more house for both of us, and, as long as it gives everybody privacy, it would be a great idea.
>
> *Janet (homemaker and mother of three)*: My folks wanted a smaller house with a swimming pool but found it was expensive to buy one in the same neighborhood. We had a beautiful home, but we didn't have a pool. The kids were young and we thought that might be kind of a nice thing to have. It just dawned on us that if we combined our resources we could get what they wanted and we could upgrade, too. So we started looking, and then Craig and Mom found this great house with both a pool and 1,200-square-foot cottage in the backyard.
>
> *Craig*: The layout allows us to have our privacy and at the same time be close enough to go back and forth. Also, if they want to entertain a large group, they'll come over here and use our place and we'll go out to a movie or do something else.
>
> *Sharon*: What made you decide to participate in three-generation housing?
>
> *Craig*: Part of the idea is knowing that it would give them a place where they could relax and grow old at the same time and also watch the kids. I remember when I was in grad school, we had a curriculum which was a mix of business, languages, and area studies. The area I concentrated on was Asia. I was always

interested in the philosophy of China. You get often three or
even four generations under one roof. They do it mostly for
economic reasons, but also the family is important to them.

Sharon: So a seed was planted back in the college days?

Craig: Yes. And the other thing is, as we met and were married, the family was always very close, my side of the family
and Janet's side of the family. When the opportunity presented
itself to merge households, we felt comfortable doing so. The
reason we didn't stay in our other home is that it didn't lend
itself to the two families living together. In fact, they prefer
smaller square footage because they like having less space to
have to maintain.

If you're lucky enough to have a cooperative relationship with your siblings, then by all means, get everyone together and talk. You'll notice that
Janet's brother was involved in arrangements described just above. When we
were handling the various problems with our brother Steve's health and care,
it was most helpful and reassuring to have other loved ones involved in the
decisions and discussions. Indeed, had our parents made it to their seventies in good health, the five of us would have conferred on the best way to
approach them. Maybe we would have asked our sister, Mary Ellen, to broach
the subject.

It may or may not make sense to have everyone gathered at a big family
meeting. It may be better to get your parents thinking about these kinds of
things with a gentle conversational nudge from the parental favorite. Finally,
another approach is simply to deliver a copy of this book as a late seventieth
birthday present.

After three such nudges or giving them three copies of this book, you're
probably pestering. But, a key thing to give your parents is *time* to consider
these ideas. We all like to ignore the inevitability of our own death. But, really
this is not much of a step beyond insurance policies and wills. It's simply a
matter of planning ahead, dealing with the foreseeable future. And, setting up
your everyday living arrangements is probably more important than all the
paperwork preparations put together.

It's always helpful to plan a difficult conversation. Again, AARP provides some very useful information about conducting the negotiations with your family members—see exhibit 6.2. One of these ways to break the ice might work for you and your family.

Exhibit 6.2. The AARP Recommends You . . .
Plan the Conversation

Approach the subject indirectly:
"I know you're taking lots of pills. How do you keep track of them? Would a pill organizer from the drug store help you?"

"John says his dad has given up driving. How would you get around when you can no longer drive?"

Be direct but nonconfrontational:
"Mom, I'm worried that you seem to be unsteady on your feet. I'm wondering how I can help protect you from falls."

"If you ever get to the point where you can't live alone, Dad, where would you want to live?"

Watch for openings:
"Uncle Joe, you mentioned having problems with your eyesight. Have you seen the eye doctor lately? Does it seem to affect your driving?"

"Gramps, after you said last week that you had trouble turning the handles on the water faucets, I wondered how you were managing with the shower."

Share your own feelings about your parents' changing life:
"You've always been so independent, Dad. I imagine it's now hard for you to ask for help. Is it?" Let your parents know they can always ask you for help when they need it.

"It's hard to see you give up reading, Mom, now that your eyesight is getting bad. Do you miss it? Would you like to try a book on tape?"

Make a list:
Family members are sometimes uncomfortable jumping right into a talk about sensitive topics, such as finances. If so, consider giving them a list of questions or concerns and schedule a time to talk. This lets them think about the kinds of help they may need and prepare for the conversation.

Dealing with resistance:
Some resistance to talking about independence is normal. They may put you off with reassuring statements or tell you to mind your own business. But experts advise:

---

continued

- Respect your parents' feelings if they make it clear they want to avoid a subject. Try another time.

- Push the issue if health or safety is at risk, while recognizing your parents' right to be in charge of their own lives.

- Act firmly but with compassion, if you decide you cannot avoid intervening: "Dad, we can't ignore this any longer. We have to deal with it."

- *Facilitators* are crucial.* Involve other people who your parents respect, such as a minister, lawyer, or a family friend. *It would be ideal to meet at their church, office, or home as a neutral venue. In a location other than your parents' home, it may be easier for all to break out of old parent-child roles and behavior sets. Such facilitators may also be able to help you borrow ideas from other families. Indeed, that is the primary purpose of our book—to provide you with others' inventive ideas and best practices about family arrangements toward stimulating your own thinking.*

- Look for community resources that can help a parent remain independent, such as transportation, home health care, meal delivery. Share the options with them.

- Hold family meetings where everyone discusses concerns and jointly develops a mutually agreeable plan. Make sure your parents feel a sense of involvement and control over their lives. Listen to their opinions and recognize their right to make decisions. Stay focused on current needs and avoid past resentments. They'll feel more in control if the meeting is in their own home. But, as we advise above a neutral location is probably best. Getting to an egalitarian discussion where all are treated as adults may be more difficult at your parents' home. This would be particularly so with a father like Archie Bunker—we quote him: "Whatever happened to the good old days when kids were scared to death of their parents?"

- Perhaps the best way to start such a meeting is for everyone to describe how they see things ten years out. Then try to invent and agree on a common story about the future. This also serves to enhance everyone's focus on the future.

- Don't try to change minds in one such family meeting. Give everyone a chance to ruminate on things overnight or over a few days. We know that the brain works more creatively as it is leaving or entering sleep. Breaks can also provide a chance for all to consult with others and/or to discuss among themselves such big changes.

- Techniques of brainstorming may also be appropriate. The key is having everyone participate, and a facilitator can be particularly helpful ensuring everyone gets a chance to talk. Humorous, even crazy and impractical ideas should be encouraged and ". . . yes, but . . ." responses forbidden. Often such crazy ideas lead to wonderfully inventive options.

- Sharing food or a glass of wine may also be helpful as long as no one has alcohol problems.

- Finally, mark momentum. The first "baby steps" are important and should be noted. Celebrate worthwhile new ideas early and often. When you acknowledge areas of agreement or work together to bridge any of your differences, you establish critical momentum and a track record of success.

Keep it positive:
Avoid role reversal. Talking to parents and helping them doesn't mean you are "parenting" them. In your talks, treat each other as equals. Be prepared to let your parents make their own choices, even if you don't agree with them. As long as they are not impaired with Alzheimer's disease or other dementia, your parents have the right to make their own decisions. Growing older does not give up that right. Even when they make what you think is an unsafe choice, it doesn't necessarily mean that they are no longer capable of living independently. If their choices disturb you, you may need to set your own limits to how involved you can be, so that their decisions don't run your life.

*We have added our own advice in italics to an excellent list published by AARP in 2004. Our comments are based on John's 2012 book with coauthors, *Inventive Negotiations*.

WHO SHOULD BE INVOLVED

The answer here is simple—everyone. It may mean convening the family from around the country or the world, but everyone should be involved in the initial discussions. The invitation list should include the sister you hate or the brother that drives your mother crazy. And, the emphasis of this first meeting is to lay out all the alternatives *without discussion*. This is crucial—*without discussion*.

Avoiding ruling things out immediately keeps everyone involved and maximizes inventive thinking.

How many possibilities are there? When our father died our mother might have moved in with any of the five of us, or any of us might have moved in with our mother—she had a big house. Now obviously some of those ten options were clearly impractical. But, at the first meeting with everyone present, all options, even the bad ones, should be put on the table.

Norma (seventy) and Roger (seventy-five) retired in Oregon on a property that includes a main house and two accessory units. They were careful to include everyone concerned in their evolving decision-making:

> *Norma*: When our daughter Jane graduated from college in California, she said she liked our area, too, and was going to look for work up here. So, she said, "Why don't we make an apartment out of the back of our house." At that point, all the kids were gone. It was just the two of us here.
>
> *Roger*: When we bought the house, we planned to have a lot done to it. The five-bedroom area was designed in such a way that it could be separated and made into an apartment with a kitchen and outside entrance. So when Jane said, "Make it into an apartment and I'll be your first tenant," that's exactly what we did. We thought, "We don't need all of this space."
>
> *Norma*: Jane's been subsequently married and has two daughters. After the kids came, we added another bedroom. Then they approached us and said, "How would it be if we built a house on the property?"
>
> *Roger*: So that's where it got tricky because, since we couldn't divide the property into two lots, we ended up with joint-tenancy ownership. We knew that this might be a problem in dividing up our estate inheritance-wise because of the other two siblings. But, after discussing it with all the kids, we just decided that we'd give it a try anyway. So they built their house. The local government did require that it be smaller in size than the main house. So they had to go by those parameters.

WHERE TO TALK

Some neutral place not at the home of anyone in your family is probably the best choice. In exhibit 6.2 we emphasize the importance of facilitators; perhaps they might provide a good neutral venue at a church or in their offices or home. It might be at a local restaurant or picnic place. The food will keep everyone there and even the big talkers in the family will have to eat, thus allowing others to contribute to the conversation. This initial discussion with all the family involved should be someplace comfortable and informal and should allow an open-ended time frame.

NEEDS AND RESOURCES

The fundamental assumption about family responsibilities made by mainstream American culture goes something like this: "When kids hit eighteen, they're on their own. Legally they're adults and neither parent nor child owe each other anything."[38] Most folks may be willing to help out with college, but in America kids are nudged out of the nest one way or another after they finish high school. And, both sides proclaim their rightful freedom. Parents congratulate themselves for a job well done and kids celebrate their freedom from parental control. Yes!

So that makes any decision to live together a negotiation between equals. "Ideally it's a negotiation among equals where everyone's feelings are taken into consideration," agrees Dr. Joshua Coleman, a psychologist specializing in child-adult relationships.[39] Both parents and grown children have needs and resources to trade. The decision-making process is really just a matter of determining and agreeing about what will be exchanged, when, and how.

We all have basic needs. Psychologist Abraham Maslow described a hierarchy of human needs:

1. At the base are *physiological needs* for food, sleep, and shelter—the things that keep us going physically. If any of those needs are not satisfied we may experience pain, sickness, and so on. Only if those most basic physiological needs are satisfied do we then begin to worry about the next level of needs, those related to our personal safety.

2. *Safety needs* are more psychological in nature and have to do with feelings of security from a chaotic world.

3. Once physiological and safety needs are satisfied, then we begin to focus on *relationship needs*. Given that we're social animals, acceptance, belongingness, and love are important.

4. Maslow argued that only when the first three levels of needs are satisfied do humans begin to focus on *esteem needs*. These include both self-esteem and the esteem of others.

5. Finally come *self-actualization needs*—simply stated, the need to fulfill one's potential as a human.

Maslow's hierarchy, while useful here, should still be taken with a grain of salt. For example, Mary Pipher, in her excellent book on elders, *Another Country*, argues that you can't always neatly categorize human needs. That is, the mind and body are connected:

> Communities keep people healthy. In 1988, James House of the University of Michigan found that the lack of social relationships constituted a major health risk, rivaling cigarette smoking or high blood pressure. Research on Roseto, a village of Italian immigrants with three-generation households, indicated that people lived longer if they stayed in Roseto than if they moved away. This increase in longevity rates wherever there is community is called the Roseto effect.[40]

Still, family members often have the abilities and resources to supply all these kinds of needs. Certainly, sharing shelter and food preparation and the financial aspects of both might be part of any exchange. Childcare and elder care would also both fall into the category of physiological needs. Or, simply sharing the chores around the household also fits the description. All kinds of offers might be made regarding sharing rent, mortgage payments, insurance, washing machines and dryers, and so on. "You cook on Tuesdays and Thursdays, and we'll cook on Mondays and Wednesdays;" or "You help out with the grandkids during the next ten years or so, then we and the grandkids will help out when you start to fall apart in your eighties."

Following are three instructive stories about how households with three generations living together can satisfy a variety of human needs:

Joan (who is in her late thirties, has a PhD, and is a financial consultant): Some years ago, my mother was living in a home in Charleston. My father had passed away in 1980. So, for almost ten years, she was maintaining the house by herself. That worked out fine. However, my husband and I began seeing that it became more difficult for her to maintain the house. She had trouble finding someone to mow the lawn, clean the gutters, and we weren't always able to help out. We did what we could. But to find people to help out was becoming more difficult. We started to project down the road what her long-term housing situation would be. We knew from a financial perspective that she would not be able to afford a long-term care facility.

When we bought this house, it had a garage with an entrance that went out to the side of the property. We thought that was kind of a natural area to put on an addition where there would be an entrance from the garage into what we called the guesthouse. There would be access to it from the house but not from the main part of our home. So we began getting some drawings in place of what it would look like. I had also talked to a few Realtors, who told me this was a positive thing to do when you go to resell the home.

From my perspective, my mother was still driving. She was mobile. She was involved in the senior center. It was an extra set of eyes that I felt was around the home environment during the day. Even though we had a caregiver for my daughter, if that person wasn't able to come or was coming an hour late, there was just another person around. We did it for that reason, for my daughter to have a relationship with her grandmother.

Eleanor (a successful Northern California interior designer in her early sixties, describes how her mother helps out): Yes she still drives but slowly. She also takes care of our kitty when we are gone. She watches over our house. It gives her a sense of responsibility. I think that is very important. She feels useful. I think the real fear of getting older and being alone is wondering, "Why am I still here? What am I good for?" Because she lives with us, she'll come down and see that I've got the laundry piled up and offer to help with it. She'll do dishes for me. Also, if I'm going to be out on an appointment and my husband is coming home, I can leave stuff out for dinner, and she will put it together for him. If I have to travel for business where I'm gone for several days or a week, she may fix his dinner every night. He'll call her when he is on his way home and say, "Mom, I'm on my way home. What's for dinner tonight?" She will cook what he wants. It's not easy for her. It's very difficult for her to move around and do things, but she has a sense of accomplishment by helping out.

Don (a recently retired air traffic controller in California, talks about the arrangement he and his wife have with their daughter and her family living with them next door in their duplex): It's really very mellow. The only problem is, we are all running out of room. I mean, the kids want to move because they want their own house. There is no way they can afford one here. They want to go back east, and we are going to go with them. You are talking about shared income now. In other words, we need to have some flexibility in how we do it. There are a lot of things we have to look at from a financial end before we make the move.

Sharon: So when you move, you are planning to do a joint venture with your daughter and her husband again, so you'll share the funding of the house?

Don: Right. Depending on the price. As necessary. It would be perfect if they could go back there and buy it on their own and we could have a place to live with them. But then finding that along with where we want to live and at the right price, they haven't hit the lottery yet. So, we'll be sharing the cost.

Just having someone in the house, next door, or at least within yelling distance adds to one's feelings of safety, no matter the neighborhood.

Beyond the physiological and safety support close extended family members can supply when they live near one another are the companionship needs. The mutual satisfaction of these depends completely on the mutual enjoyment of one another's company—liking one another. For most American families this means sharing entertainment experiences—television, movies, sporting events, and such.

Elisa and Neal explained to us how this "liking" stuff works, and how it's fun. They're both in their midthirties. She's a stockbroker and he's an accountant in Cleveland:

> *Sharon*: So what made you decide to live with Elisa's parents in this apartment above their garage? Whose idea was it?
> *Elisa*: I've always known that we could move in here. So, it was just one of our options. I like being close to my family. It's a good way to get started financially and get a house fast, too.
> *Neal*: We looked at other choices and in the end we realized it was the best, especially since we wanted to get a home soon. If we had to pay money to rent a place, it would prolong our inability to get our own house. It's nice being rent-free.

Over half of the people we interviewed said that their families have been involved in multigenerational living arrangements before. So a history of extended family living can be an indicator of those who later decide to live together again:

> *Sharon*: Had you heard of others, your parents, participating in a similar living arrangement?
> *Elisa*: My parents lived with my grandma for a few months.

Neal: I know my parents lived with my mom's brother and his wife for a while. It was a rough situation because they were all in the same house. It wasn't a separate thing, like we have. So, when my mom heard that I was thinking about doing this, she said to just be aware that it's a large family we would be living with. She recalls having to deal with her brother, who had a lot of kids, and they didn't have a separate type of entrance or kitchen like we have. So she was a little concerned. I let her know that it was a completely separate home that we were going to be in, a separate living area. She said, "That sounds like a good deal."

And, if things work out best, living with extended family members should also help satisfy one's esteem and self-actualization needs. For example, among the benefits of helping with elder parents might be the esteem-building gratefulness of those parents and your siblings, or the self-actualization of helping and supporting family members. Mary Pipher says about assuming responsibility for the care of those we love, "It is not just a burden, but a joy to help those we love. It is a chance to stay connected, to return love, and to grow ourselves."[41]

EXCHANGING INFORMATION

So, once families have listed all the potential living arrangements, the next step is to trade information about what needs and resources might be associated with each arrangement. Frankness and realistic estimates of what folks have to offer one another are key. Write all of these considerations down on paper and let everyone involved review them. List the advantages and disadvantages of each living arrangement being considered. Once all the information is on the table, literally, then it's time to make a choice.

We must also add one caveat here about information exchange. Depending on how communicative family members are, it may be important to augment their descriptions of their needs with observations of their limitations. Accompanying loved ones on doctors' appointments or shopping trips may be more than just helpful but also informative. Observing meal preparation or gardening activities at home are other examples of learning about needs by just "being there." It may also be quite useful to compare notes with siblings or other close relatives and friends.

We've excerpted a useful checklist of things to consider in making decisions about moving in with elder parents (exhibit 6.3). Virginia Morris's book, *How to Care for Aging Parents*, provides more details. In chapter 13 we add the notion of "caregiving contracts" to her lists.

Exhibit 6.3. A Checklist from *How to Care for Aging Parents*[42]

- Their safety
- Your limits
- Costs
- Location
- Loneliness
- Future care
- Can you get along?
- What about the rest of the family?
- Do you have the space?
- Is your house equipped for this?
- How much attention does your parent need?
- Do your lifestyles meld?
- What are the advantages?

Compatible lifestyles are key as described by Colleen, a retired school administrator in Michigan:

> *Colleen*: Because I had decided not to move into my vacation home, I thought I should move in with one of my kids. Well, with the four having such different lifestyles, I knew

I could get along best with my daughter. And, she had just lost her husband in a car accident and has an 8-year-old son. She suggested we get a place together since she was gone a lot with work and I generally stay around home writing and doing other kinds of things with community groups and such.

If you've started early in this process, at the recommended seventy years plus one month, then you also have time to experiment with different living arrangements. No matter how carefully folks have considered what living together again might be like, some things (good and bad) are simply impossible to anticipate. However, we also want to raise caution here. Obviously in most cases it will be impractical to add kitchens or find duplexes during such an experiment. And, we know that seemingly trivial privacy considerations can make big differences in how households work. For example, imagine living with your three generations together in a 6,000-square-foot house versus a small apartment. The physical environment can be a powerful influence on how folks get along. So, be careful and note that it will take some imagination to look beyond such temporary environmental obstacles. But, the key point here is that more information will be created during such experiments that can better inform ultimate decisions. So, try things out if you can.

Following are a series of illustrative stories about trying things out. We'll begin with Dorrie, a fitness counselor, and her husband, Tim, a retired architect. They share a divided house with his daughter in Northern California:

> *Dorrie*: Well, a number of years ago, Tim's daughter had three children and was in a difficult marriage living in Fresno. We found that when the children were very young, she would come and visit us on the weekends and bring them with her. Then she would come on vacations and stay and would also spend Thanksgiving with us and the kids. She would stay a little bit longer each time. We knew that things were not good in their relationship. It was a real strain. We could tell that she needed to get away to a safe place, a haven to come to with the kids.

One summer she asked us if she could come and spend an extended vacation during the summer. We said, "Sure." I looked at Tim at that time and said, "You know this extended vacation might indicate that we should start cleaning out the extra bedrooms downstairs." Sure enough, she came really with the intention of just getting away for a while to clear her head and have a little break for the kids. I think underneath there was a definite possibility of a breakup in her marriage, but I don't think she was ready to admit it to herself at the time. But psychologically we started to gear ourselves up for the possibility that by the time school started in the fall, we would have a family of four living with us. That's what happened.

Tim: We are fortunate to have a rather large house with six bedrooms and five bathrooms, designed so that it is totally separate between the two levels. In fact on the first level, which is where they stay, there is a complete kitchen and family room, along with two bathrooms and three bedrooms. It lends itself very well to having a second family of four people stay with us. In fact, there is even a separate driveway so they can come and go without our even knowing it.

Todd and Lynne, both in their midthirties, own two nursery schools near Denver, Colorado. They also took an incremental approach to living with Todd's parents:

Todd: Actually, my mom and dad moved up here about a year and a half ago. They moved in with us in the beginning until their house, which had renters in it, was vacated. They stayed for three months and it worked out very well. Now they are planning to sell their house and we are going to build a new house in the back of our property for them, too.

Lynne: During the time they were living here with us, it was such a pleasant experience to be able to lead separate lives but also come together for family meals, as well as share the house-work and the kids. That's when we said, "When we build our new house out back, might you consider buying this house from us?" So for a while that was the question. We would be about a hundred yards from each other. Since then, the situation has changed for them. They want to go more to simplicity, to downsize to something more reasonable at their age and be even closer. So we'll sell this house. That is the plan. We will live in our new house, and they will live in, quote, a "guesthouse."

Sharon: So what made you decide to participate in three-generation housing? Was it based on the successful experience that you had just having them nearby, or were there other reasons?

Todd: We purchased this land with the intention of being able to take on whatever we needed to do for the family. It was a very good deal. I looked at it and said, "I don't know what their retirement is going to be. They might end up here anyway, so we might as well plan for it." Either set of parents, we don't know who might show up, could be in the future guesthouse. Eventually, when we are old, maybe we will be in the guesthouse, and the kids can take over this house. Also, we never know if my brother might show up one day.

Lynne: It wasn't until they came here and we lived together that the message to us was very loud and clear: "We are here to support you." Once that message sunk in, it was an obvious win-win situation. That's when we really started talking about it, when they moved here.

Without question, our favorite story about trying things out is that of Helen, a real estate agent, who in her early sixties began experimenting with housing arrangements during visits to her daughter. Here's Helen's story:

Helen: I've tried out a variety of options. I've tried staying in a hotel, but it was expensive and too far away. Next I rented an RV to park in their front yard, but it was not insulated very well and that didn't work. In the middle of the summer, I asked if any of my daughter's friends had an extra guest bedroom that I could rent within walking distance. That wasn't a comfortable option for her. Then I started looking for houses nearby. So for two years I looked. The house next door came up for sale, and I could see it had a lot of potential for a long-term investment. Also, three months before I bought that house, I had a medical emergency and became acutely aware that I might need somebody to take care of me. I might need to have a place where my daughter could look after me. If I have a rental, I can easily live next door for six months, depending on what I needed. It would be easy for her, and I could be involved with the grandchildren.

What I am doing right now is renting the home out. First I went and fixed it up. It had two bedrooms and one and a half baths, and I could legally convert it to three bedrooms, two baths, making it more valuable. I added a full bathroom with wheelchair access width and a shower that has a three-inch sill, which I figured I could get over easily. I also put in handrails.

I decided I would rent the house short term. I do know my daughter is committed to staying in Arizona until the kids are out of high school and that is another seventeen years. Another benefit this gave me was a project to do while I'm there that is not family related, so that I have something I can do on my own and be independent.

So that was the sequence—first the trailer and then the house. Originally, I helped them buy their house with the understanding that it would be large enough that we could put in a mother-in-law unit someplace or there would be an extra bedroom. Once they got in the house, they changed their minds. They loved it, but they decided that they did not want to put in a mother-in-law unit. It would block their view, and they would not have enough play space in the backyard. It was perfectly fine for me to stay in the guest bedroom for a while. Now they have three children so that is not possible.

Now I am back to using the RV, and that is a little bit better for me. What I like best is being able to walk out the door and have privacy when I need it. The other thought I had, when I bought this house, is that there is a large area where my RV could be stored to the right of the house. But I really don't feel good about the RV, so I haven't really found a total answer yet.

RULING OUT OPTIONS

Finally, it is very important to recognize that some situations simply do not work out. For example, it is often impossible to overcome conflicts about geographic preferences.[43] Knowing when to say no or when to give up is important. Having carefully considered the options often brings a kind of peace.

A young mother shared a story about the dilemma that she and her husband are facing about how to care for their respective mothers. Both women are difficult personality-wise. Her husband's mother yells at the children and is very demanding. Lorraine's ten-year-old son commented after a visit from his grandmother last summer, "Mom, she is so mean to me." It seems the woman would yell at him a lot for minor things. Lorraine's own mother is very negative and finds something wrong with almost everything.

Her husband is adamant that he does not want his mother, who now lives in Texas, to come and live with them. His mother had intimated she would like to relocate to join them. Lorraine said her husband's brother and his wife moved to a house in Texas, five minutes away from his mother. Shortly thereafter, they moved to a place three hours away, just to get away from his mother.

What should this couple do in these situations? Right now, Lorraine's husband is sending his mother money to help her out. Surely, the number one priority should be their own immediate family, and the mother should absolutely not be allowed to come and live with them. They can continue to send her money and get the other siblings to help out as well. We did not talk about what to do with Lorraine's mother.

In some cases, ADUs and close proximity to the grandkids will not be preferred by some. For them, independence, privacy, and separation from noisy kids will be more important than the convenience of proximity. A friend's nanny, Isabel, told us the story about her oldest daughter, Maria, who has just moved back to their home with her four-year-old son. Isabel's daughter and her husband had been living for twelve years with his grandparents in a separate apartment in their home. Her husband worked with his grandfather in a business owned by the grandfather. In exchange, he received a salary and they enjoyed free rent in the apartment in the grandparent's home. Also, they were told, "When we die, everything will be yours."

Unfortunately, the emotional cost of living with them was more than Maria could stand. It seems the grandmother had a key to their apartment. She would find out when they were going to be out, and, without asking, would enter their place to look around. Maria's housekeeping was simply not up to the grandmother's standards. Not only would the grandmother give her a verbal scolding for not being neat, but she would tell the neighbors that Maria was a lousy housekeeper. Moreover, if Maria went bike riding with friends, she would be criticized for "not being a good mother" because "she should be home taking care of her son." Bottom line, Maria could no longer take the grandmother's continual interference in her life.

According to Isabel, Maria's husband is perplexed about what to do. The grandparents have told him that, if he leaves, he "will lose everything . . . not receive an inheritance from them." Logic suggests that, if he wants to keep his marriage, he needs to find other work and a new place to live. Sometimes proximity is not a good thing in living with extended family. Sometimes the best decision is to live somewhere else.

CONCLUSIONS

For many of the folks we've interviewed, the decision-making was relatively simple. The fact that you're reading this book suggests this isn't necessarily the case for you. We've tried to outline a road map you might follow to engage your family in an exploration of all the options for best managing the needs of the aging seniors in your family. And, of course, all families are different in size, wealth, geographical constraints, interaction style, and so forth. That's exactly why we present so many different stories here.

The keys are creativity, communication, and getting an early start. As Anne Frank so eloquently put it in her diary, "How wonderful it is that nobody need wait a single moment before starting to improve the world." Perhaps the best place to start is with your family!

PROXIMITY AND PRIVACY: LIVING TOGETHER IN HELPFUL WAYS

The kitchen mediates between power and submission and love and hate and all the other dynamics of living day by day.
—Betty Fussell

There are many helpful ways to live together and apart at the same time. By far, the two most important considerations are a separate entrance and kitchen. It may be a cliché, but the kitchen really is the heart of the home and is traditionally run by the female head of the household. As we learned in some of our interviews, two women trying to manage one kitchen can present serious problems.

In one case, a woman shared the story about her experience living with her mother-in-law. Laura is American and married to a Chinese man from Beijing. He is one of four children—the only son. The prevailing custom in Chinese culture is for the oldest son's parents to move in with him and his family. The young couple recently had a baby, and his widowed mother flew out to California from Beijing to help out. Unfortunately, no time limit was set on her visit. The first problem to surface was that his mother does not speak English, only Mandarin. Not only was Laura unable to communicate with her husband's mother, but also the mother-in-law began to take over her kitchen. Laura began to see all kinds of Asian foods she had never seen before. Without asking, her mother-in-law threw out Laura's cooking pots and replaced them with her own. Along with the pots, she threw out Laura's snack foods, including her cookies. Ouch! When queried about this by her son, she said she thought the cookies were stale. After a few months, mom was asked by her son to return home to Beijing. Laura said that things might have been different, if the mother-in-law had her own place with her own kitchen.

In another case, a woman from Pennsylvania told the story about her mother-in-law coming to live with her, her husband, and their two children. Kathy said that she and her husband both worked and needed help with child-care. Although the mother-in-law was given a wing of their house to live in, she gradually took over the entire house, including the kitchen. Kathy began to feel like it wasn't her home anymore. She told us that she and her husband almost got a divorce over this conflict. However, they eventually built a cottage in the backyard for the mother-in-law, and things have been fine ever since, especially since she now has her own kitchen.

The importance of privacy was also more generally demonstrated in a study of multigenerational living, commissioned and reported by *Builder* magazine. Researchers from San Diego–based Marketscape Research and Consulting spent days in people's homes asking questions and observing how folks actually lived in their houses. The following quote well makes our point:

> Not surprisingly, privacy is a major concern. While the families spend a lot of time together in the kitchens and living areas, each member feels a significant need for a place he or she can be alone. As one grandmother who has her own suite put it, "I've been living alone for four years. I wanted privacy; they're here when and if I need help. That part was very important."[44]

These stories illustrate that *proximity* and *privacy* are two key words to think of when you begin the process of deciding what type of housing to use for extended family living. Once you've made the decision to live together with family members, there are a variety of ways you can. Options include houses with ADUs, duplexes, town houses next door, two or more condos in the same building, family compounds, or cohousing developments. Certainly, houses next door, behind, or across the street from each other, as well as those a few blocks away, can also work.

ACCESSORY DWELLING UNITS

Suitable for one or two people, an accessory dwelling unit (ADU) is a self-contained dwelling, usually installed in the surplus space of a single-family home. It can also be a detached building or a portable unit on the same property. Minimally, it features an outside entrance, a bedroom, a bathroom, and some type of kitchen. In addition, some units may have a living room and an outside patio or deck. At most, an ADU shares an entrance, a yard, and parking with the primary residential unit. It is subordinate to the host home in size and appearance, often invisible from the street. There are many other names for this type of housing, including granny flat, sonny flat, in-law apartment, guest suite, cottage, life-cycle unit, second unit, studio apartment, bonus unit, *casita*, carriage unit, *ohana*, and efficiency apartment.

The ADU is one of the most versatile housing types. It can offer homeowners a good investment with a healthy rate of return; furnish housing for family members (especially elder parents); or provide flexible living space for adult children or grandchildren or even for a nanny, tenant, or caregiver. ADUs can also function as home offices and improve security in the home. This flexibility provides a tremendous advantage to household structure. In our society, which values both community and privacy but provides few choices between those two extremes, the ADU would allow an extended family to live together and apart at the same time.[45]

One Southern California woman has realized these benefits. Susan is divorced and lives in a small residential community. Several years ago, she came up with a novel way to age in place with a multigenerational living arrangement that utilizes a remodeled garage on the same property as her house. At first, she used this ADU as a rental to supplement her income. Then, she allowed her daughter and son-in-law to live in the unit while they both worked on their graduate degrees and subsequently established their careers. After they started their family, Susan traded places with them. While she had the apartment remodeled, she lived in the big house with her daughter and family and found it difficult. She said, "When you're sharing a house with four bedrooms, and you're in one of them and the kids are using the others, it's hard. But, by the time I moved out to the apartment, it was much better. I'm very separated in the sense that I don't even hear the grandkids crying during the night." Here's a story she shared that underscores the benefits of separate living quarters:

> *Susan*: By the way, I just became aware that my daughter's mother-in-law is expecting her own daughter and husband, and their three little boys, to come and stay with her. They now live in Arizona but are moving out here. She was looking forward to sharing space with them for a couple of weeks; then they were going to either rent or buy a place. She's just discovered that they're not planning to buy a house here until the house in Arizona has been sold. Meantime, all the kids will be living with her and her new husband. She is suddenly much more bothered than I thought she would be. It's going to be awfully crowded in her three-bedroom house. Actually, it's four bedrooms, but her husband uses one of them as an office, and he works at home a lot.
>
> Someone said to me, "Oh, she's all upset, and she's really just going to have what you have." And I said, "Oh, no, not at all. We don't share the same roof. I don't hear them wake up. I can go home to my little place and do exactly what I want, play my music loud at night." It just reminded me of the extent of that difference. I mean, my kids can walk over and visit me. That's lovely. But the separation, even sound-wise, I think is quite important.

In another instance, a childless couple has come up with an inventive way to make use of the downstairs ADU at their beach house in Northern California. They loan it out as free vacation housing for their "extended family" of school-teachers. Here's Dan's story of how and why they choose to:

Sharon: What led you to offer your unit to schoolteachers as free vacation housing?

Dan: We have a friend who is a retired local schoolteacher, who lives nearby. We also know another teacher who lives in Los Angeles and stays with us when she comes to visit her brother, who lives in a studio apartment close to us. She typically brings a schoolteacher friend of hers, because our unit is really big enough for two people to stay in comfortably. After we got these three teachers together, they became a circle of friends. Then, among my clients, I have quite a few schoolteachers, and a lot of them are single. A couple of them are divorced and have children. Since their children would be with their fathers on the weekends, they would have an opportunity to get away. However, they don't have the money to spend on something like that.

One day, I thought, "What a great way to give back to schoolteachers!" I think they are the most important people on this planet for what they do. And I thought, "I know these people." So, we let them come and stay for free. We don't charge them. The only prerequisite for them coming is that they just totally enjoy themselves and not think about anything. They don't need to feel obligated at all to call us or knock on the door. We just want them to think that it's their own private little getaway.

It's been so great because I wanted the downstairs apartment to be used a lot more than it had been. By the way, our retired schoolteacher friend helps us out with the reservation process. The teachers who want to use our unit will call her to see when it's available. She also opens up the place for the guest teachers, saying, "This is your place for the weekend." We've had a lot of her teacher friends stay here, too. The other neat thing is that they've all been so considerate about leaving the place clean.

Sharon: Have you heard of anyone else who has offered free housing to teachers?

Dan: No. But I really hope more people will open up their hearts and do the same thing. My basic philosophy in life is: What goes around, comes around.

Sharon: Along with feeling good about making a donation to teachers, do you see any other advantages to having an accessory apartment?

Dan: Definitely. Since we've had the separate unit, when we've had our other friends, not schoolteachers, come and stay, it is just so wonderful for all of us. When you do stay with people . . . and I think everyone has had this experience . . . you try not to inconvenience your hosts. In turn, the hosts do their best to entertain and take care of you, and you are both being inconvenienced. I think that's another facet to this thing, just the convenience that having separate quarters brings. You can have your own privacy and really enjoy your friends more.

MOBILE HOMES

Included in the category of ADUs are mobile homes, trailers, or manufactured housing. More than twenty million Americans now live in these types of structures.[46] Mobile homes can be useful in many ways. For one, they can serve as places to live when visiting family members.

Jack and Mary, a retired couple who live in Arkansas, spend a good deal of their time traveling in their mobile home to visit their four children and grandchildren, who reside in Delaware, Michigan, Washington, and Texas. They typically stay with each child for two months at a time. They can either park in the yards of the children or in nearby trailer parks. Their mobile home allows them the freedom to have their own things in their own place. Furthermore, when the grandbabies start crying or the teenagers start playing loud music, they have a detached place to which they can escape. This is yet another example of the benefit of separation to get away from noise.

DUPLEXES

Duplexes are two homes sharing interior structures, such as a wall or a floor and ceiling, in two-story units. The floor plans of these homes may be identical or different, but usually they offer very similar amenities. Owning a duplex allows the same flexibility as an accessory apartment, in that one of the homes can provide housing for family members, a nanny, a tenant, or caregivers of elders. In fact, duplexes are gaining popularity as adult children are opting to live near aging parents. This home style is ideal for providing semi-regular care to otherwise independent family members. Duplex homes allow each family to retain complete privacy, while proximity makes shared errands and frequent visits easier. Also, since a duplex has two separate addresses, there is no need to sort the mail at the end of the day. Utility bills are separate, too, making that aspect of living together less complicated.

One Northern California woman who co-owns a duplex with her daughter and son-in-law spoke about the advantages of this type of housing. Elena is a high school counselor, who has shared a duplex for the past twenty years with them and her grandchildren. Here's what she had to say:

> *Elena*: After my divorce, I was looking for a small place that I could buy. The places where I wanted to live were so expensive, more than I could afford to pay. At the time, my daughter and her husband were living in an apartment, and I suggested that we find something together. I was willing to buy a house with maybe mother-in-law quarters. That way we could combine our resources. Although they didn't have any money, his parents wanted to help out. They are lovely people, by the way, and so is my son-in-law. So, we looked and looked. Nothing fit until I found this duplex and fell in love with it. It is not the kind of duplex where the two homes are separated by garages. It is L-shaped with the garage in the front and my doorway around the side. But their entrance is on the opposite side, way behind the garage.
>
> *Sharon*: So you have the privacy thing, then.

Elena: That's right. But they do not have an attached garage like I do. I have a single-car garage and they have a double-one that is separate. Their place is not only bigger, but they also have all this space on the side and behind their house, where they can barbecue and entertain. Occasionally, I use it for entertaining, too.

Sharon: That's a nice advantage. Are there other ways living together has been helpful to you?

Elena: Oh, there are lots of other benefits. If something breaks, like a plumbing problem with the toilet, my son-in-law is available to fix it. Many times, I don't even have to ask him . . . he will offer. Being by myself, I do rely on him. I also remember when he and his parents helped paint the inside of both of our units. Then, one time, I had car trouble and they were right there to lend me one of their cars. A while back, I ordered a computer and he put it together for me, and my daughter taught me how to use it. The longer I live here, the more I appreciate their willingness to help out.

Also, I'm here to help them. When we first lived together, if they were going somewhere, I would babysit the cats. I would go over and feed them. Then, later, after they started having children, I would babysit the grandchildren in the evenings. I was right there. They felt good about it, too, because they didn't have to get anybody to look after the kids. I like to help them with the garden, too. Mainly I pull weeds. Another thing my daughter likes about me living next door is she can always help herself to whatever she needs and just leave me a note. Actually, that is neat for both of us because it works both ways. We have keys to each other's places.

Sharon: So it has been a big help to you having the family so close.

Elena: Yes. I feel connected; I don't feel like I'm living alone.

Sharon: Together and apart at the same time.

Elena: Right. I would recommend it. You have to have an open mind.

TOWN HOUSES

A town house is one of a group of two- or three-story houses of similar architectural treatment, usually joined by common sidewalls. Two town houses next door to each other can offer many of the same amenities as a duplex. A young Chinese woman, who lives now in Los Angeles, told us about the benefits of living in the town house next door to her parents and brother. Lan is married, works as a manicurist, and has two small children. A year ago, she and her husband bought their town house and a few months later bought the one next door for her parents and brother. Here's what she had to say about the mutual support and emotional well-being that close proximity has to offer them:

> *Lan*: Having them live so close to us makes it easier for them and easier for my kids, too. My parents can enjoy my kids every day, any time they want. Likewise, my kids feel the same way about their grandparents. They can help me out with my children, and I can help them go to the supermarket and doctor's appointments. I drive them, since they don't drive. Also, my mom has diabetes. I know what she should eat, tell her, and check on her to make sure she knows. Because she doesn't speak English, she never talks to anybody. So if I know something, I'm going to tell her. Since they don't speak English, I'm there more to help them out.
>
> *Sharon*: Was it your idea to live together or was it theirs?
>
> *Lan*: My idea. I'm the one who brought my parents here. I'm responsible for them. I wanted to make sure my parents are happy. If they live far away in China, I'm just nervous. They have retirement income there but no one to look after them when they get older. I brought my brother to the U.S. to help me look after them. It's better to bring them now, so they can help with my kids.
>
> *Sharon*: What I'm hearing from you are positives. But do you ever wish they weren't next door?
>
> *Lan*: No. Someday I would like to buy a bigger home with maybe five or six bedrooms, so my parents could stay in one of them.

Sharon: You could also buy a house that's big enough that you could create a little apartment for them, where they have their own place with an outside entrance and separate kitchen. That way, it's like what you have right now. It's called an accessory apartment. A lot of people are using them now to house older parents.

Lan: That would be great.

Sharon: The neat thing about that is, after your parents are gone, your children may need to come home and stay for a while. We have over 30 percent of American adult children ages 18 to 34 now living at home. That means three in ten. So if you had a little apartment as part of a big house, then you could use it for your adult children. It could become rental income. At some point you could say to the children, "Let's switch. Dad and I will live in the apartment and you can have the house."

Lan: Perfect. You feel good when you can take care of your parents. You always expect your kids to do that, but I don't know about the kids that are born and grow up here. If they see what we are doing now, I think they will do the same thing for us.

Sharon: Children do observe what happens. We have an expression, "What goes around, comes around." So what you do, you get back. Would you recommend your living arrangement to other people?

Lan: Oh, yes. A lot of people say that my parents are so lucky. When they go to learn English at their school, they meet a lot of other parents there. They invite them to come over. When they are all here, sitting around and talking, they tell my mom how lucky she is to have so much room and a daughter next door, too. They love that. They say that they want that, too.

As sensible as duplex arrangements can be, and even though restrictions are being lowered in some states, construction of duplexes continue to languish.[47] We predict duplexes will become a good real estate bet in the near future.

CONDOMINIUMS

A condominium is an apartment house with individually owned units, typically referred to as condos. The condo owners in the complex share in joint ownership of any common grounds and passageways. They elect a board of directors to manage the operation and maintenance of these co-owned facilities. Families who live in the same condo complex, whether next door or on a different floor, can have many of the same benefits as duplex and town house next-door owners. Beverly, a Southern California Realtor, gave us an example of how this works:

> *Beverly*: Over lunch, a friend who also works in real estate told me about an elder client who wanted to sell her home and move to a multigenerational condominium complex. She not only wanted one for herself but also a separate condo in the same building for her divorced 60-year-old adult son. My friend was sure the son wouldn't be interested in moving from his house to a condo, but she followed up with a phone call to him. Surprisingly to her, he was receptive to the idea. Ultimately, he did sell his home and move into a condo in his mom's building. He said it is working out very well. When he travels on business, Mom will look after things for him, water his plants, etc. He doesn't have to worry about maintaining his former house and managing the pool service, the cleaning people, etc. Also, he is nearby if Mom needs help with something and to check in on her.

CONDO CONVERSIONS

These days, a lot of apartment buildings are being converted to individually owned condominiums. A friend told us about a widowed grandfather who sold his big house and bought a small apartment building with four separate apartments. He was able to convert them into separate condominiums, one for himself and the three others for adult grandchildren. Over time, he is gifting the units to them, so they will own them individually. In turn, they will be there to help him out as he gets older.

Condo conversions are being done more as a way for young families to achieve home ownership, as well as to provide affordable housing. Be aware, however, that some municipalities discourage this practice by charging high fees for conversions and some don't even allow it. Consequently, before exercising this proximity option, be sure to check the financial and legal details. You also may want to consult with an attorney regarding these issues. Also, please see chapter 13.

FAMILY COMPOUNDS

A family compound is two or more separate houses on the same property. We spoke to a young woman who lives in Southern California in a family-owned subdivision compound with her husband and four children. Karen is an attorney and real estate broker. Her family developed the property to include three lots adjacent to each other on the same hill. On one lot, there are three structures, including the main house (rented out) and two detached apartments. On the two other lots, there are two additional houses built like duplexes. On all of these properties, in a total of four structures, live two brothers and four sisters with spouses, their mother, and twelve grandchildren. Karen told us about the advantages of having such close proximity with so many members of her family:

> *Karen*: My parents purchased the original fifteen-acre property thirty years ago. My dad, who is now deceased, had the idea that our family members could settle around one another. As the property was sold off and subdivided, different family members purchased the property from my parents. At this point, I co-own a one-acre parcel with my sister. On this property there are three different structures. There is a guesthouse, there is a granny unit, and there is the original house that was built fifty years ago that we rent out. My sister lives in the guesthouse. It is a freestanding unit; she has her own kitchen and shower. My 70-year-old mother lives in another unit with my 45-year-old sister, who has multiple sclerosis. My sister is

very homebound and has her own caregiver, since my mother still works full-time, twelve to fifteen hours a day.

Sharon: So are the guesthouse and the granny unit the same thing?

Karen: No, they are not. It's interesting, three structures but two legal residences. My sister's guesthouse is more like a recreational facility, not a traditional home. So my mother, sister, and brother live in the granny unit, and my other sister, who co-owns the property, lives in the guesthouse.

Sharon: She co-owns the property with you?

Karen: Yes, and I don't even live on the property. We bought it ten years ago and I never moved on to it. We were already in a situation that we were happy with. We live on an adjacent property that my mother also owns. On that one, we have a house that's divided into units. We have the one side. My sister, her husband, and two children live in the other half. They have their own kitchen and bath.

Sharon: Like a duplex in a way?

Karen: Yes, it is. It is something like that. It really is a single residence, but they have their own living area, their own kitchen, and separate entrance. We come through the back and they come through the front. I live in the other part with my husband and our four children. We've lived there for fourteen or fifteen years now.

Sharon: And the three pieces of property are adjacent to one another?

Karen: They are all touching, all around the edge, on a hill. We all share the same swings, a swimming pool with a Jacuzzi, a trampoline, and even a tree house. The kids run up and down the hill from the three houses. They play with each other practically all day. They are in somebody's house, over next door, or up at Grandma's house. The dream my dad had has come true.

Sharon: What do you like about your housing situation? What do you like about living so close to everyone?

Karen: For me, it's ideal; I love it. I think it's because I love being around my family. I continue to grow as a person in the same environment where I grew up. I have so much freedom. Most of all, I love that the cousins can grow up knowing each other.

Sharon: Would you recommend your living arrangement to others? Why or why not?

Karen: You know, in my family every person is so completely different. Because we are four married and two single siblings, that means a lot of different interests and people at different stages. People are financially in different places. People are religiously in different places. Fortunately, the spouses are very easy to get along with, amazingly so. I think that is why it works. I think, if we can do it, others might be able to also.

We also talked to a friend about how her married sister and adult children live together on a 34-acre farm in Kentucky. Three of the four adult children have separate living quarters in this family compound living arrangement. A son has built his own place on the property for his wife and their three-year-old child. He was careful to have a legal agreement over ownership of their home drawn up between himself and his parents, who own the farm. A daughter and her husband, who have spent lots of money for fertility treatments in order to have children, have moved into the main house on the property. They plan to live there temporarily in order to recoup some of their expenses for the fertility treatments by not having to pay rent on an apartment. Fortunately, the daughter is now pregnant with her first child. Another daughter, who is unmarried with a little girl, has moved into a trailer home she placed on the property. As for our friend's sister and her husband, they live in a remodeled cottage on the property. In a variety of ways this extended family has successfully achieved proximity with privacy.

In yet another case, we spoke with a young man who is planning on joining his three other brothers on a family "colony" compound in Hawaii. One brother owns the property and is inviting each of the three other siblings to build their own homes, all with attached *ohanas* (guest units) for family and friends. Here's what Mike had to say about how they were planning to manage privacy in their future arrangement:

> *Mike*: We plan to have a central sort of communal area that all the houses will share. It will include a small structure with a meeting place, an exercise room, and a barbecue pit. But, we will make sure that our individual homes are arranged so that there is privacy if we want it. In other words, we won't be forced to be with everybody all the time and have our own space when we need it.

Actually, Mike's planned family compound with the central communal area has similar elements to another type of proximity-with-privacy housing known as "cohousing."

COHOUSING AND KINLESS AMERICANS

Cohousing refers to a cooperative living arrangement planned and used by both extended families and non-related people who want to live in a communal development together. It features a cluster of single-family houses around a common building utilized for shared meals, childcare, and guest facilities. The residents own their own units and divide duties for maintenance, gardening, and other chores. Most are intergenerational communities in urban centers or next to mixed-use developments.

There are a number of cases where members of an extended family have chosen to join non-relatives in cohousing developments. Once again, it would be important to do your homework to determine if this type of housing is right for you and your family. The Cohousing Association of the United States is a good place to start. The website, Cohousing.org, says that "cohousing communities combine the advantages of private homes with the benefits of more sustainable living, including shared common facilities and ongoing connections with neighbors. These intentional neighborhoods, created and managed by residents, offer an innovative solution to today's environmental and social challenges." Indeed, these cooperative living arrangements can offer long-term savings through energy efficiency, as when neighbors share a car.

This topic of cohousing leads directly to a topic not covered in detail in the two previous editions of our book: elders who have no family. However, we are quite impressed with Paula Span's recent article in the *New York Times* about kinless seniors and we have excerpted from it here:

> Several demographic factors have fostered increased kinlessness. Baby boomers have lower marriage rates and higher divorce rates than their parents, and more have remained childless. The rise of so-called gray divorce, after age 50, also means fewer married seniors, and extended life spans can make for more years without surviving family. "All the pathways to singlehood have grown," said Dr. Deborah Carr, a sociologist and researcher at Boston University. Among older couples, cohabitation has increased as an alternative to marriage, but those seniors are less likely than married couples to receive care from their partners. Those in committed relationships who don't live with their partners are less likely still. In addition, seniors who are Black, female, and have lower levels of wealth have particularly high rates of kinlessness.
>
> The growing number of kinless seniors, who sometimes call themselves "elder orphans" or "solo agers," worries researchers and advocates because this group faces numerous disadvantages.[48] A study of middle-aged and older adults in Canada found that those without partners or children (this study included no data on siblings) had lower levels of self-reported mental and physical health and higher levels of loneliness. They were less likely to participate in activities like sports, cultural or religious groups, or service clubs—a predictor of later cognitive impairment.
>
> Kinless Americans die earlier. Dr. Margolis and her coauthors, using data from the Health and Retirement Study, found that a decade after respondents' initial interviews, more

than 80 percent of seniors with partners and children had survived, compared with only about 60 percent of those without either. At the end of life, researchers at Mount Sinai in New York reported, people without partners and children had received fewer hours of caregiving each week and were more likely to have died in nursing homes.

"Getting old is hard under the best of circumstances and even harder if you're going it alone or with weak social ties," Dr. Carr said.

On the other hand, meet Dr. Joan DelFattore, 76, a retired English professor at the University of Delaware. Like some solo agers, "I had a sense from an early age that I simply didn't see myself as a wife and mother," she said. Preferring to live alone, "I went about constructing a single life," she said.

Dr. DelFattore objects to the perception that older people without immediate family are somehow needy. Dr. DelFattore is in good health, still writes and researches, and she teaches a graduate course every other fall. She stays in near-daily contact with a group of friends, walking several times a week with one of them, and remains close to cousins in New Jersey, with whom she spent Thanksgiving. She takes an active role in several local organizations. And she dislikes "the cultural perception that old people being without immediate family has to mean that you're needy, you don't have support."

Sociologists call that strategy "substitution"—turning to friends and neighbors for the connections and sustenance that families traditionally have provided. In Mount Lebanon, PA, for instance, Celeste Seeman, who is divorced and childless and has lived alone for twenty-five years, has befriended neighbors in her apartment building. When one had surgery recently, Ms. Seeman, 65 and still working as an embroidery machine operator, walked the neighbor's Chihuahuas, did her laundry, and called her almost daily for weeks. "I hope that what goes around comes around," Ms. Seeman said. Because she has outlived her family, after caring for her parents until their deaths, there's no remaining relative to provide similar help if she needs it herself. "I'm frightened about it," she acknowledged, then added, "You can't dwell on stuff. It might not happen."

A study of sole family survivors, the last members of the families they grew up in, found that, for unclear reasons, they were also disproportionately likely to lack spouses or partners and children, and thus were doubly vulnerable.

Of course, having family is no guarantee of help as people age. Estrangement, geographic distance and relatives' own declining health can render them unwilling or unable to serve as caregivers. Still, "our system of caring for the aged has functioned, for better or worse, on the backs of spouses and, secondarily, adult children," said Susan Brown, a sociologist at Bowling Green State University and an author of the study of sole family survivors.

Relying on substitutes has limitations. About two-thirds of older Americans will eventually hit a rubber-meets-the-road moment and require help with the activities of daily living, such as bathing, dressing, and using the toilet. "Friends and neighbors may help with meals or pick up a prescription, but they're not going to help you in the shower," Dr. Margolis said. Dr. DelFattore has prepared for that possibility by buying insurance for long-term care years ago, so that she can hire home-care aides or afford assisted living. Few Americans have done that or can afford the costs, yet most will also be unable to pay for sufficient care out-of-pocket and don't have incomes low enough to qualify for Medicaid.

"Policies tend to lag behind reality," Dr. Carr said. "There was the belief in past decades that older adults would be married and have children; that's what the classic American family looked like. It no longer does." In the absence of any broad public program, experts suggest a variety of smaller solutions to support kinless seniors.

Shared housing and cohousing, providing safety and assistance in numbers and community, could grow, especially with public and philanthropic support. The village movement, which helps seniors age in place, might similarly expand. Revised family-leave policies and caregiver support programs could include friends and neighbors, or more distant relatives like nieces and nephews.

However governments, community organizations and health care systems begin to address the issue, there's little time to waste. Projections indicate that kinlessness will increase greatly as the population cohorts behind the baby boom age. "Younger people are less likely to marry and have children, and they have fewer siblings" as family sizes shrink, Dr. Brown said. "How will they navigate health declines? We don't have a good answer. I'm not sure people are paying attention."[49]

A growing number of kinless elders are getting roommates. One study reports that between 2006 and 2016 the percentage of American elders sharing their homes with non-family members grew 88 percent.[50]

THE HOUSE NEXT DOOR

Living next door to family members can have benefits similar to those of other types of housing already discussed in this chapter. Certainly, the extra space between the homes and separate ownership can make things easier, too. Linda, a woman who lives in Northern California, is delighted to live in the house next door to her in-laws. Linda is married, has four children, and is a homemaker and civic volunteer. Her husband grew up in the same house where his parents are now living on a small lake in the countryside. He liked the setting so much that he suggested to Linda that it would be a great place to raise their family. Twelve years ago, the house came up for sale, and his parents let them know about it. They bought it and have lived there ever since. Here is what she had to say about the "wonderful arrangement" of living so close to her in-laws:

Sharon: Please describe the physical layout between the two properties.

Linda: Years ago, my in-laws bought the lot next door to give them more space. So our house is actually on the other side of that empty lot. I think it was my mother-in-law's idea to put a walkway between our two homes, just knowing that there was going to be a lot of foot traffic back and forth. It's helpful because my husband is currently managing the family business. My father-in-law is still involved somewhat but not in day-to-day operations. So I would say probably four evenings a week after work, my husband will wander next door and they will have a chat about some business. Then usually family issues come up and there is an update on that.

Sharon: What do you like about your housing situation being so close?

Linda: Well, probably on a selfish note, it's so nice to have Nanna there if I need to park a kid somewhere and run out with another child. She is more than happy to do that for me. Just their influence on my children and the fact that my kids have such a close relationship with their grandparents is wonderful. Just as an example, Nanna is instructing my 7-year-old on how to play the flute. He and my 12-year-old will be playing the ukulele that his grandmother taught him how to play and will be in the talent show. So it's time to rehearse, and they go over to Nanna's. It's just very cute. It's the older generation passing on skills and talent to the younger ones. It's really wonderful.

Sharon: Any other things that the other children do specifically with their grandparents?

Linda: Well, the family ranch is nearby. My mother-in-law is still part owner of that operation. There are horses out there and my oldest, Lana, and my youngest, Kelly, like to ride. I'm not a rider. So Nanna picks them up and off they go to the ranch, which is five minutes away. So that definitely is something that she has facilitated and passed on to them.

Sharon: What about Grandpa? Does he take them fishing?

Linda: My husband does that. Grandpa is the gardener. When he is out in the yard, that usually spurs the kids on to go out. "What are you doing? Can I help?" As I said, we do a communal garden between the two houses. Grandpa has always gardened that patch of yard, but in the last two to three years, his interest has dwindled. So then we have come in and picked up on it.

Sharon: What do you grow? How does that work?

Linda: We grow corn, tomatoes, and squash. We started growing our own pumpkins and decorate our home for Halloween. That's a big deal here. It comes alive on Halloween. We needed the corn stalks for that, so we've kept up the corn crop.

Sharon: In what ways do you help your in-laws? Do they travel very much?

Linda: Yes. They do travel. It is interesting how their lifestyle suits the arrangement we have with them. They have a beach house in Carmel and then a cabin in Boulder Creek. Both homes are thirty to thirty-five minutes away. So it's not unusual for them during the winter months to throw their stuff in the car and go to the beach for two nights. In the summer, they will go up to Boulder Creek for weeks at a time and park themselves up there. Then, they are in Hawaii for two weeks out of the year. They like other venues, and they like their time together without the grandkids. That's important to them, too.

Sharon: When they are gone, do you help them with the mail?

Linda: Sure. Mail and watering the plants. And they do the same for us. That's a real plus. We go to Hawaii for one week out of the year together as a family. Then there is one week in the summer when we piggyback with them to the cabin. But other than that, our vacations typically don't overlap. So there is that neighborhood watch, close-up and personal, that goes on.

Sharon: Would you recommend your living arrangement to others?

Linda: Certainly. As long as the personalities are such that you can live side-by-side.

HOUSES ACROSS THE STREET AND BEHIND

Another couple, Lily and Tom, not only have her widowed mother living in a house across the street, but his parents also live in a house right behind them. The latter home is on a separate lot with its own address on a different street. They've added a connecting gate on the common fence between their homes. This arrangement works well for everyone right now. Eventually, their adult son and his family will probably live in one of the homes.

HOUSES NEXT DOOR ON CUL-DE-SACS

A cul-de-sac with no through traffic can be a great place for raising children. Think of that environment with grandparents nearby to help with babysitting. A young couple, Sam and Margaret, bought a house in a new development on a cul-de-sac for themselves and their three small children. They each told their respective parents what they were doing and invited them to consider buying the houses next door, one on each side of them. They did and have lived happily together now for the last five years.

CONCLUSIONS

There are certainly a number of helpful ways that extended families can live together. Having proximity with privacy is the primary key to success. Both Laura and Kathy talked about the importance of separate kitchens. Susan discussed the value of her detached ADU when it comes to noise, as did Jack and Mary with their mobile home. Dan feels good about allowing schoolteachers free use of his ADU for vacations. Elena mentioned the benefit of separate entrances in her duplex housing arrangement. Lan is pleased about the mutual support and emotional well-being that the close proximity of town houses next door has to offer them. Karen is especially delighted that her family compound allows cousins to grow up with each other nearby. Mike is pleased with the design features of his family compound that allow for proximity with privacy. Linda extolled the mutual benefits of living in the house next door to her in-laws. Sam and Margaret enjoy the close proximity of both sets of parents living in houses next door to them on a cul-de-sac. Finally, Lily and Tom are so pleased to have their parents nearby to help them out when needed. The plight of and options for kinless folks are also addressed in this chapter—cohousing seems an important consideration.

Our next chapter talks about extended family living in other countries, as well as within different ethnic or racial groups in the United States. Examples from American history are given, and a view of related data from the U.S. Census Bureau is provided.

CHAPTER 8

OTHER TIMES, OTHER PLACES

The family is the oldest, most firmly grounded human institution. However great the changes may be in the proportion of the population that is married, in the age of marriage, or in the number of years people live within the family, whatever the size of the family may be, however much or little time members of a family spend together, and whatever else they may do individually, apart from all the others, still the family survives.[51]

—Margaret Mead and Ken Heyman

As Margaret Mead and Ken Heyman put it so eloquently, yes, "the family survives." But its form varies from place to place and from time to time. As conditions change, family structures adapt. And throughout history, family residences have been built to accommodate these changes.

The apparent purpose of this chapter is to acquaint the reader with the variety of household structures (both physical and interpersonal) that have existed in different ages in the United States and in different locales around the world. Of course, our discourse is not exhaustive—we don't have the space here. But, the options we list below do serve our deeper purpose for this chapter. That is, we wish to open up your thinking toward creating your own best family and housing arrangements. The white-picket-fence thinking of the recent American past simply will not serve the immediate American future.

THE CHANGING AMERICAN FAMILY

As mentioned in earlier chapters, we see several forces converging to make multigenerational housing a preferred solution to the financial, demographic, and societal pressures of the baby boomers' retirement years. We can already see the changes happening. Indeed, a most interesting set of predictions were made about the changing American family in 1991 in William Strauss and Neil Howe's book *Generations.* Their prescience is remarkable. The authors labeled four generations:

1. G.I.-born (1901–1924)
2. Silent-born (1925–1942)
3. Boom-born (1943–1960)
4. 13th-born, aka Generation X (1961–1981)

The aging Silent will be in a renaissance of the American extended family. More than at any other time in American history, 65-year-olds have parents still living. Nor can the Silent count on their own children to leave home once and for all. Run the 13er "boomerang" child syndrome on fast-forward, and picture a continuing stream of young adults abandoning small urban apartments and returning to the large home of the Silent parents. Sooner or later, many a 13er live-in child will drop the hint, the parent will relent, and the master bedroom *coup d'état* will occur. The typical G.I. parent, who scrimped long years to afford household comfort, would never give in so easily. But the Silent are a softer touch. Having been empty nesters rather early, they will attach less value to the privilege of living alone in a big home. Besides, the Silent will be culturally compatible with their children in ways the G.I.s were not. Around the turn of the century, these 65-year-old rock-and-rollers will get along just fine with their 35-year-old post-punk children.[52] Grandparents will welcome the chance to help nurture a new generation of children—a task they realize they performed too young the first time around. Silent authors will do to the "art" of grandparenthood what they once did to the "art" of sex: They will scrutinize it endlessly, making it the subject of countless books, films, plays, songs, and paintings. And they will professionalize it with consultants, seminars, and global conferences.[53]

In order to better understand the changes we see happening in American families today, it is worthwhile to view them in the greater contexts of history and other global patterns. We start with the first family structures, then move to historical ones in the United States, and finally on to how families manage themselves in other countries.

THE FIRST FAMILY STRUCTURES

As best we can tell, the first prehistoric family households were formed by bands of hunter-gatherers. Reference to the San peoples give us a glimpse of how these original families might have worked, lived, housed themselves, and handled their elders. Hopefully you viewed *The Gods Must Be Crazy*. James A. Michener provides a bit more detail in his description of Gumsto's clan in his historical novel *The Covenant*:

> The clan for which he was responsible numbered twenty-five; more would prove too difficult to feed; fewer, too vulnerable to attacks from animals. His consisted of himself as leader, his tough old wife Kharu, their sixteen-year-old son Gao, plus assorted males and females of all ages and all possible relationships. The safety of his clan was his obsession . . .
>
> His immediate responsibility was to feed his clan, and this day he would mount an attack on the rhinoceros, kill it or be killed by it, then gorge his people with one gigantic meal and move them off to some better site. As he reached these basic decisions, his small brown face was wreathed in a contented smile, for he was an optimist: There will be a better location.
>
> Leaving the dying lake, he went to the living area of his

clan, which consisted of absolutely nothing except a halting place beneath low trees. The terrain of each family was outlined in sticks and a few piled rocks, but there were no huts, no walls, no lean-tos, no paths, no shelter except grass rudely thrown across a framework of interlocked saplings. And each family's area contained only enough space for members to lie in hollows scooped out for their hips. The few possessions had been meticulously selected during centuries of wandering and were essential and tenderly prized: loincloths and skin cloaks for all, bows and arrows for the men, body powders and small adornments for the women . . .

There were weaknesses in the system. Since the husband had to be much older than the wife, there was in any group a surplus of old widows whose men had died at the hunt or been killed by falls when searching tall trees for honey. These elder women were welcome to stay with the band as long as they could function; when they could no longer chew or keep up with the march, they would be placed in the shade of some bush, given a bone with meat clinging to it, and one ostrich egg, and there they died in dignity as the clan moved on.[54]

Such a form and function rendered some family problems easily solved. Housing might be changed to accommodate new kids, and so on, simply by moving about a few rocks and sticks. And, health care decisions about elder members boiled down to which ostrich egg to leave behind with them. There was no yelling at kids about TV, video games, or smartphones. But, the constant worry about starvation perhaps made life on the Kalahari Desert less fun than here and now.

FAMILIES IN HISTORICAL AMERICA

Steven Ruggles, professor of history at the University of Minnesota, reported in an NPR interview that in 1850 some 75 percent of folks over age sixty-five lived with their adult children. That number dropped steadily to a low point of 15 percent by the 1990 census and has again picked up in the most recent census. The thorough research that underpins James Michener's exhaustively detailed storytelling makes it a great tool to demonstrate here corroborating details relative to Professor Ruggles's historical facts:

Maryland

So for the first time she sailed across the river to Peace Cliff and walked up the oyster-shell path to the unpretentious, restful house that stood on the headland, and as soon as she saw it she understood what the brothers meant when they said *telescope*. The humble house built by Edward Paxmore in 1664 was still sturdy, but after his death the growing families of his four children merited additional space, so a larger block of four rooms had been added, with a higher roof line. And when the boatyard had prospered, a real house had been added, with an even higher roof line.

The result was a house tall and solid to the left as one approached it, joined by a lesser middle section, which was joined by a noticeably smaller third. The three buildings resembled a collapsible telescope. "A giant could shove them together," Rosalind said approvingly as she studied the design. "It's neat, efficient, pleasing to the eye, and perfect for this cliff."[55]

Michener also described in this novel what family meant for slaves in America, also using descriptions of the Steed Plantation for it:

The pitiful fact about slavery as it existed on the Steed plantation was its banality. On white and black alike the heavy encumbrances of custom pulled everyone down to a mournful level in which the most extraordinary situations were accepted as inevitable. An unbroken chain of black men and women was purchased for the plantation or bred there, and they existed through the centuries without family names, or recorded histories, or education, or variation, or hope. The male field hands formed an interminable succession of Toms, Jims, Joes; at the big house classical names were preferred, for these gave a kind of distinction to social life: Pompey, Caesar, Hannibal, Napoleon, Brutus. Women in remote fields often bore names that were rarely spoken by their white overseers: Pansy, Petty, Prissy, Pammy, Puss. Generation after generation were judged to be alike: treated alike . . . dressed alike . . . ignored alike . . . and buried alike.[56]

Besides this strange reckoning, Michener also reports that the slave owners took a census and counted their wealth at the same time (see table 8.1):

TABLE 8.1. THE STEED SLAVES

	MALES			FEMALES	
CLASSIFICATION	NUMBER	VALUE ($) EACH	NUMBER	VALUE ($) EACH	TOTAL VALUE ($)
Infants, 0-5	44	0	47	0	0
Children, 6-13	135	300	138	250	75,000
Prime, 14-52	215	2,000	161	1,800	719,800
Older, 53-66	72	1,200	65	300	105,900
Ancients, 67-	16	0	21	0	0
Total	482		432		900,700

Michener's *Chesapeake*, while epic in scope and fictional, teaches the fundamental in the history of family in America that, in the 1800s, landowning Whites lived in flexible housing—they had the space and often the means to expand in the agrarian society of that time and place. Meanwhile, during the years slavery was practiced, enslaved Black people in America suffered; their family relationships depended on the whims of their owners, and elders were literally valued at zero.

We provide another example of how writers of fiction can, with skill, interweave historical fact about the history of the family so that it is subtle, entertaining, yet informative.

Texas/Mexico

Now we head farther south and west to the border area between Texas and Mexico, and to the mystical love story of Tita and Pedro in Laura Esquivel's *Like Water for Chocolate*. There, family structure brought objections, then questions, and eventually tragedy. The 1992 movie based on the book is also wonderful. Just recently the story has been retold by the American Ballet Theatre. (For those of you that recall the book and movie, in the 2023 ballet rendition the entire wedding party cast vomits into the orchestra pit, not in the local river. John was wondering how they would handle that particular scene.)

One afternoon, before Mama Elena told them they could leave the table, Tita, who was then fifteen, announced in a trembling voice that Pedro Muzquiz would like to come and speak with her . . .

After an endless silence during which Tita's soul shrank, Mama Elena asked: "And why should this gentleman want to come to talk to me?"

Tita's answer could hardly be heard: "I don't know."

Mama Elena threw her a look that seemed to Tita to contain all the years of repression that had flowed over the family, and said: "If he intends to ask for your hand, tell him not to bother. He'll be wasting his time and mine too. You know perfectly well that being the youngest daughter means you have to take care of me until the day I die." With that Mama Elena got slowly to her feet, put her glasses in her apron, and said in a tone of final command: "That's it for today."

Tita knew that discussion was not one of the forms of communication permitted in Mama Elena's household, but even so, for the first time in her life, she intended to protest her mother's ruling. "But in my opinion . . ."

"You don't have an opinion, and that's all I want to hear about it. For generations, not a single person in my family has ever questioned this tradition, and no daughter of mine is going to be the one to start."

. . . Still Tita did not submit. Doubts and anxieties sprang to her mind. For one thing, she wanted to know who started this family tradition. It would be nice if she could let that genius know about one little flaw in this perfect plan for taking care of women in their old age. If Tita couldn't marry and have children, who would take care of her when she got old? Was there a solution in a case like that? Or are daughters who stay home and take care of their mothers not expected to survive too long after the parent's death? And what about women who marry and can't have children, who will take care of them? And besides, she'd like to know what kind of studies had established that the youngest daughter and not the eldest is best suited to care for their mother. Had the opinion of the daughter affected by the plan ever been taken into account? If she couldn't marry, was she at least allowed to experience love? Or not even that?

Tita knew perfectly well that all these questions would have to be buried forever in the archive of the questions that have no answers. In the de la Garza family, one obeyed— immediately. Ignoring Tita completely, a very angry Mama Elena left the kitchen, and for the next week she didn't speak a single word to her.[57]

So at least as depicted in one novel, along the Rio Grande at the beginning of the last century, birth order determined elder care roles. That is, Mexican American culture solved the problem by designating the last-born girl as the responsible one. This is in contrast to Chinese culture, for example, which demands that the eldest son take on the responsibility of his parents care in his home. The Chinese solution also involves the difficult wife/mother-in-law interaction. But, at least the constraint of celibacy as in the de la Garza family is not added to the burden.

California

Esquivel's poetic descriptions of family life along the old Rio Grande seem to be confirmed, in our family, by the facts of John's and Emily's own California ancestors. They are sixth- and seventh-generation Californians on their mother's side of the family. It seems their third-great-grandfather died in his youngest daughter's house and care sometime past his one-hundredth birthday. His obituary read:

> José Maria Amador, who was born in 1781 on the site of the City of San Francisco, died in Gilroy on Tuesday, at the home of his daughter. He was the original owner of Rancho San Ramon, covering the site upon which Dublin, Alameda County, stands; but for many years he lived at the Mission San Jose and at Watsonville. He has been married three times, his last wife surviving him. He also leaves seven sons and two daughters. (from the *San Francisco Bulletin*, June 18, 1883)

Shortly before Amador died, he delivered an oral history at the behest of Thomas Savage at the Bancroft Library at the University of California, Berkeley. The old pioneer's accounts of life on the rancho in the San Francisco area, including the slaughter of Native Americans, the early days of the Gold Rush, and the day-to-day activities of Mission San Jose, can all be found on the shelves there today. Savage provided the following preface to the book:

Don José Maria Amador of Watsonville, CA

One of the main objects I had in view in visiting Santa Cruz in June 1877, was to see this ancient Californian, said to have been born in 1781, that is twelve years after the foundation of the first mission in California, and only about five years after that of San Francisco.

I had been assured that Amador had a clear head, an amiable disposition, and a large stock of information which he would not withhold.

My disappointment was great on discovering that he had moved away from Santa Cruz years before, but was living in Watsonville. I went to see him, and found him on a small farm about four and a half miles from town, in great poverty under the care of his *youngest daughter* [our emphasis] who is married and burdened with many children. Amador is also quite crippled from the effects of paralysis which attacked him two or three years ago—the house was such as is found inhabited by the poorest class of Californian rancheros.

Such was the condition of the man after whom Amador County (California) was named, of the son of one of the original founders, Pedro Amador.

He had heard of Mr. H. H. Bancroft's labors in collecting material for a History of California, and did not hesitate one instant in furnishing what he remembered about the past of his country during the Spanish and Mexican domination.

I rode to his dwelling place every morning, and returned to town in the evening, during the seven or eight days, which were industriously employed by me in recording what he dictated—all of which appears in the following pages under the title *Memorias sobre Historia de California.*

Amador's memory was quite fresh and had it been possible for me to make a longer stay in that vicinity, I doubt not that from time to time he would have supplied me incidents, anecdotes, as they came to his mind, to fill up many more pages. As it is, his contribution may be called a substantial one.

—Thomas Savage, for The Bancroft Library, 1877

Sharon, John, and Emily are obviously proud of their deep California roots and often recognize the cultural influences of their Mexican/Spanish forebears. Indeed, we note that Mary Ellen, the younger sister in our family, was headed in the general direction of caring for/living with our own elder mother. But, Mom died suddenly, choosing to live by herself in her own big home against our protestations.

New York

Now back to the East Coast for another "first family" story and to where American history offers another classic example of both how to, and how not to, practice multigenerational living. For example, a few years after Franklin Delano Roosevelt and Anna Eleanor Roosevelt (his childhood friend and fifth-cousin) were married, his mother offered to build them a house. According to Blanche Cook in her biography of Eleanor Roosevelt, mother-in-law Sara not only directed the planning of the Siamese-twin house but also ran both homes after they were constructed:

> On each floor, sliding doors gave Sara full reign of both houses. On the parlor floor, the dining rooms and drawing rooms could be opened onto each other to create a spacious party environment. On the bedroom floor, the children's floor, and the servants' floor, there were connecting passage-ways. The house was designed so that Sara could at any time intrude herself on every level into her children's lives. One never knew, Eleanor wrote, "When she would appear, day or night."
>
> Shortly after they moved into the new six-story town house, Eleanor sat in front of her dressing table, looked into the mir-ror, and wept. She cried and cried, until Franklin appeared to find out what was delaying her for dinner. "I said I did not like to live in a house which was not in any way mine, one that I had done nothing about and which did not represent the way I wanted to live." Franklin made no effort to console his wife or comprehend her pain. He announced that he thought her "quite mad" and assured her she would "feel differently" as soon as she became calmer.[58]

Apparently, Eleanor survived her mother-in-law once she became "calmer." Or, maybe it was after the move to the governor's mansion or the White House?

Some of the folks we interviewed also provided some interesting comments on families in America's past:

Tony: My house in Hartford was built in the 1920s in a neighborhood where the typical design included entry into a front hall which had an open stairway going up. In the front hall there was a French door leading to the parlor. At the top of the stairway there was landing and another French door. The reason for that design was so that if, for example, the breadwinner lost his job, then instantly the family home could become a two-family house. They could rent out one part, so that they did not have to lose everything they had.

Greg: Do you know much about the Amish? They have what they call *grossdaddi* houses. ("Grandfather" in German.) They will build a little house for the grandparents and systematically trade. As the younger generation's family expands, the older generation moves into the *grossdaddi haus*. Do you know the guy who makes granny flats, Ed Guyen, of Coastal Colony Corporation? He's never sold them on the West Coast. They are manufactured houses that you put on treated posts in the ground and put cement around them. He happened to live in Lancaster County [Pennsylvania], where the Amish live. He actually had Amish folks building these things for him. He sort of introduced me to this *grossdaddi* thing. As a matter of course, they trade in terms of family size. It's compelling from a marketing point of view.

Michener's description of the Chesapeake telescoping house was representative. Taken together, all of these examples show us that the American household is constantly changing. Sean Mitchell of the *Los Angeles Times* not only tracked some of the most recent changes, but he also provided a bounty of new ideas that will stimulate new options for the design of housing to fit your own multigenerational family (also see chapter 10 of this book):

The Interior Landscape—Space

How big a house do you want? How big a house do you need? Americans have been trying to reconcile the answers to these two questions for as long as banks have been extending mort-gages. Complicating the responses are family size and level of affluence, personal taste, fashion, and the ever-changing ways in which we live.

Through the years, while garages and bathrooms have mul-tiplied and kitchens have grown in size and stature, living and dining rooms have all but disappeared. Outdoor space has been colonized, media centers have infiltrated, and the home office has nearly supplanted the practically quaint idea of an extra room for guests.

In the master-planned communities designed by Irvine architect Art Danielian, homeowners are rediscovering the modes of a century ago when the family, including grandpar-ents, lived above the store. His 2,500-square-foot Spanish-style homes in the new Pasadera development in Palm Springs include a 240-square-foot detached *casita*, or little house, designed as a space for work or hobbies, "or a place for the mother-in-law," says the architect.

This design shift is directly influenced by the changing demographic of home buyers. Twenty-five years ago, tra-ditional families represented 67 percent of the residential market, says Danielian, compared with today's new house-holds in which 75 percent "are childless families—either empty nesters, divorcees, late bloomers, or singles."

Yet as the median family has stabilized at about 3.15 during the last twenty years, the median size of the single-family home in the U.S., as measured by new construction, has bulked up from 1,560 square feet to 2,340 during the same period, according to the National Assn. of Home Builders. In 2021 the average square feet of new single-family homes had grown to 2,534. "That's enough space for a family of four if you do it right," says Kurt Beckmeyer, an architect in South Pasadena. "But I have a lot of clients who really want big. I'm working on an 11,000-square-foot house right now."

"We're coming back slowly I hope from the excesses of the last 20 years in overscaled homes," says Duo Dickinson, a Connecticut architect and a leader of a downsizing movement to persuade Americans to think smaller in the face of such realities as available sites, swelling building codes and rising construction costs. "People have valued cubic footage over community, and extreme mediocrity has been rewarded with gigantic price tags."

Even one hundred years ago, the need for privacy was a consideration, and many early twentieth-century homes were designed with thick pocket doors that could seal off one large space from another.

"The notion of public versus private space has long been with us," says Robert Timme, dean of the school of architecture at USC. "And it has changed as a result of things happening in social customs. Once, the kitchen was seen only by the cook or the woman of the house. But when people no longer had domestic help, breakfast rooms were added. And when cooking became part of the conversation, the great room was wrought. The den and the living room got married and became one room," he says.

In the tract homes that spread across the nation after WWII to provide housing for returning GIs and their baby-boom offspring, the den was also opened to outdoor light and the formal dining room was sometimes sacrificed to the new open floor plans, borrowed from Frank Lloyd Wright and other modernists.

In this country, the notion of living more efficiently in a smaller space goes back more than 150 years to the American writer Catharine Beecher, a pioneer in the field of home economics who favored utility over decor and put forth the significant idea that a small house, because it was easier to take care of, could be a more comfortable house—understandable from a woman's point of view since women were expected to clean and maintain it.

"Design is powerful and people deserve to take control of their spaces, but I don't see that happening on a big scale," Lockley says. Instead, he has noticed that clients are preoccupied with resale value, which often inhibits them from tailoring a house to their personal needs and style. "A lot of clients are almost frightened by the next buyer," he says. "People tend to look at their houses as financial instruments rather than as homes."[59]

FAMILIES IN OTHER COUNTRIES

Family forms and functions vary substantially around the world, even within individual countries. Consider the Belgian executive who lives with his mother, wife, and kids in a home in Brussels that his family has owned for the last five hundred years. Then there's the common practice of the high-income folks in Cairo buying an apartment house and filling it up with the extended family—grandparents, married siblings, cousins, and kids. Or the Japanese mother caring for her two children, pretty much by herself, often co-sleeping with them at night. Meanwhile her husband catches up on sleep during his four-hours-a-day commuting via train. And, there's the American family in California, where both parents work to support their cars, closets, and kids in college, all the while worrying about aging grandparents halfway across the country in Texas.

Even the ratio of male to female children is affected by culture. For example, the percentage of boys aged one to six years old is 52 percent in India, while in China, the percentage aged one to four years old is 55 percent. Obviously these ratios have long-term implications for families and societies. Moreover, the historical favoritism of boys is deep-seated in such cultures, as demonstrated by the Chinese *Book of Songs*, circa 800 BC:

When a son is born
Let him sleep on the bed,
Clothe him with fine clothes.
And give him jade to play with . . .
When a daughter is born,
Let her sleep on the ground,
Wrap her in common wrappings,
And give her broken tiles for playthings.

All these cultural differences lead directly to differences in how children think and behave. For example, individualism is being taught the first night the American infant is tucked into her own separate bassinet. Values for egalitarianism are learned the first time Dad washes the dishes in front of the kids or Mom heads off to work or the toddler learns that both Grandpa and little brother are properly called *you*. In the last case, most cultures have at least two words for *you* that must be learned to be used properly. So a child in Spain learns almost immediately that social hierarchy is important—*usted* for some people and *tú* for others.

ELDERS' YEARS AROUND THE WORLD

Yes, the form and function of the family varies around the world. But, the fast aging of the American population is by no means unique. Table 8.2 well illustrates how some countries are actually ahead of the United States in this regard.

TABLE 8.2. RETIREES (65+ YEARS) PER 100 WORKERS

COUNTRY	2010	2030
United States	18.2	27.0
Germany	25.0	34.5
China	11.2	20.4
Japan	26.3	33.4
Russia	16.3	25.6
Brazil	10.5	17.2

Source: U.S. Census, International Database, 2010.

We should certainly be watching Germany, Japan, and China as they man-age their aging population ahead of us. For example, the Japanese are leading the development of elder safety surveillance technologies.[60] They are now sort-ing out the privacy issues with such innovations, and we should be watching them (irony intended). Now let's take a quick look at how folks around the world organize their families.

Ireland

What happens when there's a shortage of grandparents? In Ireland today, 11.2 percent of the population is sixty-five years of age or older, while in the greater European Union the percentage is 16.8. Big families were the norm in the 1950s in the heavily Catholic Republic of Ireland, and now several siblings are available to take care of the relatively small elder population of today. Imagine yourself with eight brothers and sisters to share the responsibilities of caring for aging parents! So, in Ireland today there is actually a shortage of grandparents. The following is a story about how one family adjusted to the problem:

> The attending physician asked, "Who's his next of kin?" Anne Gallagher blurted out, "I guess I am." And ultimately the words made it so.
>
> Seventy-year-old Dick Madden lay in bed in a Dublin hos-pital ward for indigents dying of pneumonia. The doctors kept him alive, but Anne saved his life. Anne is trained as a nurse but now is perhaps Ireland's greatest connector. As founder of a peace-building organization that she named Seeds of Hope, she seems to know everybody on the island, North and South, Protestant and Catholic, ex-prisoners and policemen, rich and powerful, and folks in the direst of straights, like Dick. She finds common interests and makes introductions and thus strengthens the peace that's held in Northern Ireland during the last decade.
>
> She also rescues people like Dick, a stranger she met on a cold and rainy street and helped to the hospital. She visited

him during his recovery. When he was well, she and her husband, Jerry, moved him into a small flat near their home in a Dublin suburb and invited him to gain strength in their own home. The Sunday suppers sustained both his body and soul. They gave him a key to their front door and he helped out with their 14-year-old son, Jared. Both Anne and Jerry work full-time, with Anne spending days at a time helping to repair community in the still-divided Belfast in the North.

Indeed, the best part of the story is the "grand relationship" that developed between Jared and Dick. Jared's a youth champion at both hurling and Gaelic football, and his biggest supporter has been Dick. He never missed a game and was the community's most ardent fan. Thus developed five years of a growing three-generation relationship. During the last year, when Dick's health failed him again, he moved into Anne's house to die. She wouldn't let him go back to the hospital. Anne, Jerry, and Jared all helped keep Dick comfortable as he faded away finally:

> So, Dick died at home, surrounded by his adopted family. Jared was holding his hand when he passed, and he kissed his forehead at the services attended by scores in his adopted community. Dick is particularly missed by his breakfast bunch and his fellow sports fans and parents. Jared misses his best friend.

So in such a way, in a land where a shortage of grandparents exists, Anne created a grandparent relationship for her son Jared. Anne's own dad had died a number of years earlier and her eight siblings take good care of her mom up in Belfast. It wasn't a conscious act, but this very personal connection she made in her own family served all very well.

Norway

At least according to *Parade* magazine, they apparently they don't have a shortage of grandparents in Norway:

A Norwegian woman is trying to auction off her father on the Web. "Giving away my dad to a nice woman in Trondheim," wrote 25-year-old Nina Melhum Gronland, who was looking to free herself of her father, Odd Kristiansen, 52. Odd had moved in with his daughter and her family after ending a long-term relationship. "Dad is tall, dark, and slim and in his best age," she wrote. "I am tired of him living with me. Furniture comes with him. Serious!"[61]

France

Adam Gopnik reports in his entertaining book about his residence in Paris:

The national craze for early retirement may be an employee's twist on an employer's gimmick, but its roots are cultural. Retirement isn't scary here. In America one unmentioned aspect of the Social Security debate is the feeling people have that to stop working is, in a sense, to stop living. It is the vestibule of death. In France there is no equivalent anxiety—and there are no great Florida-style gulags for elders. One of the striking things about Paris is that it is filled with old people who actually look old: bent, fitted out with canes, but dining and lunching and taking the air and walking their small, indifferent dogs along with everybody else. The humiliations visited upon old people in America—dressed up like six-year-olds, in shorts and T-shirts and sneakers, imploding with rage—aren't common here. The romance of retirement is strong. The right-wing *Figaro*, for instance, though editorially opposed to the move for very early retirement, ran a series of pieces about the "young retired"—people still in their forties and fifties who have managed to stop working. The series described people who at last have time to "reflect"; it was written in exactly the same admiring spirit that an American daily might use for a series about old people who are as busy as all get-out.[62]

Belgium

European economists decry the lack of mobility in their labor force. Folks just won't move to follow the jobs. Indeed, the family of a friend at a Belgian university has lived within 500 meters of the same spot for 500 years—that's immobility at its worst, or perhaps best? The story is related by Jean-Paul, the forty-five-year-old father of two:

> *John*: You talked about three-generation households being more common in Belgium. Can you talk about the rest of Europe and about the economic sense of the lack of mobility and desire to stay in one place? In the States, we are all commuting.
>
> *Jean-Paul*: I have the feeling this is more of a Catholic thing that at least one child stays at home. I'm telling you this because I had some Dutch girlfriends and the moment I started talking about relations, future, and marriage, the opinion of their parents was that there are two moments when children should leave the house. One moment is when they start to study, they go to another city, and they don't come back anymore. The other moment is when they get married; then they should move out. I saw this happening much more in the Netherlands, particularly in the north. There, more people are Protestant. So I think it's a little more . . . maybe an old-fashioned Catholic thing where you stick together, where the family has to be closely connected. Maybe it's more of a Protestant thing that you say families are important but not that important.
>
> *John*: What do you think the advantages are of having three generations in one household?
>
> *Jean-Paul*: Since we were living in a very large family house with a lot of space, there was also a lot of emotional space. I think in our modern culture this is an important condition. If you don't have that condition, it doesn't work. It's completely impossible. A lot of times this practical stuff creates a big limitation.

In our house, we don't use the same bathroom or the same kitchen. We have a totally independent living level on the first floor and a totally independent living level on the second floor. If we would have a little bit of an intense situation, my wife would live completely downstairs without going upstairs and my mother could live upstairs without going downstairs. That gives a big psychological advantage.

John: You talked about the relationship between your mother and the kids already. But can you see anything that affects the kids' behavior and values and things like that? Maybe in Protestant Europe the kids don't have the grandparents in the house or even in the province. They seldom see them and there is no passing on of the values, etc.

Jean-Paul: That is where that wonderful, old, wise person comes in. It's not a threat; it's not a policeman dictating to you what to do. It's an old, wise person who says, "I have no power anymore. Allow me to show something of my experience." Then they go out of the room and they suddenly see their parents differently. I remember that from my grandmother until my father died. My grandmother was 99. She did not live in our home, but it was always wonderful to talk with her.

John: She lived right in the neighborhood? So did you go there in the afternoons?

Jean-Paul: She lived very close by. I'd visit her once a week, Sunday or . . . I remember that sometimes I would talk with her other times as well.

John: Is there anything you want to add on this topic?

Jean-Paul: As I said, I think it's wonderful, but it's difficult because there is no standard recipe to do it. For people who have their parents in the home or one of their parents, it's a wonderful tool to teach yourself how to handle people in general. Then, when you look into a company, an organization, you see all kinds of variations of people there. It makes you sometimes a little bit more wise.

So, Jean-Paul lives in the house of his ancestors with his mother, wife, and two children. The arrangement has its ups and downs, but it all seems quite natural for all. The benefits are there for all three generations. And, such an arrangement is common in many areas of Europe, particularly so in the Catholic areas. Indeed, when we lived in Spain (Sharon in the 1970s and John in the 1990s) we saw Spaniards living at home well into their twenties—usually not moving out until marrying, if then.

China

Peter Hessler, in his wonderful book *River Town*, compares how things work in rural China and America:

> The families I knew in Fuling were arguably closer than the average in America, because individual members were less self-centered. They were remarkably generous with each other, and often this selflessness extended to good friends, who were also drawn into tight social circles. Collective thought was particularly good for elders, who were much better cared for than in America. In Fuling I never saw older people abandoned in retirement homes; they almost always lived with their children, caring for grandchildren and doing what they could to help out around the family farm, business, or home. There was no question that their lives had more of a sense of purpose and routine than I had seen among elders at home.[63]

Our own observations twenty years ago in Beijing's Hutong District also demonstrate the emphasis the Chinese put on family and how housing has been adapted accordingly. The term for this old district in Beijing comes from the Mongolian word *hottog* (water well). Originally, villagers built their homes around convenient sources of water. *Hutong* literally means a narrow lane or alley. In fact, it is the passage between homes called *siheyuan* (a compound with houses built around an inner courtyard). Before 1949 these courtyard housing compounds were used by extended families, including some servants.

However, after the communist takeover, these high-income houses were converted to multifamily apartments with huts filling in the courtyards to save on
precious space.

We visited a family living in the district in August 2003, shortly after
the SARS travel ban was lifted, allowing tourism to begin again in Beijing.
The quarters were tight, Mr. and Mrs. Xin living in a large 20x20 room that
included their bed in one corner and dining and entertainment area in the
other. There was a separate small kitchen area for cooking and food storage.
They shared bathroom facilities with the ten other families living in their compound. Both were retired and in their seventies and had lived in the house
since 1949. They had raised a son there and now their teenage grandson was
visiting. He often stayed there, as well. They had a large color television and
a microwave oven, both beside the kitchen table. The teenager, like so many
Americans his age, had a cell phone in his pocket. That day the Xins were also
caring for a neighbor's six-year-old son. The boy obviously had the run of the
house and kept Mr. Xin laughing.

Before the Beijing Olympics in 2008, there were pressures to demolish the
hutong districts, which many believed to be important cultural treasures. Some
were saved by Beijing's new millionaires, who bought the compounds from the
multifamily residents, cleared out the courtyards, and reestablished the traditional, extended family compound idea. But, the land is precious and only 260
hutongs with 2,000 siheyuans survived the redevelopment projects, this despite
sit-in protests by middle-aged and elder residents like the Xins.

Perhaps the most interesting challenge facing the Chinese these days is not
housing redevelopment—that's proceeding at a breakneck pace. The real conundrum for the society will be the consequences of the one-child policy on elder
care during the coming decades. They are fast headed toward a demographic
scenario where one child is supporting two elder parents and four oldest old
grandparents. The good news is that the prospective grandparents are investing
big time in their "little princes," and the latter are enjoying the blessings of four
"grand" relationships.

Finally, it is worthwhile to include a few wise words from anthropologist
Edward T. Hall's still-pertinent book, *The Hidden Dimension*:

Fixed-feature space is one of the basic ways of organizing the activities of individuals and groups. It includes material manifestations as well as the hidden, internalized designs that govern behavior as man moves about on this earth. Buildings are one expression of fixed-feature patterns, but buildings are also grouped together in characteristic ways as well as being divided internally according to culturally determined designs. The layout of villages, towns, cities, and the intervening countryside is not haphazard but follows a plan which changes with time and culture.

Even the inside of the Western house is organized spatially. Not only are there special rooms for special functions—food preparation, eating, entertaining and socializing, rest, recuperation, and procreation—but for sanitation as well . . . [64]

Actually the present internal layout of the house, which Americans and Europeans take for granted, is quite recent. As Philippe Ariès points out in *Centuries of Childhood*, rooms had no fixed functions in European houses until the eighteenth century. Members of the family had no privacy as we know it today. There were some spaces that were sacred or specialized. Strangers came and went at will, while beds and tables were set up and taken down according to the moods and appetites of the occupants. Children dressed as, and were treated as, small adults. It is no wonder that the concept of childhood and its associated concept, the nuclear family, had to await the specialization of rooms according to function and the separation of rooms from each other. In the eighteenth century, the house altered its form. In French, *chamber* was distinguished from *sale*. In English, the function of a room was indicated by its name—bedroom, living room, dining room. Rooms were arranged to open into a corridor or hall, like houses into a street. No longer did the occupants pass through one room into another. Relieved of the Grand Central Station atmosphere and protected by new spaces, the family pattern began to stabilize and was expressed further in the form of the house.[65]

CONCLUSIONS

Except for the United States during the last fifty years, three-generation house-holds have been the norm around the world and throughout history. Different cultures have solved the problem of caring for elders in different ways: For San it's ostrich eggs and shady spots, for Hispanic families it's been the youngest daughter, and for the Chinese, the eldest son. Here in America in 2024, we are blessed with the freedom to set up households pretty much any way we want if we allow ourselves to think creatively about how best to organize our families and our housing.

Room for Thought 8.1.
Is It a Tsunami or an Earthquake?

In 2009, 178 million Chinese were over 60. That figure could reach 437 million—one-third of the population—by 2050 . . . "It's a demographic tsunami," says Joseph J. Christian, a fellow at Harvard University's Kennedy School of Government who specializes in housing issues for seniors in China. "The whole multigenerational housing model has disappeared."[66]

UNLIKE an earthquake, a demographic disaster does not strike without warning. Japan's population of 127 million is predicted to fall to 90 million by 2050. As recently as 1990, working-age Japanese outnumbered children and elders by seven to three. By 2050 the ratio will be one to one.[67]

CHAPTER 9

DESIGNING AND
REMODELING

*Virtually everything man is and does is associated
with the experience of space.*

—Edward T. Hall

Sharon and John's cousin Frank is a retired writer who planned ahead for himself. He currently lives alone on Kangaroo Island in Australia, while his daughter lives with her family 1,000 miles away in Sydney. When Frank goes to visit her, he likes to stay for a few weeks. With his daughter's permission, he had an apartment with a separate kitchen and its own entrance built onto her house for himself. Frank paid for it and gifted it to her. He is pleased to have his privacy, along with peace and quiet during his long stays with his daughter, her husband, and their three active children. Eventually, Frank will move there permanently, when he can no longer take care of himself. Until that time, he plans to visit his daughter and her family and stay with them in his own attached apartment.

Whether you are thinking of remodeling your home to add an ADU for your elder parents or adult children, or even planning ahead for your own future needs as Frank did, you can accomplish this in a variety of ways. In many cases, a separate dwelling unit can be carved out of your home or added to it. You can extend existing bedrooms, close off walls, or convert surplus garage, attic, and basement space. If your single-family home site has the land or space, you also can build a cottage in the backyard. Furthermore, if you live on property with an existing barn, you can convert it into housing for family members. Given the American preference for privacy and independence, the ADU is a type of architecture that allows families or individuals to live together and apart at the same time.

HOME CONVERSIONS

Research indicates that one-third of American houses have the space to add an accessory unit. Patrick Hare, a national expert on ADUs, took data from the 1987 American Housing Survey and determined that 32 percent of all single-family homes with five rooms or more were occupied by two persons or fewer. The term *rooms* does not include basements, garages, or attics, all of which offer additional space for accessory units. On the basis of those figures, he concluded that 32 percent or almost one-third of American homes have the potential of creating new ADUs.[68] As both the size of new homes and elder population have increased during the last three decades, the numbers of homes that might accommodate an ADU have ballooned, as well.

The relatively minimal cost of creating a dwelling unit out of existing interior living space makes it more affordable than other types of remodeling projects that involve extending walls or raising the roof to add a second story. For instance, for as little as $10,000 to $20,000 in material costs, an outside door can be added to a single-story home, a laundry room can be converted to a small kitchen, an existing bedroom can be used as a living area, and another existing bedroom and bathroom can be used as such. The apartment can be made private with the installation of a wall with a lockable door at the beginning of the hallway leading to it, effectively closing it off from the rest of the house. Because these types of units use existing space, they typically can be installed for one-third the cost of constructing a standard rental unit.[69]

Indeed, there are a variety of ways to add a second living unit to an existing single-family home. Inspiration can be found with renovation television/online programs and books, for example Michael Litchfield's *In-Laws, Outlaws, and Granny Flats*. Additionally, Patrick Hare also includes drawings of a split-level house lower-level conversion; a two-story house second-floor conversion; and a town house basement conversion in his book, *Creating an Accessory Apartment*.

When working with an architect or designer to remodel your home to add an accessory unit, there are a number of ways you can prepare for the initial meeting. You will want to think ahead of time about your space needs, lifestyle issues, and home layout. Also, figure out which family member will be the project manager. Noreen, a Northern California architect, had this to say about working with one of her clients:

> *Noreen*: When I worked with Paul, he wanted to modify his existing single-family home so he could live there with his daughter, her husband, and their child. The young family was to live in the main house, and Paul would have his own private apartment with a separate kitchen and entrance there, too. They did want to have the two units connected with a door, as well, to be convenient and provide easy access to his grandchild and the public area of the main house. It allows 5-year-old Gail to come over to see him when she wants to, without having to go outside.
>
> When I first started working with them, we talked about their space needs. How did both families want to use their public and private areas? We determined where people would sleep and work. Paul wanted a room with a big table where he could spread out drawings related to his work. It also has a foldout hide-a-bed for guests. His son-in-law, Tom, also needed a separate office to work in. As I said, they both wanted their own kitchens. Paul did not want a dishwasher. His bathroom has a shower. His daughter wanted a tub for young Gail's bathroom. We installed plumbing for a shower in the tub for her to use when she got older as well.
>
> When working with clients, we also look at lifestyle issues. Those who live in California are inclined to want "California casual"—a combined living, dining, and kitchen room. In the East, lifestyles tend to be more formal and separate.

In addition, we see how the house is laid out. Do they want the laundry room in the house or in the garage? Where do they want the sleeping, work, and play areas?

Also, we research building code requirements. For example, in some municipalities, if a second unit is added, fire sprinklers are required throughout the house. Off-street parking also comes up, along with square footage requirements. Furthermore, in some cases, the owner has to live on the property if a second unit is put on it. That has to be part of the title.

Sharon: What about noise issues in remodeling homes when a second unit is added?

Noreen: We put in sound insulation between the floor joists. Any connecting walls or floors call for sound insulation. Also, floor coverings are important. Carpeting is obviously quieter than wood or tile floors. Also, the installation of quieter plumbing pipes with insulation is important. Room furnishings, such as draperies and upholstered couches, can also affect sound.

Sharon: Do you have suggestions for people considering remodeling their home to add an accessory apartment?

Noreen: Don't be afraid to go to a professional beforehand for guidance. You're talking about quality-of-life issues. I've talked with clients who have a baby on the way or a mother-in-law about to move in with them. Plan ahead; don't be frozen into inactivity.

Lina, a divorced seventy-year-old secretary with an insurance company, paid for an apartment addition to her daughter's home in Connecticut. Lina's daughter, husband, and their two children live in the main house. She was originally planning to go to Florida to live after she retired, but her four adult children did not like the idea of her living so far away by herself. After a medical incident left Lina hospitalized for two months, they finally talked her out of it. Here's what she had to say about her involvement with remodeling her daughter's home to accommodate her joining the family:

Lina: My problem was the housing in the area was so expensive, particularly for a single person with a limited income. A friend suggested I sell my house and use the proceeds to build an apartment attached to my daughter's home. My daughter thought it was a great idea. The folks at City Hall didn't object as long as I lived in it—it couldn't be built as just a rental unit. The place is about 1,000 square feet with a kitchen, a living room, and a half-bath downstairs. Then, I have a bathroom and bedroom upstairs. I put my washer and dryer upstairs as well. Also, I have my own separate entrance.

Sharon: You paid for the remodel. Did you have choices on what color to paint the walls?

Lina: Yes, I designed it. I have a friend who is an architectural designer and she helped. I was very careful to include my daughter and son-in-law in the process. I would ask, "Would you mind if I did this or if I added that?" I think it's a whole-house look. It's part of their house. I want them to know and to feel that this is their house, even though this section is mine. I just try not to be a pain.

Sharon: Anything you would change about your addition?

Lina: Yes. I don't have a basement or a garage. So even though I have a lot of storage spaces, there are some things I don't have places for. I miss the space. On the other hand, maybe that's good because then I don't clutter too much.

Sharon: But storage space is still something to think about in terms of making an addition to a home. If possible, be sure to create more storage space.

Eric, a young college student living in Wisconsin, told the story of his parents adding an upstairs apartment with two bedrooms, a kitchen, and a bathroom to their home for his grandfather to live in. It has an outside entrance and worked until the grandfather could no longer use the stairs. He then decided to move in with another family member nearby. Eric helped his grandfather move out before he moved into the ADU himself and started to remodel it:

Eric: I like the fact that it's something I can fix up. You know, if you rent a place you're not going to fix it up. So I try to upgrade it, since I know it will help my parents.

Sharon: So you are actually helping out by doing a little bit of remodeling stuff?

Eric: Yeah, we put in a new kitchen sink and new flooring, stuff like that. I like doing it. I am learning a lot by fixing up the place.

Sharon: Well, it's kind of a win-win situation because you're helping out, but you also get to live there.

Margaret, an interior designer living in Illinois, remodeled her current home to include an accessory unit for her mother with a small wet-bar kitchenette, a living area, two bedrooms, and a bathroom. It includes a stairway but also the space to add an elevator, should her mother need to use one in the future. Here's what she had to say about it:

Margaret: We originally considered getting a condo for my mother that is just a short distance from here, within the neighborhood. Then, we got to thinking about how difficult it would be to have to run back and forth all the time. Also, the condo would not be a single story for her. She would have to go up and down the stairs so many times because the bedrooms are all on the upper level, and the living space is down on the ground level. Since we have a very large house here to start with (3,600 square feet), we thought, "Why not add on to this?" It certainly made sense in terms of investing the money here rather than buying another place. It would increase the equity in our own place. She would be close at hand, and if anything came up, we would be right here.

So, we built an addition of about 1,500 square feet so my mother could come and live with us. We did that in 1999. It took about eight months to get everything in order. We moved her here from Los Angeles. She loves her little place with us. It gives her privacy; it gives us privacy. She can come down when she needs to. She used to eat every meal with us. But now she has to watch her sodium intake and, in order to control that, she fixes her own meals and eats all of them upstairs.

Sharon: Anything you would have done differently?

Margaret: Well, there is one thing I probably would have stuck more to my guns on. When we first wanted to build this addition on our house, we encountered problems with the property line on one side of the house, where we were planning to push out and do a one-story addition. There was a question about the property line and who owned from the ridge of the hill down to the water, which is not usable to anyone, really. But there is a setback. If you couldn't use that as a setback, then you had to come back another ten to fifteen feet from that edge of the hill. That wouldn't have allowed us enough room to put the addition out in that direction. I would have waited a little longer and pushed a little harder to have that happen as a single story for her. Then she could have had an exterior entrance and would feel a little more independent, as well as not have to go up and down the stairs.

Sharon: You have covered the base, though, with your idea of providing space for an elevator that could be installed if needed.

In a further example, a middle-aged couple who live in Illinois remodeled their home and put in an ADU for the wife's parents downstairs. Her parents were invited to come and live with them and did so. Subsequently, the mother developed a medical problem that required her daughter's help on a daily basis. Because of the living arrangement they had set up ahead of time, and because the daughter worked out of her home as an editor, she was easily able to help her mother. Also, her parents did not need to suffer the additional anxiety and stress of moving to a senior facility.

COTTAGE ADDITIONS

When possible, for privacy, it is preferable to have completely separate living quarters on the same property.[70] Many people are building a detached cottage or guesthouse on their property to allow aging parents or adult children to join them now or in the future. Todd and Lynne own and operate two nursery schools in Colorado. They are building a large house for themselves and their two young daughters and also plan to include a cottage for Todd's parents. Originally, his parents were going to buy their current house from them and live nearby. However, his parents have since reconsidered. They want to simplify their lives, to downsize to a new and smaller place that doesn't require the expense of remodeling or as much upkeep. Todd explained how they are including their parents in the process of designing the guesthouse on their new property:

> *Todd*: Actually, my stepdad is a professional home designer and is not only designing our house for us but is also planning the guesthouse. So, it will be entirely what they want for themselves. We still need to check with the city about the possibilities. There might be a limit to what we can do.

A young Northern California couple planned ahead for their parents' future care by building a cottage in their backyard. In the meantime, it has become a revolving-door guesthouse, with different family members and friends living there for several months at a time. Diane is a young homemaker and community volunteer. Here's what she had to say:

> *Sharon*: How did you get involved in building it?
> *Diane*: It started out with the idea of having an extra bathroom and shower for the children near the swimming pool. But, knowing my dad was ill and that my mom would be coming more often for long periods of time, we also wanted a space for her to stay. So the guesthouse idea came up and we drew up plans. They were approved by the town. We decided to put in a Murphy bed instead of making it a full-time residence or guesthouse. It became an extra space, kind of a hangout place for the kids. But then it could be used for someone to stay for a short

period of time. Along with the living area and a foldaway bed, it has a little kitchen and a bathroom with a big closet.

Sharon: Anything that you would change if you could about the guesthouse?

Diane: Add a washer and dryer. But, I think if we do that people would stay too long.

Another young couple living in Oregon put in a guest cottage for his mother, who babysits their daughter while they are traveling for their work. Jim and Christine, along with his mother, Madeline, talk about how they worked together to design and build the cottage:

Madeline: We met with the builders and looked at apartments and different floor plans to try to figure out what was too small, what was too big, and try and get some ideas. Jim and Christine then came up with the final floor plans. They did a great job. I was able to bring with me my important furniture pieces and be surrounded with my things. They even designed a wall at an angle to accommodate my favorite antique carved wooden chest from China.

Christine: When Madeline moved into her new cottage, almost all of her original stuff went with her. So she now is surrounded by 95 percent of it.

Sharon: What about wall colors for the new place? Who made those selections?

Jim: We encouraged her to pick out all the colors as well as the carpets and the flooring. The only thing that we selected was the cabinets.

Sharon: So that gave you more of a sense of it being your home?

Madeline: Yes, it is 800 square feet. It has one bedroom, a living room, a kitchen, a bath, a laundry room, and a very large walk-in closet off the bedroom, which is almost big enough to fit a bed. It also has a small covered patio. The cottage is absolutely lovely.

GARAGE CONVERSIONS

It is possible to convert a garage into an accessory apartment. However, before doing so, it is advisable to hire an architect or building designer to conduct a feasibility study. You will want to determine if there is enough space available on your lot for a "habitable living area" addition and whether the conversion will conform to all building codes required by your local planning and zoning office. Also, you may want to request a zoning classification for the site, along with papers describing zoning regulations and the application-and-approval process.[71]

Be aware that one of the issues that comes up with garage conversions is where you will park your cars in the future. Do you have enough room for tandem parking, that is, one car parked behind another? You would need 20 feet in front of the garage for an extra parking spot or "20 feet from the leading edge of this parking stall to the front property line."[72] Will cars evicted from the old garage have no place but the street to park? What impact would this have on your neighborhood? You might want to talk to your neighbors beforehand to see what they think of your plans.[73] Also, you may be required to have covered parking for one or more cars located at least 20 feet in from the front property line. If there is enough space available, you could consider building a carport in front of the former garage or somewhere else on your property. Be sure to find out what your city requires in the way of parking, including setbacks, number of spaces, and building dimensions. Typically, the minimum width for a single-car garage is 12 feet.[74]

If you are considering converting a portion of a two- or three-car garage into a studio apartment, there are special conditions that must be met when constructing a wall between the new room and the remaining garage. The new wall must meet fire-resistant building codes that are even more strict than those for an interior wall in a house. Moreover, in some cases, a garage cannot open directly onto living quarters, so you won't be allowed to put a door between the new room and the garage. Again, look into what your city's planning department requires.[75]

In short, although there are not a lot of code requirements for a garage because it's just a storage area, there are many code requirements for a space that will be inhabited. It has to be both safe and comfortable to live in. Besides the basic structural, electrical, and plumbing requirements, there are also "habitability" codes that regulate ventilation, natural light, insulation, floor covering, and minimum room sizes.[76] To be livable, your apartment must be weather-tight, well ventilated with windows, heated in winter, and furnished with comfortable lighting and flooring.

In many instances, people are converting garages into apartments for rental income. In one case, Helen, a single Northern California Realtor, remodeled her garage into an apartment with an outside entrance, bedroom, living area, kitchenette, and bathroom. It has the potential for many uses. She uses it now as a rental, but, in the future, someone could live there and take care of her. Likewise, a single friend of ours has remodeled her garage into a smaller, 400-square-foot "sonny flat." Our friend's three-bedroom home was becoming too cramped for her bookkeeping business and two teenage children, so she created the new studio apartment for one of her sons. When he moves away, she plans to use the unit for rental income.

Susan, a divorced college professor in Southern California, initially had her garage made into an apartment and rented it out for income. When her daughter and husband needed a place to live while completing their graduate degrees, she offered the space to them. Subsequently they had a baby. Here's what she said happened next:

> *Susan*: It soon became evident that the three of them over in this little tiny apartment and me in this great big house was kind of silly. So, there was a point when they moved into the house, and I moved out to the apartment. But that transition was relatively difficult. When you're sharing a house with four bedrooms, and you're in one of them and the kids are using the others, it's hard. But, by the time I moved out to this apartment, then it was much better. And I'm very separated in the sense that I don't even hear the kids crying during the night. Furthermore, I had sort of lost interest in keeping the big house up. I didn't want to remodel or make any serious changes. Whereas, with my new apartment, I've had a great time remodeling and having everything new and bright and shiny and lovely.

Sharon: You did remodel your apartment yourself; you put in a sunroom.

Susan: Right. Then I put in one of the storage walls, which is beautiful and made out of maple. Then I did a completely new kitchen and finally finished the floors to match the ceramic tile floor in the sunroom. That's been kind of fun and makes it really nice.

Sharon: How would you describe the physical layout of your apartment?

Susan: The main apartment was sort of the bedroom and kitchen. That's where I've done most of the remodeling. Also, there's a bathroom beyond that. It's more like a Pullman kitchen. It's not a big kitchen, but it's very well laid out. You walk through my sunroom into what you might call my sitting/living room/kitchen. I had a whole wall installed for storage. That's what you end up being short of when you go from a big house into a cottage. By the way, my sunroom is the place where I entertain.

It's also possible to build an accessory unit above a garage. A young couple living in Utah have benefited from her parents making this type of addition to their home. Brenda, an elementary school teacher, and her husband, Joe, a Realtor, are living there rent-free in order to save money to buy their own place. They described their living situation:

Brenda: Well, it's an apartment right next to my parents' house. We have one bathroom. We moved in just after we got married. We've been here for about six months.

Joe: It's above the garage. It's attached to the house, but it has a separate entrance. It's attached by a walkway. We have our own kitchen, living room, central area, bedroom, and bathroom. It has lots of light and high ceilings, like a quaint little château.

Sharon: Was someone living here before you?

Brenda: No. Relatives would stay here when they came to visit. Five years ago we had a couple living here who babysat.

Sharon: What about the washer and dryer? Do you use their washer and dryer?

Joe: We have our own downstairs in the garage. Her family set that up.

Sharon: Do you have any friends who are also living with their parents to save money?

Brenda: I have a lot of friends who have lived with their parents when they got married, mostly in separate basement apartments with their own kitchens.

Joe: A lot of the basement apartments are big. It's just a very common thing. In our town, it's very difficult to find ADUs because of restrictive zoning. But, I'll get a lot of calls from people on an ad just because it has a mother-in-law unit. That would be the thing that drew them. If you are listing a house, that's always a major draw. A place with a mother-in-law unit is bound to be nice and big, and people like that. It seems like more parents are getting them for their adult children or the other way around.

Paula, an administrative assistant living in Northern California, and her husband recently converted their garage into an apartment for her mother and niece. Her mother had just sold her home and plans to move out of state once she retires. She needed a transitional place for a couple of years. She also wanted to have a place to stay when she comes back for visits with her daughter. The unit has a living area, one bedroom, a bathroom, and a small kitchen. Paula talked about why and how she remodeled her garage:

Paula: My mother was about to retire and said to us, "Well, you have a garage and it's detached. It has a bathroom in it. Why don't I fix it up and stay in it?" My husband and I were already thinking about doing that anyway, just so that we'd have an extra room separate from our three kids. They are only

11, 8, and 6. We wanted a little hideaway place for us. So, we decided to move forward with it.

My mom and my husband worked on the project together. They came up with a plan and hired a contractor to do the work. It's a two-car garage and it had a half-bath, which was just a toilet and a sink. We had to install a shower and the kitchen. Fortunately, the plumbing was already there, since we had our washer and dryer out there. She has her own little yard. We have our own backyard, so it's really convenient in a way.

BASEMENT CONVERSIONS

In a town near Boston, a sixty-three-year-old grandmother was able to convert a walk-out basement space in her home into a place for her grandson and his wife to live in while they both attended a local community college. For an investment of about $7,000, including building permits, she hired a contractor to make the conversion, complete with a kitchenette and separate entrance. To make ends meet, she did need to charge them a small rent each month to help pay the cost of utility bills. Fortunately, her area is zoned for multifamily houses and rental apartments are legal.

Lou Manfredini, in an article he wrote about basement conversions for *USA Weekend*, provided a series of tips:

1. Check building and fire codes for windows and safety exits other than stairs.
2. Add plenty of light via windows if possible.
3. Floors and walls should be built with space/insulation between the usual concrete and the interior of the unit.[77]

OTHER CONVERSIONS

Not only can garages and basements be converted to ADUs, but also you can create housing in barns, stables—even chicken coops. Across the country, unused farm structures are deteriorating, collapsing, being torn down, or finding new life in being transformed into housing. Although we did not personally interview people who had made such conversions, we found numerous examples on the internet. *This Old House* (*TOH*), a home-remodeling TV show, has featured several ADU remodel episodes the past couple of years, further indicating the increasing national trend for this type of housing. Two articles you can read online—"Barn Storming" and "A Cottage in Concord"—describe how the *TOH* crew turned a two-story barn in Massachusetts into an in-law apartment for a couple's parents.

In short, barn conversions can be very rewarding but also more expensive than building a new house. To keep in line with modern-day regulations, they almost always need major structural alterations. Furthermore, in most cases a lot of work is needed to meet roofing and insulation standards. Nonetheless, a nicely done barn conversion can be a lovely sight and give the owner a great sense of accomplishment and pride at completion.[78]

GREEN BUILDING

There are affordable ways to remodel and build these days to conserve energy, reduce waste, and improve air quality. During the last decade, "prices for such things as installing photovoltaic solar panels on the roof for pollution-free energy or using recycled materials and sustainably grown wood are getting close in cost to the conventional alternatives."[79] Depending on where you live, incentives are available to help reduce costs. In some areas, state and federal incentives can bring down installation costs by as much as 50 percent. For example, in 2006 the federal government began to give 30 percent tax credits for residential solar installations, according to California Solar Center.[80] In addition, during the same time period, the federal government offered tax credits "for energy-efficient air conditioners, heat pumps, furnaces, water heaters, windows, and insulation."[81]

Using recycled or salvaged materials is often less expensive than using new materials. Not only can green systems and materials save money to begin with, but they can be cost effective in the long run:

- Radiant heating systems can save space and costly framing labor by not needing big chases and additional furnaces that might be needed for forced-air systems.

- While cellulose insulation (made from 90 percent recycled newspapers) is initially more expensive than fiberglass, installation costs less because there's no need to provide air spaces around the insulation.

- Cotton insulation costs more than fiberglass, as do most environmental materials; however, environmental materials save on energy bills in the long run.

- The easiest and cheapest way to save on energy bills is to add insulation in attics and walls to avoid artificial heating.[82]

In fact, homes constructed with sustainable building products can save up to 90 percent of monthly utility costs. These zero-energy homes "generate their own electricity with photovoltaic systems and reduce energy consumption through on-demand hot water heaters, radiant roof barriers, high-efficiency furnaces and appliances, tightly sealed ducts, extra insulation, and low-E windows."[83] Installing fluorescent light fixtures is another option. "They use one-fourth the energy of regular lighting and last ten times longer."[84] Also, you can put light switches in rooms "that can be programmed to automatically turn off the lights when sensors show no one is in the room."[85] Furthermore, installing ceiling fans in key living areas can cut down the need for air-conditioning. Likewise, programmable thermostats will save on utility bills. Certainly, converting unoccupied rooms of a large house into an apartment for extended family living can help reduce energy and resource consumption in general.

POLICY ISSUES

There are a number of factors to investigate before moving ahead with plans to add an accessory unit. Included are local codes or regulations, zoning, permit processes, tax, and insurance issues that can complicate your project. The first step is to check with your local building department to see if the conversion or addition is feasible for your property. Are accessory units allowed? How are they classified? What are the tax ramifications? Most cities define an accessory unit as a space that has its own entrance and kitchen similar to that of an apartment. Different municipalities have different regulations regarding their installation and use. Depending on where you live, some cities encourage the building of such units, while others put up barriers against constructing them. Requiring extra parking for automobiles can be one of the biggest barriers. Other obstacles include minimum lot size, setback requirements, and requirements about what percentage of a lot can be covered with living space. For example, the city of Los Angeles requires a minimum lot size of 7,500 square feet, while neighboring Pasadena requires double that. Also, check to see if there are limits on the number of occupants and rules about lease terms.[86] The good news here is generally around the country the regulations are being relaxed as demand grows for ADUs.

Depending on your needs, you can select a licensed architect, a designer, or a design/build contractor to work with on your project. It helps to get referrals from friends who have had positive experiences. You can also contact the American Institute of Architects (AIA), the American Society of Interior Designers (ASID), and National Association of the Remodeling Industry (NARI) for referrals. Be sure to look for someone who has remodeling experience. If that person happens to be from outside your area, make certain that individual consults your local building department for requirements before drawing up your plans.[87]

When working with a home architect/designer, it is wise to determine your budget for the project in advance. The cost of adding a unit can be far more expensive than just adding a single room. Be sure to allow for the extra costs of putting in a kitchen with the required electrical and plumbing work, along with the possible installation of separate utility services. Also, your unit may require additional insulation between ceilings or adjoining walls, depending on municipal codes. According to Leo Cram with the Missouri Gerontology Institute, the costs of a home conversion vary significantly based upon:

- the amount of remodeling work required,
- the ratio of do-it-yourself to contracted-out work for materials and labor,
- the amount of prior furnished space available, and
- the luxury of the living accommodations provided.[88]

Once you have your detailed architectural plans in hand, and if you are not already working with a design/build contractor, you will need to select a licensed and bonded home remodeler to do the work for you. One source for finding these people is your own homeowner's insurance company. You can request a list of local contractors that they recommend. Once again, NARI provides information and referrals to people who want to remodel their home. Also, you can ask your architect/designer or friends for recommendations. It's a good idea to get price quotes from more than one builder and compare them, making sure they are bidding on the same items. Take the time to go look at projects your prospective builders have done.[89] Another thing to consider is hiring a contractor you would like to work with, someone who is a good listener and has a professional business. It is very important to establish solid lines of communication early on. It helps to provide as much information as possible to the contractor with drawn-up, detailed plans at the beginning of a project. You will want to write down the details of any communication with your contractor, so if disputes do arise, there is a reference to what was agreed upon.[90]

After you've selected your remodeler, it's a good idea to hire an attorney to draw up or review the contract. Make sure the contract specifies the start and completion dates.[91] It's important to allow adequate time for construction. Many homeowners underestimate how long it will take to build a unit before they can begin to use it. If you want to save time and know the budget in advance, you may want to consider working with a designer/builder/remodeler instead of an outside architect.

Before attempting any home improvements, whether they be plumbing, electrical, or structural, you (or your contractor) will need to obtain the necessary permits from your local building department.[92] Finally, after the work is completed, be sure to follow up with the required inspections by your local building department. *Good luck with your project!*

CONCLUSIONS

Certainly, there are a number of ways you can add a self-contained living unit to your property. You can reconfigure space inside an existing single-family dwelling or add on to it. Spaces that have the greatest potential for conversion include attics, basements, and garages. You can also build a new cottage in the backyard or remodel an old barn. Examples have been given of all of these conversions. Finally, policy issues related to building ADUs have been outlined, and they are changing fast. It's important to find out what your local municipality requires before starting your project. The good news is that restrictions are being reduced over time.[93] Most prominent among many examples are California's new laws (since 2022) mandating that local restrictions allow higher-density building, including for ADUs.[94]

On the other hand, if you should decide it is not feasible for you to become involved in remodeling your home, what other options do you have to house family members? Our next chapter discusses how to find and buy housing with accessory units. You will learn about the innovations that are already happening in housing and developments around the country.

HOW TO FIND, BUY, OR BUILD HOUSING

We have bigger houses and smaller families,
more conveniences, but less time.

—George Carlin

For many, the remodeling option described in the last chapter won't work. This chapter is about finding and buying or building properties with contiguous residences. We've divided the chapter into four main topics. First, we discuss finding existing homes with attached, adjacent, or neighboring units, giving special attention to the stories of motivated citizens who are succeeding in changing restrictive twentieth-century statutes and regulations. Next, we consider how residential real estate developers are anticipating the needs of the baby boom generation. Third, we take a look at the lucky folks that can afford to custom-build three-generation housing. We close the chapter with a quick summary of the restrictions local governments and other authorities place on three-generation housing.

THE EXISTING STOCK OF MULTIGENERATIONAL HOUSING

We'll start with the stories. The people we've talked to have been quite creative in their searches for roofs for their extended families. Their stories fall roughly into three categories:

1. Some folks looked for and found two adjacent units.
2. Others just moved in with family with big places and stayed.
3. Several just bought the house next door.

Adjacent Units

Nancy: We lived in a large home for thirty-five years and it came to the point where we would have to redo a lot of the house. It was getting tiring. We were tired of taking care of the garden. We decided we were going to sell the house. Our son-in-law was very much a part of this whole decision because I would not have done this with just my daughter and me working something like this out. An in-law thing can be a very difficult thing. We were going to buy a small house in our neighborhood and our son-in-law said, "Let me look for a home with a guesthouse and see if maybe we can find something that will fit us all."

We found this. We saw several others that were not appropriate at all. I remember walking in the door here and saying, "I could live here very comfortably." Everything turned out right. The original owners didn't want to move right away. We weren't in any great hurry. It was October. Prices were coming down a little even though this was before the big rush. By the time we purchased it, it was a wonderful buy for us and the timing was great. We had a huge estate sale. We sold most of our furniture, just walked in, and have enjoyed it so much ever since.

Families with Big Places

Here are stories from members of three families lucky enough to have big places:

Kathleen: When I graduated from college, I came back to Los Angeles. My parents had initially bought an apartment building in Santa Monica that had a little house in the front and an apartment building in the back. They did it mainly for my older brother to have a place to live. He was also finishing school, and he was back East. He had met a girl and ended up deciding to stay back there for a while. So, when I graduated, I took one of the units, and then I got married. My younger brother ended up moving into another unit while he was at UCLA because he couldn't get housing. Then he got married and lived there. Next my older brother came back from New York and moved into another unit. He was not married at the time. So we were all three siblings living together again.

Then my husband and I ended up buying our little house two years later and moved out. My brothers were still living there. In fact, my younger brother moved into the little house in front that we had used. Then he proceeded to have children. When he and his wife were looking for a house, they started looking in our area. It just so happened that the house right next door to us came up for sale, and they bought it a year ago.

Marian: I lived with my parents in a house in Indianapolis. When I was 5 and my sister was 3, my grandparents (my mother's parents) asked if they could build a house next door to us on the property. They did. So we ended up with a family compound, combination yards and that sort of thing. As time went on, we all appreciated the advantages of the setup.

Dorrie: Our house was designed with an in-law quarters downstairs. The family who lived there before and built the home had the mother-in-law living in it. They had teenage children who had their separate bedrooms upstairs. So that is how they designed the house, with the upstairs and downstairs as two separate houses. Tim and I loved the location and many things about the place. We just decided to take the size along with everything else. Little did we know, fifteen years later, we would have our daughter and her three children move in with us. We now all live in every inch of the house.

The House Next Door

Sylvia: We finally got a place near the lake. My in-laws mentioned, "Keep us abreast of any homes that go up for sale. We would love to move out to the lake, too." My mother-in-law grew up on a family ranch where there were three families on a compound. So that situation was one that she's very familiar and comfortable with. So anyway, the neighboring home came up for sale. It was a private matter. It was never put on the market. It was just by word of mouth that we heard that our neighbor wanted to sell her home. They negotiated a deal, bought the house, but didn't move in right away. They had renters in the home for a year or two before they actually moved in. *Dana*: When we were looking for a place for my grandmother to live, we basically went to our neighbors and said, "What is it going to cost us to get you to move?" They had two children and it was a small house. We had heard that they were getting ready to put on a second story. We decided we better jump on this. It worked out so well for them because they were given the opportunity to buy a much bigger, better house. We paid them significantly more dollars to move. So they benefited and we benefited even more because we really needed that house. I wanted my grandmother to be close by.

So, we described three basic types of existing housing: contiguous houses/duplexes, compounds, and houses with cottages. Most folks we interviewed didn't work through a Realtor, but some did. And, of course, calling a Realtor in your neighborhood of choice will provide you the best information about how to find your particular preference. And such options vary substantially by neighborhood depending on land prices and the house's age. If you're interested in buying either of your next-door neighbors' places or perhaps the one across the street, one of the three will typically come up for sale about once every four to five years.[95] So, those opportunities are precious. You'll generally find houses with *casitas* in older neighborhoods where they've been added over the years or in new, upper-end housing tracts built since the late 1990s. In the latter case, builders have been recently giving buyers the option of a third garage or a *casita* with a separate entrance in homes of more than 3,000 square feet. Such options are the subject of the next section of this chapter.

HOW RESIDENTIAL DEVELOPERS SEE MULTIGENERATIONAL HOUSING

The housing boom peaked in 2006 at 537,000 units sold. During 2009–2010 home sales declined to less than 200,000 but rebounded to 391,000 by 2021.[96] The new-home builders can see the baby boomers retiring but are still figuring out what they'll want in the way of housing. Those who don't recognize the generations-uniting trend we are talking about in this book mostly build and advertise for recreational needs like hiking and biking (in addition to golf), along with broadband communication facilities allowing continued home-based employment. Many builders are still making the mistake of planned isolation of the generations. Even in Orange County, California, considered by some to be the housing innovation center, most of the new communities are segregated by unit size and so on. In other words, the creative mixing of small units with large ones, attached with detached, and owned with rental units remains taboo. They're putting the 1,200-square-foot single-story units in separate villages from the 2,800-square-foot family homes, even if both kinds are in the same development. In the upper-end developments—3,000 square feet and larger and over $2 million—granny flats are listed as options, but even then they don't often include kitchen facilities or separate entrances. And, worst of all, in high-density California billions of dollars are being wastefully invested in *upstairs* "artists' studios" that well accommodate the boomerang kid but make absolutely no sense for the future flood of grandparents who will have trouble with all those stairs.

Luxury home builders, such as Toll Brothers, have offered "multi-gen options" ranging from $12,000 to $36,000 in their new homes. Competitor Pulte Homes offers detached *casitas* in its new developments in Nevada and Arizona at around $30,000. Toll Brothers has recently started to mix housing types, including larger single-family homes and smaller single-story homes aimed at older folks. An executive there reports, "We have master plans across the country where there is both product for the growing boomer family (and for) parents who might be retired at this point. That wasn't the case five years ago. Now we do a lot of that because of market demand."

Andrew Kochera, senior policy adviser at AARP's Public Policy Institute, suggests that Toll Brothers's high-end innovations will spread: "A lot of the features that start appearing in the upper-end homes tend to drift down toward other homes in the market. Large kitchens and bathrooms started in upper-end homes, large window casings, all those sorts of things gradually filter down as builders increasingly try to offer those to other people."[97]

AN INTERVIEW WITH EXECUTIVES AT STANDARD PACIFIC

John had the good fortune to talk with two executives at Standard Pacific, one of the leading residential builders in the country renowned for their innovations, high-quality homes, and excellent consumer satisfaction. Below are the comments of Scott Stowell and Ralph Spargo:

> *John*: What I'm seeing in the current stock of new housing are the granny flats, or at least there is a downstairs bedroom. The one place I'm thinking of is in Turtle Ridge, where you walk up a set of steps and there is an office area that could be a separate bedroom.
>
> *Scott*: We have an option for that.
>
> *John*: So you must have done market research to come up with that. People are asking for that kind of option?

Ralph: Yes. But primarily for us it is because we think that potential customers are doing it because their married children might come to stay with them for five years.

John: So you are recognizing that kids are coming back.

Scott: That's the bigger trend that we see versus the one you are talking about, which we think will happen later. We're not seeing a whole lot of that yet—the parents moving in with their kids. It's probably happening a little bit.

Ralph: Let me just comment on that real quickly. The challenge that we are also going to have is, twenty years ago when lots were much bigger, it was easier to do that. Today, especially in California, as land gets really expensive, lots are getting smaller and smaller. We are not nearly as flexible as we were when we were putting in pool houses. That's going to be a challenge. The land use is going to be the limiting factor. Things are going to become more vertical.

Scott: I think what you are seeing more of now is the adult children who have just started their families, who have trouble finding a house to live in around here. So some of it is necessity-driven. The baby boomers don't want their kids to move to Temecula where they can buy a house. They would like them to stay here. If they don't, they're not going to see the grandkids as much as they would like to. So I think a lot of that is happening, even before the grandkids arrive.

Ralph: Right. They're investing in their kids now. We are seeing a tremendous transfer of wealth from baby boomer parents to their children. They are going to transfer the wealth anyway at some point in time. They're gifting it now so the kids can buy a home and be close, versus moving inland to Riverside County or out of state to Phoenix, where the housing is cheaper.

Scott: Del Webb puts out a report every year. Historically, the seniors they focus on have retreated to the large retirement communities to get away from everybody. Now Del Webb is reporting some important changes. In their most recent survey, 30 percent of boomers would prefer retiring to an urban community. Another 29 percent would prefer a mixed community that included a multigenerational neighborhood. Also, more than half would be "happy to help" if either their parents or children needed to move in with them.

Ralph: The report talks about being an empty nester for a long period of time. Male baby boomers are more likely than female baby boomers to indicate they will be happier once their children leave. But it's only less than a quarter; only about 20 percent of the people want to see them leave. The other 75 percent don't.

John: There are a lot of nasty terms floating around in the popular press, like "boomerang kids." So how long ago did you notice this trend?

Ralph: We probably have been seeing it for ten years.

Scott: I would say that at least for us at Standard Pacific, division presidents, along with the marketing staff, really have a lot of influence on the design principles used in our housing. We look to trends plus our own experience with our sales people. But I would say that probably ten years ago, we were designing houses that had both an office and a guest room downstairs. This gives enough flexibility that you could have a parent move in with you and be down on the first floor, if they were handicapped or couldn't negotiate the stairs. And you didn't have to give up your home office or den to do that. Then the third-car garage option allows people to combine that space with the guest room and make it into a suite. You could have the room plus a converted third-car garage and create a whole guest suite that would include a kitchenette.

Ralph: So we've been designing houses for flexibility to accommodate families that needed to come together.

John: How about universal design?

Scott: We are looking at universal design where it makes sense. There are certain elements of universal design that are really bordering on handicap design, being able to lower cabinets and things like that. Things like how you situate tubs, how much turning space you give in bathrooms, how wide your hallways are—these kinds of things are fairly easy to integrate into a house. In fact, in many cities, we're actually required to prepare a list of what universal design things there are in our homes. And, other new laws are coming into effect on these issues.

Ralph: For example, there's a new California state law . . . I'm not quite sure how it's going to affect things, but all municipalities are going to have to have some acknowledgment of what elements of universal design builders have included. It's not going to tell what they have to include, but they have to tell people about what they have done. Things like backing for grab bars. We do a lot of that anyway: raising plugs to sixteen inches rather than twelve inches, lowering switches from fifty inches to forty-six inches. I mean, some of these things are very subtle, and it just takes a little bit of attention to detail. But it isn't a major change in the design process.

Scott: We hired Ralph to help us build our active adult business. So we are focused intently on designing housing for this baby boomer generation that we know is going to buy different housing. We have not been as focused on designing houses for their kids to accommodate the parents moving back home. However, if what you are saying is really right, we probably need to be thinking more about designing houses for families that can accommodate parents coming home. We do that already but maybe not to the extent that you are suggesting.

Ralph: I agree with the whole thesis that the baby boomers are going to change the way the market works all over. The numbers are bearing this out. What we are trying to do is figure out what that means because we know it isn't just one answer. It's not just, "Why don't you go build them a seniors' community out in the desert." I think the numbers already show only 10 percent of that population want to do that. Most of those are government workers that have got their retirement pensions. They don't want another job. Most of the baby boomers don't see themselves in classic retirement. They're going to rejuvenate, reinvent, redo, re-create themselves in other ways. How we accommodate that is where the opportunities are.

Scott: Let's say you are 70 years old and go back and live with your kids. You can invest in your grandkids or your great-grandkids perhaps or help out at home. That's going to put tremendous pressure on families' abilities to get along.

Most recently, Scott Stowell founded a new real estate investment company. The firm was an early investor in Modal, a new start-up that specializes in building backyard ADUs. See Livemodal.com for details.

As their comments suggest, the folks at Standard Pacific are looking toward the future housing needs of baby boomers and their extended families. In particular, they are noting and responding to the changes in the preferences and needs of American families:

1. The fading attractiveness of senior communities

2. The appeal to many of multigenerational arrangements

Others are noticing, as well. On the first point, Strauss and Howe, in *Generations*, wrote: "'Seniors Only' living communities will become more uncommon and controversial, perhaps even objects of legislative or judicial attack."[98] On the second point (and much more recently in time), an AARP study reports that 80 percent of adults over the age of forty-five agree it's important to live near their children and grandchildren.[99] When asked in a poll sponsored by Century21.com about whom folks would prefer as next-door neighbors, more than half said, "A family member."[100] And, at an early 2000s conference of architects and builders sponsored by *Residential Architect* magazine, topping the list of fifteen (then) emerging trends in home design was "Housing should accommodate more activities, types of people, and living arrangements, and it should be multigenerational."[101] Finally, also in the early 2000s, researchers at Vision Group reported that nearly half of the Americans they interviewed thought they would have parents or other relatives living with them over the next ten years.

Further, as we see toward the end of the chapter, the new-home builders generally complain that outdated zoning and building codes restrict their creativity in responding to the changing demographics and preferences of their customers. Despite the obstacles, many developments in the last decade or so around the country demonstrate the wonderful ways that residential builders and architects are able to accommodate the revolution in American housing arrangements.

Granny Flats Add Flexibility and Affordability

Accessory dwelling units (ADUs), as we know, appear under many aliases—granny flats, garage apartments, carriage houses, ancillary units—and they almost invariably show up on a checklist of what sets new urban communities apart from conventional subdivisions. They are by no means ubiquitous, but developers from diverse projects report that granny flats have become a popular amenity and an important selling point.

From a developer's perspective, ADUs provide an extra tier of housing options—affordable units that can attract people from diverse age and income groups. Another benefit is safer and more lively alleys. With more "eyes on the street," children and adults are more likely to use the alley for play and socialization.

Moreover, "accessory units are an easy way to get more people in the same area and therefore support low vehicle miles traveled and all of the good environmental outcomes from density," says developer Bob Chapman. "Accessory units offer density without making the street appear overbuilt." In the infill project Trinity Heights, which Chapman is developing in Durham, North Carolina, with architect Milton Grenfell, garage apartments have been added to fifteen of the twenty-four single homes. Because Chapman and Grenfell want to encourage builders—who generally have no experience with granny flats—to construct ADUs, they offer a financial incentive. Instead of charging builders a per-lot fee, the developers ask for 17 percent of the home sale price. For the ADU upgrade, however, builders are assessed only 6 percent of the sales revenue.

Despite high-impact fees, ADUs have been very successful in Prospect, North Carolina—out of the approximately 110 homes completed, forty have finished garage apartments. Builders usually include an unfinished shell above the garage and charge about $50,000 for the average upgrade. Most units are in the 650-square-foot, but one 950-square-foot unit has been built over a three-car garage.

DESIGNING AND BUILDING YOUR OWN MULTIGENERATIONAL HOUSING

Depending on where you live and the extent of your family's resources, building your own three-generation housing may make the most sense. A few of the folks Sharon interviewed for our book have done that and also suggested design features. In two separate interviews, first, we hear from Sarah, and then Paul's family:

> *Sarah*: When his dad and Carl built this house on a cul-de-sac, the plan was that Carl would live in the lower-level apartment with the kitchen. His parents would live above in the main house until we got married. Then we would switch with them and his parents would go downstairs.
>
> *Paul*: Structurally, I wish this house had more [sound] insulation. I really believe people ought to be able to live within reason the way they would like to live. Unfortunately, if they want to play their music louder, our home is not well enough insulated from floor to floor for them to do that.
>
> *Charlotte*: Yes. Walking on the floor sometimes wakes them up downstairs.
>
> *Stacie*: Every time.
>
> *Paul*: Not in bare feet. But if we walk with shoes on, they hear it.
>
> *Stacie*: Just adding to the insulation thing, it goes both ways, from upstairs to downstairs and downstairs to upstairs. We can hear conversations, almost to the word, that my parents have together downstairs, particularly at this end of the house. Despite the fact that there is a locked door, there is not much privacy.

Indeed, it's no wonder the long-crowded Japanese culture avoids shoes worn in the house. It's a matter of cleanliness but also noise! But, such cultural matters are the subject of chapter 12.

We discuss the latest thinking on Elder Cottage Housing Opportunity (ECHO) housing in chapter 11. Another interesting approach is prefabricated housing. These differ from manufactured housing because while the pieces are built in a factory, the houses are assembled on the lot. Note this description of one "put together" by Michelle Kaufman, a San Francisco architect:

> The house that emerged was a long, low-slung, understated dwelling—a marriage of Californian warmth and Japanese precision—with a slanted roof and a long wall with a series of 8-foot-wide sliding-glass doors that can open onto a view or close off the interior from the elements. Louvered panels slide into place over the glass to create protection from the sun while still letting the breeze in. With only 1,344 square feet, the home includes a long great room that includes a kitchen, an eating area, and a living room, as well as two bedrooms and two baths—one with his-and-her stainless-steel basins and a giant slate shower.[102]

And, if you have the financial resources you can really have some fun, as did one family in Northern California, described in the *San Francisco Chronicle*. It's a great story, so read on:

A Full Table

It's 5:55 on a Sunday afternoon at the house in Fairfield. Five-year-old Grace Curry walks around ringing a small bell to summon everyone to dinner.

By 6 p.m., they're all seated around the dinner table: Grace's parents, Bernadette, 37, and George Curry, 42; her brother, Jack, 3; her aunt and uncle, Teresa, 41, and Steve Lavell, 42; their children, Jennifer, 15, Michael, 13, and Danny, 11; and her grandparents, Gretchen, 70, and Joe Shilts, 72. The family dog, Roxie, also shows up. They all live in a 6,800-square-foot house on 4.8 acres along the Putah South Canal. The Shiltses live downstairs, and each of the other two families has an upstairs wing.

The idea for the family compound started after Joe was diagnosed with Parkinson's disease in 1999. The five Shilts daughters had all moved out and married, so the Fairfield house where they had grown up was too big and too much work. In the meantime, the Currys and Lavells were outgrowing their Fairfield homes.

Teresa Lavell came up with the idea of everyone living together. She and Steve had moved all over the world while he was an Air Force pilot. After he had completed his service, "She said, 'We're moving back to Fairfield, and then we're going to live together,'" Gretchen Shilts said.

Three of the Shilts daughters and their families had moved away, but the three Fairfield families were already spending time together, "so there was a natural integration of our lifestyles," Bernadette Curry said.

The search for a site began in 2000 and ended with the purchase in November 2000. Next the family settled on an architect, Jacobson, Silverstein & Winslow in Berkeley. "We spent hours not only talking with them but also poring over books" to get ideas, Gretchen Shilts said.

Finding financing for construction was difficult. The family invited loan officers to lunch to explain the dream, but possible default was a worry. Finally a loan officer from First Northern Bank agreed to lend the money. "He caught the vision," she said.

The project cost $1.4 million—the equivalent of $466,666 per family—for the land, design and construction except for the pool, landscaping and solar panels.

The Shiltses used some of Joe's retirement money to buy the land, and all three family groups pitched in for the down payment after selling their houses. They own the house as joint tenants, and each family contributes to a joint account that pays for the 15-year mortgage and other shared costs. Although the new house is unique, Joe Shilts estimates that buying three new Fairfield houses suited to each family's needs would have cost "at least twice what we paid." New single-family detached houses in Fairfield can cost anywhere from about $600,000 to more than $1 million.

If the families had built three separate houses, they would have had to buy three lots because city zoning allows only one house on the lot they have. Shilts estimated that three lots would cost a total of $100,000 more than they paid for their land. Construction costs would have totaled nearly $500,000 more.

The entryway is flanked by a hall spanning the center section. The hall is lined with bookshelves beneath large windows on the outer wall and openings into the great room with its two-story-high ceiling. On the left end of the great room is a conversation area with a fireplace, TV, piano, a window seat and another wall of windows overlooking the backyard, which has decks, pool, lawn and a dry, grassy hillside sloping down to the canal.

The center of the great room is dominated by a long dining table that can seat up to 20. It was the first joint purchase because of "the communal value of sharing a meal," said Bernadette Curry.

This table also has allowed the family to have Thursday night soup suppers during the winter. They started with friends and neighbors who sometimes brought others along, making for lively discussions. "It was a way to have a wider community," George Curry said.

Each family chose the colors for its living area. Colors and other details for the communal areas were collaboratively chosen. "It was work," Gretchen Shilts said. Everyone would meet around the Shiltses' dining room table to make decisions during construction.

Collaboration is a huge key to the success of this living arrangement. Families take turns cooking dinner for a week at a time. Everyone is on his own for breakfast, lunch and Friday dinner, which often winds up to be leftovers or pizza. The family that cooks also plans the menus and does the grocery shopping.

Housekeeping tasks for the communal areas are divided eight ways and rotate weekly, excusing Joe and the Curry kids. Each family takes care of its own area.

Eating dinner together at 6 p.m. is "quite an experience for the young people," Gretchen Shilts said. It gives everyone a chance to talk about the day.

It's also a chance to head off conflicts, she said, noting that the family spent a lot of time talking about that issue before moving in. The family also tries to have regular meetings for everyone, but the kids are excused when finances are involved. "The chemistry is here to make it work. We have the commitment to one another," said Gretchen, a nurse who works on call as a lay Catholic chaplain with North Bay Hospice.

In planning the house, "we saw it as a marriage of families" and a way "to be there for Mom and Dad," Steve Lavell said. "This isn't an experiment. We're going to make it work."

George Curry agreed. "No matter what happens, we can work it out. It's a more impressive family than it is an impressive house."[103]

We have a few more suggestions. Chapters 7 through 12 of this book are intended to stimulate your creative juices when it comes to designs for living. HGTV online has some 21,000 house plans you can explore, including twenty-six for accessory units and 615 duplex units. If you find one you really like you can buy the detailed plan for around $575. But, it's just fun to cruise around their "virtual neighborhood" for ideas. The HGTV website will add useful options to your plans. Finally, having written all this about designs, three design features are crucial: avoid stairs, allow for separate kitchen facilities, and provide separate entrances.

FIGHTING THE CODES

Any innovation is disruptive. Even though the successful ones improve life overall, some folks will always see them in a negative way. It is certainly no different with innovations in housing. Everybody in the business complains about the codes—zoning and building—that inhibit flexibility and creative solutions to the changing demographics and lifestyles of Americans. Here's a representative taste of the comments from folks we interviewed:

The Families' Views

Joe (a Realtor): Here in our town, it's very difficult to get ADUs because of restrictive zoning. But I'll get calls from people all the time. They'll inquire about an ad just because it had a mother-in-law unit. That was the thing that drew them. If you are listing a house, that's always a major draw. People are interested in these units for their adult children or their elder parents.

Lina: A friend of mine said, "Why don't you try and have your daughter buy a house that already has the unit in it?" That is what they originally tried to do. But they couldn't find anything with a unit that was within their price range. So that's when they bought this house that had the space to add one. Then they had to go through the normal procedures with the town hall. The town didn't mind it being an in-law suite but didn't want it to be used for rent.

Nancy: Our town fought us adding on an in-law unit. In fact, when we were moving in here, they were very restrictive. The town said you could only live in them thirty days out of the year. They did not want people living in places like that.

COMMUNITY ACTION

In order to adjust the housing stock of the country to reflect the baby boomers' retirement and the associated growth in extended family living arrangements, changes will be required in long-existing and mostly local housing and building codes and associate ordinances. The main battle line in this political fight is over ADUs. Public debate and political battles are being fought, won, and lost around the country over making changes in codes that not only allow for, but actually promote, the construction of ADUs in existing neighborhoods and in new developments. Below we report on recent events primarily in crowded California, the "neighborhood" we know best. Hopefully restrictions in your area are less onerous, but we do know that similar issues are being discussed around the country. We just hope with more civility!

THE FUNDAMENTALS OF THE DISAGREEMENT

According to housing expert Martin Gellen, ADUs produce two kinds of problems. The first concerns physical impacts, such as increased parking and traffic and architectural changes that are seen as disruptive to a neighborhood. The second relates to social and cultural issues. The ADU deviates from the traditional way of looking at housing, family, and the neighborhood. It stands for a change in the way the single-family house is used, a departure from the conventional meanings connected to residential zoning categories.

Residential zoning gives a community control over its social and economic composition and gives continuity to the character of a community. American zoning caters to the separation of single-family housing from apartments. It does so in order to retain a system of land use that favors a perceived "natural progression": that is, climbing a ladder from renting an apartment to the ultimate goal of owning a home. However, today that traditional mindset is being challenged by both changes in family structure (particularly the growth in multigenerational family living arrangements) and the economics of housing. Still, people's beliefs about housing and family have stayed somewhat fixed; ADUs challenge these beliefs.

Moreover, there is a historical problem that needs to be overcome. Even though today accessory units are seen by many as an attractive housing alternative, they were once viewed as an indicator of neighborhood blight. Years ago, they were found only in run-down areas. But even if its connection with urban blight could be eliminated, the ADU would still be shunned. Since it allows multifamily use of a single-family home, it violates the sanctity that many people attribute to the single-family house and neighborhood. This cultural perception has been difficult to alter and has acted as a deterrent to ADU zoning. Indeed, a 2022 article in the *Los Angeles Times*, "Despite the Sprawl, L.A. Is America's Most Overcrowded Place," continues this culturally based (perhaps racist) attack on multigenerational living.[104]

When the rational basis for exclusive single-family zoning is examined, an important question emerges: What public purpose is served by preventing individual homeowners from adding accessory units in answer to changing lifestyles and economic needs? In fact, zoning regulations "must have a substantial relation to the health, safety, morals, comforts, convenience, and general welfare of the community." If so, then "zoning is to a large degree an instrument of social policy and must therefore serve legitimate social ends." Zoning needs to serve the needs of the people and keep up with the times.[105]

BARRIERS TO THE CONSTRUCTION OF ADUS

The San Francisco Bay Area's Double Unit Opportunity (DUO) Program has developed the most comprehensive listing of specific deterrents to creative housing options.[106] One-half of all DUO clients dropped out of the program without filing for a second-unit permit. Many who did not proceed were discouraged by the required additional parking; limits on the accessory apartment's size, type, and occupancy; deed restrictions; and the cost of fees and permits. Building costs were another important deterrent; many were shocked at the cost of construction in general. Elements of all the obstacles described below are mirrored in the comments of the stories reported above.

1. Additional parking is the single factor most likely to block planning approval of a second-unit project. Zoning and building regulations specify the number of additional spaces required, along with size and their location on the lot. Feasibility is also determined by the local

topography and lot size. Unfortunately, with few exceptions, most Bay Area ordinances require two or more additional parking spaces for a second dwelling. DUO found this requirement to be unnecessary, as its clients owned an average of 1.67 cars per household, with 1.3 cars owned by tenants living in completed DUO units.

2. Unit size and type can be restrictive deterrents to building second units. All ordinances define minimum and maximum unit size, generally from 300 to 700 square feet, and mandate that the addition be subordinate to the primary dwelling. Some municipalities use a 10 percent cap on the floor area for the second unit, discouraging such buildings in homes of less than 3,500 square feet. Others prohibit detached units, which doesn't make sense on a large suburban lot, where a well-designed unit could easily be placed.

3. Cities often place occupancy restrictions on ADUs. The most common is to require that the homeowner live in either the main or second dwelling. This requirement means that the owner must record a deed restriction limiting future use of the property, causing some to drop the project or proceed illegally. In other cases, either the homeowner, seniors, family members, or servants must occupy the unit. Some communities also limit occupancy to low-income tenants and set rent levels. Such controls have the effect of limiting the use of the new housing and reducing the future salability of the property.

4. Use permits can act as major obstacles to building ADUs. Even though a second unit tends to be a small remodeling project, it typically receives greater scrutiny because it is considered to be a new dwelling. In most cases, those adding an ADU must apply for a use permit before applying for a building permit. The use permit application requires secondary materials, including a map of the neighborhood, site plan, along with floor plans and elevations. In some instances, there are additional requirements for "engineering surveys, soil and seismic safety reports, and detailed descriptions of vegetation and other environmental features." For even more information on such issues, see Report_SFDAS_Affordable Housing Overview October 2021.pdf online.

TAKING ACTION AT THE COMMUNITY LEVEL

Former California Governor Arnold Schwarzenegger "terminated" legislation (Assembly Bill 2702) that promoted ADU construction in California. Despite such major reversals, a growing number of local communities around the country have changed codes to allow for and even promote ADU construction: Boulder, Colorado; Westport, Connecticut; Montgomery County, Maryland; and Santa Cruz, California, are often mentioned. Building *cross-community coalitions* has been crucial in getting codes changed in these and other areas. You will need to recruit partners such as affordable housing groups, local chapters of Parents Without Partners, the AARP, and other associations with self-interests such as real estate agents, remodelers, architects, new-home builders, disabled advocates, home health care agencies, hospitals, bankers, and environmentalists. Back in California, more recently, Governor Gavin Newsom has reversed the trend by attacking local restrictions against new construction.[107]

The DUO well describes what to ask for in changes to codes:

- Exempt second-unit applications from use-permit and public-hearing requirements if they meet the development standards of the ordinance.
- Require a *maximum* of one additional parking space per bedroom in the new unit.
- Allow tandem parking.
- Allow parking in the setback areas.
- Reduce the size of the parking space to compact-car standards.
- Eliminate occupancy restrictions and deed restrictions on properties with second units.
- Allow all types of second units (conversions, attachments, and detached) as long as they are in scale with the existing house and lot.
- Eliminate arbitrary limits on unit size.
- Assess second units in accordance with their size and scale, not as new single-family dwellings.
- Consider waiving or reducing fees as an incentive to second-unit development.

Two local examples provide an optimistic glimpse at success: First, the Bridle Creek development in Pleasanton, California, offers a detached second unit on the same property as the single-family home. The sales manager for the complex said that the City of Pleasanton required the developer to provide twenty of the 111 units with ADUs in order for the project to be approved.[108] In cities like Pleasanton, where there is space for new housing developments, the inclusion of ADUs as part of these developments is a strategy that can increase affordable housing for these communities. Certainly, such a requirement would help the town meet its affordable housing quota, required by California state law.

Second, what about communities that are built out or don't encourage large new-housing developments? The town of Woodside, California, fits that category with its 5,600 people and 1,000 horses. It recently took a look at ADUs, some even in barns, as an answer to its affordable housing needs. In June of 2000, residents were surveyed about their interest in creating new rental units. Some 3,000 mailers drew 560 responses, a response rate of almost 20 percent. These responses provide a profile of residents' thoughts about extra living quarters. Key points included:[109]

- A total of 209 properties contain 244 accessory living structures; sixty-two are being rented now, with most of the others being occupied by guests, family members, or caretakers.

- Fifty-seven of the additional living quarters are attached to the main residence, 176 are detached, and eleven are in barns.

- Eighty-three respondents are interested in building new accessory living quarters, fifty-nine of which might be for rent. Another 110 said they might be interested.

- Respondents suggested incentives for building new living units: 185 want clearer information on the town's rules, 201 would welcome fee waivers, 175 support floor-area allowances, sixty-six want units in barns, and sixty-six would welcome low-interest loans.

- Some respondents worried the additional units might hurt the rural quality of Woodside and impact traffic, parking, and the environment.

The planning commission considered this survey information in its proposed amendments to ordinances controlling accessory living quarters and rental units. The proposed new rules balance more flexibility with more restrictions on the overall level of accessory buildings allowed on a lot. Proposals that would allow more flexibility include:

- Allowing living units in barns, at least for people taking care of livestock.
- Allowing rental units of up to 1,200 square feet instead of the present maximum of 720 square feet.
- Allowing rental units in the R-1 zone (smaller lots of mostly half an acre or less) to occupy 30 percent of the main building instead of the current maximum of 10 percent. Detached units still would not be allowed.

Proposed additional restrictions include:

- Only one accessory living unit on lots smaller than three acres.
- Reductions in both size and number of accessory buildings on lots smaller than three acres.
- Requirement that the owner live on any property with a rental unit—either in the main house or the accessory unit.

Proposed amendments that clarify many definitions and provisions of the current ordinance include:

- Requirement that accessory living quarters contain a full bathroom with interior access from the main room, and a sink and counter space in a separate room with outlets for kitchen appliances.
- Requirement that the unit must be at least 400 square feet in area.

Ultimately, amendments that are approved will be used to update Woodside's housing element when complete. The town staff believes some of the proposed modifications to rules for ADUs could help the town obtain state certification for its housing plan. Woodside's state-mandated quota is to provide forty-one units of housing affordable to people with low or moderate incomes between 1999 and 2006. As of August 31, 2006, the town had exceeded its quota and issued permits for fifty-six accessory units.

It can be done!

MAKING YOUR HOME ACCESSIBLE TO SENIORS

*Planning is bringing the future into the present
so that you can do something about it now.*

—Alan Lakein

So many of us are living now in Peter Pan housing—built as if no one ever ages. The typical single-family house is designed for people who will never grow old. It is not a good place for someone who can't drive, use stairs, or do simple household maintenance. Most of us will lose some, if not all, of these abilities before we die. In fact, these days we all have a long *disabled* life expectancy.[110] Our discussion here is not exhaustive. This is particularly so because building codes and standards change over time and across states, counties, and cities. So please check with qualified professionals in your area on these topics.

Consequently, in making your home accessible to seniors, it is important to include design features that can meet future disability needs.[111] For example, an ADU installed above a garage that would require the occupant to climb stairs would not be functional for a mobility-disabled person. In any case, stairs present a major obstacle to those with walking difficulties. Also, for a person who uses a wheelchair, it would be important to install 36-inch doorways to allow for passage. Adding grab bars in bathrooms near the shower and toilet would be another option. Moreover, kitchens can be set up with lower counters, and bedroom closets with adjustable double-hung clothes racks and lower shelves, for people using wheelchairs.

An alternative to remodeling an existing house is to design and build a new one to meet the requirements of a disabled individual. John's aunt, Alice Graham, did just that by having the wisdom and foresight to plan ahead for her impending need to use a wheelchair. She helped design and had built a small, two-bedroom, single-story home that includes a level front entry without stairs, wide doorways, grab bars in the bathroom, and low counters in the kitchen. She lived in this house with her son for several years before her death at age eighty-six and certainly benefited from those innovative features, which enabled her to perform the routine activities of daily living.

UNIVERSAL DESIGN

Faced with a growing population of people advancing in years and disabilities, designers and builders are finding a growing market for—and growing legal pressure to incorporate—universal design features in new or remodeled homes. Universal design "is used to describe products or environments that accommodate people of all ages, sizes, and abilities, and allow them to live and function independently. This is accomplished by eliminating or modifying those features that may be obstacles or dangers for the user, while also adding considerations for their safety, comfort, and ease-of-use."[112] It is intended to benefit all people throughout their life span at little or no extra cost. In fact, universal design features are generally no more expensive than traditional features, if incorporated by the designer at the conceptual stage.[113]

Along with 36-inch doorways and wider hallways, home builders are beginning to brace walls for the later installation of grab bars. Curb-less showers are being constructed with sloped floors and a 5-foot radius that allow for walkers or wheelchairs. Lever-style handles are being installed as doorknobs or faucets. Unlocking doors is being made easier with keyless systems that use a keypad or magnetic card. Homes are being constructed on one level without steps inside or out. If stairways are constructed, they are being made wide enough to allow for a power wheelchair track system. In some cases, space is being designed for a future elevator. For example, an executive at home builder Pulte Group, Inc. reports, "Lately we work to deliver the elevator shaft as a possibility for conversion down the road with removable floor plates . . . and stacked closets on the first and second floors."[114] Kitchens and bathrooms are being planned with adaptable counter levels, including removable drawers to allow space for future wheelchairs. Other features include storage space at lower levels and good lighting throughout the home. All of this is being done in ways that look attractive and not institutional.[115] Ultimately, universal design is intended "to reconcile the artistic integrity of a design with human needs in the environment."[116]

Eleanor is a professional American Society of Interior Designers (ASID) interior designer who has incorporated universal design in a number of in-law units. Eleanor built an attached apartment for her in-laws when she lived in Southern California with her husband and son. They were with them for almost a decade. She told us why they decided to live together and how they did it. Her stories and suggestions are very useful, if you are considering making your home accessible to seniors:

> *Eleanor:* My in-laws had moved to Arizona, and my mother-in-law was not in good health. She was almost ready to be in a wheelchair full-time. We felt it was time to bring them closer to us, so we moved them into our home. We created a 700-square-foot addition onto our home that had a separate exterior entrance and was all on one floor. It was self-contained and had a bathroom, kitchen, dining area, and living room. They also had two small bedrooms because they wanted their own privacy from each other. They liked to watch different TV programs and also had different sleeping times. One liked to read, and the other was more of a television person. We decided to build it as a handicapped ADA-compliant type of a unit, also utilizing universal design principles.

Sharon: In your professional life as an interior designer, have you had many requests from clients to build new homes with accessory units?

Eleanor: Yes, I have consulted with many families who have considered doing this. I think there are a lot of questions that people don't think to ask themselves. If you are going to move your in-laws or your parents in, what is the situation? Are they ill? If Mom or Dad is already in a nursing home, you may have to equip your house in a certain way to accommodate them. If they have certain types of problems, you have to think ahead about special design needs before you do the construction. Also, if there are health considerations, it's much less expensive to prepare the house for that when you build than it is to go back and retrofit. Retrofitting is very difficult sometimes.

Sharon: So, if possible, plan ahead.

Eleanor: You really do need to plan ahead. Make sure the design includes features and fixtures that allow for your parents' changing needs. Your parents may be fine now, but in another five or ten years, they may have special needs. At the time you build a new home, incorporate such elements as blocked walls to handle grab bars, heavy-duty carpet that stands up to wheelchair or walker use, and wide doorways and halls. Pocket doors take up less space. Also, you can install the light switches and thermostat lower on the wall so they can be reached by someone in a wheelchair. Lever handles on doors are easier, too. All those things need to be considered; otherwise you could be facing an expensive remodeling project down the road.

Sharon: Anything else you'd like to add?

Eleanor: One interesting thing that I haven't mentioned is the story about a friend of ours who came to see the apartment that I did for my in-laws and brought her father-in-law with her. He made some comments about it that I thought were

very revealing about how well the place works for older people. He said, "I love this place. I love being able to stand in
the kitchen and reach things on both sides without having to
move. I like knowing that there is a grab bar all the way down
the hallway in case I need it. I like being able to stay all on the
same level."

Joan lives with her husband and their child in South Carolina, and they
built an addition for her mother onto their home. Here's what she had to say
about why they decided to live together, and how they created a separate in-law
unit to accommodate her mother's needs:

Joan: My mother was living in a home near Charleston. My
father had passed away ten years earlier. She had maintained
the house by herself. That worked out fine, until my husband
and I began seeing that it became more difficult for her to find
people to mow the lawn, clean the gutters, and so forth. We
did what we could, but we weren't always able to provide much
help. We started wondering what her long-term housing situation would be. We knew from a financial perspective that she
would not be able to afford a long-term care facility. My father
was ten years older than her. He was a blue-collar tradesman
in Manhattan. So she basically was on Social Security. It's very
much the plight of people from that generation. So we were
looking at it from the perspective that she could not afford
assisted living.

When we bought this house, it had a garage with an
entrance that went out to the side of the property. It was a
piece of land that we never knew how to landscape because it
was not really that wide. We thought about putting in a pool.
But we also thought that it was kind of a natural area to put
on an addition, where there would be an entrance from the
garage into what we called the guesthouse. There was access
to it from the house but not from the main part of our home.

Sharon: Have people called on you for advice since you've done it?

Joan: Some people have, yes. They've come and they've looked. I've talked to them about how to care for an aging parent and how you plan for it. In terms of planning, since my mother had her own house, we tried to plan it so that some of her furniture would fit into her new surroundings. Since she wasn't completely selling everything and starting new, she was able to pull from her past. That worked quite well. We probably have a little bit less than 1,000 square feet. We were able to put in a fully equipped kitchen, a living room, a dining room area, a utility room where she has her own washer and dryer, along with a bathroom and a nice-sized bedroom. In the bathroom, we planned ahead. We put in a tub and later we also put in a grab bar. From the design perspective, I think it's important that the materials you use hold up well and are easy to care for. Think about what type of countertops to use for a vanity. Try to use products that you don't have to replace, that are dependable.

REMODELING

According to the National Association of Home Builders Remodeling Council, as the baby boom generation has reached retirement age and has begun to look at issues of home safety and comfort, remodeling needs are changing dramatically. In response to this rising demand, the organization has begun a training program for remodelers to do the kinds of home modifications homeowners require as they grow older in their homes. The first fifty Certified Aging-in-Place Specialists (CAPS) were awarded credentials following training sessions in Orlando, Florida, in May 2004. Today these specialists are now equipped with the marketing, technical, and customer service skills required to make a home accessible to seniors. Jobs for these specialists range from placing grab bars and adjusting counter heights to creating first-floor master suites and installing elevators. (For more information go to Nahb.org.)[117]Also, the NAHB offers a Directory of Accessible Building Products through their website.

Entryways

For proximity with privacy, we encourage you to build an independent entryway for any addition to your home. In order to make it user-friendly for seniors, where possible build a covered, well-lit, and level entry.

Fumbling with keys, packages, the mail—all can distract and unbalance someone entering or exiting a home. In addition to providing lighting at entryways, be sure to have a table, bench, or other surface nearby for putting things down.[118]

Where space is tight, you can also install a shelf for packages on a wall near the front door.

Eleanor created a separate entrance and flat pathway to the street for her in-laws' apartment. This allowed guests of her in-laws, as well as the Meals on Wheels driver who delivered her lunch, to access their place separately. They didn't have to traipse through Eleanor's house. Joan had a similar story to tell about her mother's separate entrance:

> *Joan*: Our housing situation works. What makes it work is that we designed it so that my mother has her own front entrance. Right now, when the caregivers come, they are not coming through our house. I think it's intrusive enough to have someone you know is around you. So they are not actually coming into our house. My mother has her own independent living and we have ours.

Ramps

We already mention the importance of 36-inch doorways to accommodate wheelchairs. If you are in a situation where you need to provide a ramp for someone in a wheelchair, there are online resources. For example, Wheelchairramp.org posts a manual for design and construction of a modular wheelchair ramp, including information on long-tread, low-riser steps to improve safe home accessibility. This site includes the manual, success stories, videos, articles, and links.[119]

Stairs

Stairs can be especially dangerous for older people. The greater hazard regards going down stairs. Tripping while climbing stairs can break your bones, but falling down stairs can kill you. Use sturdy handrails on both sides of all stairways, if possible. Since carpeting can increase the risk of slipping, removing it can be helpful. Also, make sure a staircase is well lit with light switches at the top and bottom.

Well-defined stairsteps that show where the edge of the tread is can help prevent falls.[120] Moreover, stair treads deep enough for the entire foot can ensure more stable footing and support when climbing steps. The tread of the step shouldn't extend out beyond the riser to avoid the risk of tripping. A stair rise of 7 inches or less can make it easier to climb steps. When it becomes more difficult to climb stairs, consider installing long-tread, low-rise steps outside your house. Doing so will decrease the amount of energy that is needed and allow for space to walk with a walker.

Stairlifts

If stairs are a barrier in making your home accessible to seniors, you might want to consider installing a stairlift. The AARP bulletin carried an ad regarding Bruno Independent Living Aids stairlifts. It states that "Bruno is the leading manufacturer of indoor curved and straight rail stairlifts . . . and now we have the only 400 lb. capacity outdoor model! Stay in the home you love!" Features listed include: "battery operated, onboard diagnostics, no stairway modifications, fast installation available, easily fastens to stair treads." For further information call 1-800-454-4355 or see Bruno.com.

However, stairlifts are not for everyone. Some individuals need help getting in and out of them. Also, carrying along items, such as a walker, can be problematic. In many cases, it's better to move yourself or your aging parent to the ground floor of your home and make sure that the kitchen, bathroom, and bedroom are easily accessible.

Elevators

One couple planned ahead for later housing needs by installing an elevator sooner rather than later. Bob and Sarah bought their home fifteen years ago in the San Francisco Bay Area, when they were in their sixties. At the time they purchased it, they remodeled and added both an ADU downstairs and an elevator. When asked why, Bob responded that it would be a place for people to live who could take care of them later in life. Also, since they had a lot of stairs, an elevator would help them now and later, too. They currently use it for hauling groceries and luggage. Had they waited until they were older or disabled, they probably would not have the energy to deal with the stress of remodeling.

Bob and Sarah are not alone in their forward thinking. The use of elevators is increasing in houses, as baby boomers have or anticipate needs. Elevators have existed for years in urban and suburban estate-style homes. But it is only in recent years that they have begun to show up more frequently in new and existing homes in more middle-class settings. Some say that the biggest reason for the increase in home elevator sales is the baby boomers' anticipation of needing an elevator down the road for themselves and more immediately for their visiting, aging parents. Although they didn't require wheelchair access, Gail and Harvey Pestine installed one in the two-story North Shore home they had lived in for twenty-four years because both had bad legs. Gail said, "We wanted to avoid eventually moving out. It was harder getting upstairs. We loved our home and wanted to stay put."

Grab Bars

Grab bars were not always as stylish as they are today. A while back, you could only find them in hospitals and nursing homes. They all looked alike and were pretty unattractive. However, today you'll find a variety of grab bars in fancy private homes and hotels. "Some are straight, while others are curvy. Some attach to the wall at both ends. You can move others out of the way when you're done with them. And grab bars now come in enough colors to satisfy every decorator."[121]

Universal design plans for the future. Even though you may not need a grab bar in the bathroom now, you can install plywood blocking in the walls to make it easier to attach a bar later. The plywood should be nailed into the studs. It should be three-quarters of an inch thick and 6 to 12 inches wide. You can also attach a grab bar directly to your wall studs.[122]

Grab bar installation should be done according to the user's needs. If the person needs a home care assistant, this also needs to be considered so that placement will benefit everyone in the household.

Grab bars must be installed according to the manufacturer's instructions. Professional assistance is necessary if one lacks the knowledge and skill for proper installation. Designer styles and colors are available.

Features to check when selecting and installing grab bars:

- "Fit" for a user's hand: A round or oval shape, one and a half inches in diameter, fits most people's hands best. Bars are also available in one-inch to one-and-a-quarter-inch diameter, which may be more comfortable for young children or adults with smaller hands. It's necessary to evaluate the user's hand.

- Safety clearance from the mounting surface: Clearance between the grab bar and its mounting surface should be large enough to allow comfortable reaching and gripping but small enough to prevent an arm from sliding down between the bar and the wall. A clearance of one and a half inches is a good guideline to follow.

- Placement: The user's physical capabilities, mobility equipment, and the constraints of the room layout will affect the shape and placement of grab bars.

Helpful considerations include:

- What range of reach is comfortable?
- Does the user need to lean, push, or pull for support with the transfer?

- Does the individual have a preference or necessity to have the grab bar on a particular side of a fixture?
- Will more than one grab bar be beneficial?
- Will horizontal, vertical, or angled mountings be best?
- Material and grip: Bathroom grab bars should be made of stainless steel to resist mold, mildew, bacterial growth, and corrosion. High-impact plastic bars and metal bars coated with plastic also meet this requirement. When installing metal bars, be sure the screws and other fasteners are of a compatible metal type to avoid corrosion where the two are in contact. Where hands will be wet and soapy, use a textured grip surface.
- Ability to support the user: Grab bars must have proper reinforcement to prevent them from bending along their length or from pulling out of the wall. Grab bars should be mounted into wall studs or support blocking, not just into drywall or tile. Some bar lengths (18, 24, and 30 inches) don't match the standard 16-inch spacing commonly used for centering wall studs in most homes. Stainless steel grab bars are typically designed to support 250 pounds anywhere along their length.

An adequate grab bar system must provide support throughout the tub and toilet areas and must be located at a height that provides good body mechanics. The grab bar should not be angled, as a falling person can slide down the bar rather than be stabilized. It's recommended to install parallel, horizontal bars along the long tub wall, one for standing and the other one for sitting in the tub.

Hallways

Be sure to install extra-wide 42-inch hallways where possible to allow for wheelchairs or the installation of grab bars. Eleanor told us about the hallway she built for her in-law unit:

> *Eleanor*: We had the hallway built extra wide to accommodate a wheelchair. We had blocking put in the wall so that it could hold a grab bar all the way down the hallway. Initially, it gave

her a place to hold on to all the way up and down this little hallway to do exercise, walking, and other movements that her doctor wanted her to be doing. We installed a full-length mirror from the ceiling on one small area so that she could see if she was standing straight.

Doors

She also described the doors she had placed in her in-laws' unit:

> *Eleanor*: All the doors were 36 inches wide to accommodate a wheelchair. We put lever handles on all of them. We installed pocket doors in the bedroom walls because that eliminates the area you need for doors to swing open.

To make it easier to open a pocket door, place a tassel on the opening bracket that can be pulled. Also, use hollow-core pocket doors, as they are much lighter and easier to open. To assist with opening a regular door, you can install a power door operator.

Windows

Sometimes it can be difficult for seniors to open and close conventional windows. According to Lew Sichelman, a nationally syndicated housing and real estate writer, "Old-fashioned hand-cranked casement windows with extra-large handles have replaced the sash-type windows most builders use today." In an article he wrote about the LifeWise Home, he quoted Chad Garner of the National Association of Home Builders Research Center as saying, "It's easier for many seniors to crank than it is to push up."

Also, you will want to consider the accessibility of window coverings such as blinds and drapes for people with limited mobility. It is possible to have blinds made with longer cords and handles to make them reachable for someone in a wheelchair. In addition, you can have motorized draperies installed for large windows.

Bathrooms

There are many innovations in bathrooms available now to people with special needs. If a wheelchair or walker will be used, it is important to have enough clear floor space to make a 360-degree turn (at least 30x48 inches; 60x60 inches is ideal).[123]

For those who have trouble squatting or sitting, it is helpful to install toilets that are about 2 inches higher than a standard toilet—about 17 inches or 19 inches off the ground versus 16 inches. Various manufacturers offer the taller version (called "comfort height") for approximately $450 to $620. Grab bars near the toilet need to be put in at a height that is easy to reach and helps with transfers. Do not use towel bars in place of grab bars, as they are not strong enough.

Also, as a temporary solution, you can put a portable, elevated toilet seat on top of a regular toilet seat. A friend has one available for her mother-in-law when she comes to visit. It is a locking, raised toilet seat manufactured by Guardian with padded arms for additional support. The wraparound foam padded armrests allow a sure grip and comfort, along with support. The device raises the seat height 5 inches above the toilet. She says it is easy to use and the locking system does not require tools. It is lightweight and made of polypropylene resin, which is easy to clean.

Vanities

For those who have trouble bending over, bathroom vanities can be raised from the standard 30-inch model to 34 inches tall. Building supply stores or internet resources can tell you where to find such models. Also, vanities can be sloped or angled to accommodate a wheelchair.

Sinks

If a wheelchair is being used in a bathroom, a sink with a vanity does not permit close access, although it can provide good counter space. An alternative is to install a wall-hung sink that can allow closer accessibility. A sink mounted no higher than 34 inches with a minimum clear knee space of 29 inches and a minimum width of 31 inches (preferably 36 inches), with plumbing out of the way, is desired. When plumbing pipes are exposed, be sure to insulate them to prevent burns. Also, a single-handed faucet control reduces the chances of scalding at the sink. This type of lever is easier to use on faucets than the traditional knobs.

A medicine cabinet or mirror placed no more than 40 inches above the floor allows access to someone seated in a wheelchair.

Bathtubs

Taking a bath used to be extremely difficult for some elder adults until a company called Premier Bathrooms came up with a solution: a walk-in tub! Their ad shows a picture of a man about to enter one of their tubs. He is quoted as saying, "It's so easy, I just open the door and step in . . . I really used to enjoy having a bath but I realized as I got older that the fear of slipping, or the effort of pulling myself up after I had finished bathing, was becoming a real problem . . . Premier Bathrooms has the largest range of walk-in bathtubs in the country, and buying one helped me regain my independence."[124]

On the other hand, there is a variety of adaptive equipment that you can use to make an existing tub work for showers and baths, including shower chairs, tub-transfer benches, tub slides, and hydraulic bath lifts.

- Wall grab bars in the front and side of the tub area are recommended at a height that makes transfers safe and which can be easily reached. Use of a grab bar on the back wall of the tub area can also be helpful. Grab bars that clamp onto the side of the tub can substitute for installed wall grab bars or be used in addition.

- Use of nonslip decals or a bathmat on the tub floor is recommended to prevent slipping.

- It is also possible to convert a bathtub into a step-through handicap shower with a cutout portion of the side of the bathtub. This will decrease a 14-inch step to a few inches. This method utilizes the original bathtub and keeps the walls, floors, and plumbing intact, which can also save money compared with conventional bathroom remodeling.

Joan told us she had both a tub and a shower installed in her mother's addition:

> *Joan*: When she first moved into the unit, she was able to use the tub and she enjoyed taking baths. Then, she got to a point where she was not able to get out of the tub. She could get in, but her knees couldn't support her enough even though we had a rail in there to get out. So the stall shower is another great thing that we put in because she can walk into it and walk out of it. We now have a person who comes in the morning and helps her with her shower and getting her laundry done.

Showers

For those who don't like bathing in tubs, another option is to replace existing tubs with showers that someone can walk into without having to step over a big barrier.

- A 60×60 inch square is the recommended size for roll-in showers (36×60 inches is the minimum). Slope the floor for a maximum of ⅛-inch per foot for water flow.

- Walk-in showers should be large enough to accommodate a shower chair, at least 36×36 inches. If a shower with a built-in seat is desired, check the location and the height of the seat for safe transfers. The seat height should be a minimum of 17 inches from the shower floor and positioned for a safe reach of water controls while seated. A walk-in shower with no more than ½-inch threshold is ideal.

- If personal assistance is needed, be sure that the size of the shower will accommodate an additional person.

- Grab bars in the front and at the side of the shower are recommended at a height that can be easily reached and used with transfers. A grab bar at the back can also be useful.

- Controls should be no higher than 36 inches to 48 inches from the shower floor.

Of course, sitting down while showering will lessen the risk of falling down. Fold-up seats attached to the wall can make a shower more flexible for multiple users. Using nonslip decals or a bath mat on the shower floor is also recommended to prevent slipping. A handheld showerhead can be installed so you can bathe while seated. An 80-inch hose mounted on an adjustable height vertical bar is preferable.[125] A hand-held showerhead is often easier to use for someone with limited mobility than a fixed showerhead.

Eleanor told us about the shower she designed for her in-laws:

> *Eleanor*: The shower was the most challenging because it was a space issue and we didn't have a lot of room. But we did install grab bars in the shower. We also gave her the ability to sit in the shower and have my father-in-law bathe her with a flexible showerhead he could hold in his hand.

However, if someone needs a lot more support than a shower seat, there are automatic pulley devices available that lift frail individuals into a bathtub or shower. They're made by companies like Waverly Glen and prices run about $4,500, including installation. Some states will even provide financial assistance to qualified families to pay for such things as lift systems.

AARP recommends that people put in anti-scalding devices to keep water temperatures low. They can cost as little as $15 and are easily installed into a showerhead or bath faucet. Importantly, they can prevent someone from being burned by scalding water.[126] A single-handle, pressure-balanced faucet control is not only easier to use than two-knob faucets but can also reduce the chances of scalding.[127] Another option is to turn down the hot water heater to 115 degrees Fahrenheit or less. The newer faucets and shower valves are anti-scalding.

Bedrooms

It has been said that people spend more money on their coffins than on their beds. Certainly, one of the biggest considerations in making your home comfortable for seniors, or anyone for that matter, is choosing the right kind of bed. One product advertised in the September 2006 AARP Bulletin looks worthwhile. It is a flexible bed that can be bent into a sitting position with a remote control. There are many other flexible bedding options out there, as well, including resources at Flexabed.com.

It's ideal to have at least a 3-foot clearance by the bed to allow enough room for transferring from a wheelchair. A bed height of 20 to 22 inches allows for more level transfers. If the bed is too low, evaluate use of furniture extenders or risers that attach to the legs of the bed frame and raise the height.

Having a roll-in or walk-in closet with rods and shelves lowered between 2 feet and 4 feet from the floor will also provide easier accessibility. Removal of closet doors or installation of pocket doors will allow easier entry when closets are too small.[128]

Closets with adjustable rods and shelves can allow for more flexibility. Also, it's a good idea to have a chair in a closet so you can be seated while putting shoes and socks on and taking them off.

Kitchens

Universal design has evolved over the past two decades in response to the growing population of elders and disabled. However, it does not require that every counter be lowered to wheelchair height. Instead, it can mean having one section of the counter lower and another higher, enabling an elder mother and adult child to prepare meals together. Our Aunt Alice and her son Sterling had such an arrangement in the kitchen they had built for the two of them to use. The concept has worked so well that recently the National Kitchen and Bath Association revised its guidelines to incorporate universal design.[129]

Workspace and Counters

For a kitchen to be a safe and efficient workspace, it is important to avoid wasted motion. You want to create a kitchen where you'll spend less time walking, turning, bending, lifting, and cleaning. If a wheelchair will be used, you will need a 5-foot turning radius in the kitchen. Also, there should be adequate lighting and counter space. Under-cabinet fluorescent task-lighting can make working in the kitchen a lot easier.[130]

An efficient kitchen is generally designed around a work triangle formed by the location of three basic work centers: the refrigerator, sink, and range. Ideally, these centers should be arranged to follow the natural sequence of work for food preparation and cleanup. Basic patterns which accommodate this sequence include: U- and L-shaped, galley, and island/peninsula work centers. Good counter space next to each of the work centers is very important. As a general guide:

- 1½-foot-wide countertop next to the opening side of the refrigerator is desired as a minimum,
- 3 feet of counter to the right of a sink and 2 feet to the left (assuming a right-handed user) is desired,
- 2 feet of countertop on both sides of the stove is ideal.

Having a countertop section at least 30 inches wide that is lower will allow for working from a seated position (approximately 28 to 32 inches above the floor with open knee space). If this is not possible, use of a high chair or stool makes it easier to sit while working at standard height counters. Pullout cutting boards can also provide a work site. When there are no pullouts, a kitchen drawer can be converted to a work surface by fitting a cutting board on top of it. Stabilization of the cutting board with nonskid materials is helpful.[131]

Better hardware now exists to make the cutting board level and rigid. If possible, the cooktop and sink should have roll-in areas available that are free of plumbing pipes or other exposed fixtures that could injure knees and legs. Examples of such are cabinets with retractable doors. Another option is an adjustable kitchen sink, such as one from Populas (formerly AD-AS), that features push-button controls to both raise and lower the sink for those standing or using a wheelchair. Information on these items can be found at Populasfurniture.com. Also, for safety, place a fire extinguisher within easy reach of the stove.

Storage Areas

Storage areas need to be at the right height for people who use wheelchairs. Unfortunately, this is difficult to do in most kitchens. The "prime reaching zone" for items in the kitchen is, for most people, reachable from the waist and the shoulders—difficult or impossible for people using wheelchairs. Typically, this prime reaching zone is devoted to workspace in a kitchen, not cabinets for storage. If you have the room, it is advisable to put in a pantry closet for storage. If not, you can add shallow shelves on top of a countertop or put in hooks under cabinets above the countertop to hang small pots and pans. Tambour doors or "appliance garages" can be used to enclose shelves on top of a counter. Also, you can install pullout shelves, lazy Susan trays in corner cupboards, and adjustable-height cupboards to allow for easier access of utensils and supplies. It's advisable to use wide loop pulls with ample finger space instead of knobs or small handles on drawers and cabinets. They are much easier to grab for someone with limited strength or dexterity.[132]

Appliances

For those with limited reach, consider a side-by-side refrigerator, front- or side-located controls on the stove, and side-mounted water faucets. Side-swing oven doors make it easier to be positioned in front of the oven for easier loading and removal of food. A pullout shelf underneath the microwave or oven creates an immediate counter when removing foods.[133]

The microwave and dishwasher should be reachable (drawer-style dishwashers are excellent alternatives that really save a person's back).[134]

Installing a microwave at counter height is recommended. Also, you might want to consider putting in lever-style faucet handles at the kitchen sink, along with an under-cabinet jar opener and electric can opener.[135]

Eleanor told us what she did for her in-laws' kitchen:

> *Eleanor:* I designed it so that they could have a cooktop and a microwave. If they needed to, they would use my oven, which wasn't all that often. At that point, my father-in-law was doing all the cooking for them because they had their own likes and dislikes. I designed their kitchen to be very user-friendly. We put in drawers below the counter, instead of cabinets with doors. When you have a drawer, you can pull it out and easily

look down into it; you don't have to bend over. We put in full-extension glides on the drawers, so that they could be completely pulled out without falling out of the cabinets. That worked really well. We put in a single-lever faucet with a pull-out spray at the kitchen sink. That's much easier to use than two-knob faucets. They had a miniature refrigerator and a mini-dishwasher as well. It looked like a doll-size dishwasher, only 15 inches wide. They also had overhead cabinets that were easy to reach, along with under-cabinet lighting.

It's also possible to put in a raised, regular-size dishwasher that can be loaded and unloaded with much less bending, if elevated off the floor 12 inches or so.

Laundry Rooms

The ideal spot for doing the laundry is on the main floor of a house, near the bathroom and bedroom(s). One solution for those who have trouble bending or squatting is to "lift appliances off the floor," according to Roy Wendt, president of Wendt Builders, an Atlanta-based construction company that specializes in homes designed for seniors. For example, instead of top-loading washing machines, one builder uses front-load washers and dryers in his homes. He installs them on a platform "to make it even easier to get at clothing. We raise them by about 16 inches," he says. "You put them on a raised platform covered in tile. It's a pretty subtle feature."[136] Also, use of these front-load appliances can make reaching inside them easier from a wheelchair. An accessible-height countertop nearby can be helpful for folding clothes as well. Good news: a lot of the new washers and dryers being sold today are not only front-loading but are much higher off the floor than older models.

Living Rooms

The "lift chair" is one of the best pieces of furniture being sold these days for people with limited mobility. A friend's mother has one that looks like a beautifully upholstered lounge chair. It comes with a remote-control device that will gently raise her into a standing position, as well as lower her to sit down. They are priced at $550 to $1,500 and can be found not only in medical supply stores but also in regular furniture stores. In some cases, Medicare or health insurance companies will cover some of the purchase cost. Pride Mobility Products is a major manufacturer of lift chairs. It even sells some of its models with heaters and massagers. For more information, see Pridemobility.com.

Here are other tips for the living room:

- Having 3 feet to 5 five feet between pieces of furniture provides enough room to move when using mobility devices. Ensure there are clear passageways and ample maneuvering space with furniture placement.

- A height of 19 to 21 inches with favorite chairs or couches makes transfers easier and more energy efficient. A firm, dense cushion can increase the sitting height. If the furniture is too low, extenders or risers can be used.

- Use of remote controls for controlling lights, as well as the TV, VCR, and entertainment center.[137]

Floors

Tripping and slipping are two major safety concerns in a home. According to AARP, in a single year, Americans sixty-five and older had some 1.8 million falls that led to emergency room visits. More than half—about 55 percent—of these falls occurred in their homes. Fewer than half—49 percent—of all dwellings with an older person who has a physical limitation of some sort have been modified at all to make the home safer. And only 10 percent of homes had made two safety improvements.

You can make floors slip-resistant by adding nonskid mats under area rugs or getting rid of them entirely. Also, it is important to eliminate potential tripping points like thresholds whenever possible, or to lower their height.[138] Floors should be level with a nonslip surface, not sunken or raised. For those who use walkers, low-pile carpeting is safest so the walker doesn't catch on deep pile and cause a fall. Ultimately, for both walker and wheelchair users, hardwood, tile, or linoleum floors are best.[139]

Eleanor described the type of flooring she used in her in-laws' unit:

> *Eleanor:* I used linoleum in the kitchen and a frieze type of carpeting in the rest of the house. Frieze carpet is trackless or track resistant. The yarns are tightly twisted in order for a wheelchair or a walker to go over it and not leave a track. It's comfortable to walk on; you would use a jute pad for a firmer walking surface. Elders are more prone to turn their ankles or trip, so this firmer surface works well for them.

Joan also gave a reason not to use wall-to-wall carpeting:

> *Joan:* Initially, we had carpeting. We put wall-to-wall over the hardwood flooring in her bedroom and in the dining area. A few years ago we took that out. Why did we do that? Not because of tripping but because of overall cleanliness of her unit. Elder people run into incontinence problems, which is a major problem. Wall-to-wall carpeting is not the way to go, unless you want to have a professional cleaner out once a month. Being able to have hardwood flooring was just great.

Lighting

Often ignored, adequate lighting is another important feature in senior-friendly homes. It is advisable to place extra lights at the edge of the bed or in the bathroom, where it's easy to fall. Added lighting near steps or the front door is a good idea, too. Illuminated rocker or touch-sensitive wall light switches are easier to use than the standard toggle light switches. Consider placing them lower on the wall, so they are reachable from a wheelchair. Today, you can even put in remote-controlled lights and dimmers, enabling you to turn on lights from your bed or chair without having to cross a dark room to find the switch. Hardware stores carry them and installation does not require an electrician.[140]

Eleanor installed overhead recessed lights in her in-laws' unit. She said this type of lighting eliminates the need for lamps and dangling cords. Also, you might want to consider installing skylights or clerestory windows. They can add natural light to a home, creating a bright and cheery atmosphere. Eleanor said that windows are not only important for letting in natural light but also for keeping people connected to what's happening outside. Windowsills that are about 24 to 30 inches above the floor allow people to see outdoors while seated or standing.[141]

In comments about the design of her mother's home, Joan confirmed what Eleanor had to say:

> *Joan*: One thing we did in the entry was put in a half wall. That allows sunlight from the front entry window to come in farther. If you have a light and airy atmosphere, that can help a person not be depressed. I think sunshine is very cheery. We did put in skylights, as well.

Color Schemes

When Eleanor designed the cottage for her in-laws, she was careful to select colors that would be visually appealing even as their eyesight changed. Here's what she had to say about color schemes for elders:

> *Eleanor*: I wanted to take into consideration the color of walls and paper, because as the eye ages, the lens yellows. Things you're looking at won't appear to be white whites. They'll be yellow. That issue of the aging of the eye is a very important issue when you are dealing with designing for elders, whether they be in a facility or in their own home. By the way, when they have cataract surgery, that opens their eyes to the point where they have white as white again, instead of creamy yellow. I learned this through my father-in-law having cataract surgery. However, if you put someone in a room and their eyes view everything through a yellow filter, the room could look very unappealing and even make

them unhappy. It changes the coloration of the foods they eat. Foods could become "distasteful" to their sight, and therefore they might not want to eat them. For example, if a carrot was made purple, you probably wouldn't find it very appealing. So, the coloration that you put in a person's home is something they are living with and seeing on a daily basis. You want them to have it either be soothing or a color that they feel good about. So, as a designer, you don't go in and say, "Well, I think such and such color would be wonderful here." You have to consider if the client's eyes are aging, and how that color is going to look to them.

In some cases, it is advisable to use bold and contrasting colors to make things easier to see.[142] You can make walls a different color from baseboards, as well as use contrasting borders on floors, around cabinets, and along countertops for extra definition and depth perception.

Communication

One of the benefits of living in an electronic age is that technology can be put to work to help us in a number of different ways. Monitors are used by many people caring for their elder parents. These can range from a simple, low-priced baby monitor to a customized setup. An easy-reach buzzer at the side of someone's bed is another alternative.[143] In the case of communicating between two separate houses, certainly a cell phone could be used—almost everyone today always has their smartphone with them, even in the bedroom at night. Another option to consider is an intercom system. If you're building a house, it's cheaper to install the wiring during construction than it is to install it later.

There are specialized devices and cell phones that help people who have difficulty hearing, seeing, moving, speaking, or remembering. With cell phones, you can turn up the volume, clearly see incoming calls, dial more easily, use hands-free calling, display conversations in text, and store numbers.

Safety

There are a number of features you can install in your home that deal with safety issues. In case of fire, the use of audible/visible smoke alarms is strongly advised. If you are concerned about doors being left unlocked, put in a security system. Also, for everyone's peace of mind, it is a good idea to have some sort of medical alert system in place. There are medical alert devices available—such as those from Life Alert—that can be worn around the neck or as a bracelet to summon help at the push of a button. Seniors feel more comfortable knowing they have a panic button for help at any time without ever needing to use the phone. More information can be found at Lifealerthelp.com or 1-800-813-3104.

Transportation

Some years ago, Dana, who lives in Connecticut with her husband and three small children, bought the house next door for her grandmother. Dana is currently a full-time mom and community volunteer. She had been raised by her grandmother after her own mother died when she was three. She talked about transportation issues related to making her home accessible to her grandmother. Dana came up with a creative way to transport her grandmother to and from their house next door.

> *Dana*: My grandmother is here at our place for breakfast, lunch, and dinner. Depending on the weather, I will either go over and get her and bring her back, which is literally sixty-five seconds, or my son will. He has an electric golf cart, and he'll use it to go get her for me. Most of the time I make her walk on purpose to get the exercise.
> *Sharon*: Would you say she's about a hundred yards away?
> *Dana*: Yes. From here to the end of the driveway. She can walk and she should walk. So I try not to cater to her.

Robotic Elder-Care Products

When we wrote the first edition of this book the outlook for robots helping out was bright. The Technology section of the May 17, 2004, *San Francisco Chronicle* featured an article about *Wired* magazine's NextFest technology expo. However, the 110 new technologies on display at the expo were not for sale. The point of NextFest was to expose the general public to new technologies (new in 2004) that usually only scientists, military leaders, or journalists would have had access to:

> Honda Motors showed off its Asimo, short for "Advanced Step in Innovative Mobility." The 4-foot-tall robot is the latest in an 18-year-long research effort by Honda to create a robot that moves as smoothly as a human . . . Honda believes there is a future market for robots that can, for example, assist elder or disabled people with daily tasks.[144]

Many of the innovations at NextFest still need a lot of work before they can become everyday consumer products, if they ever do.

On the other hand, according to an earlier March 5, 2004, article in the *San Francisco Chronicle*, robotic elder-care products are gaining popularity in Japan. High labor costs are helping the trend gain acceptance in a nation that has the world's most rapidly aging population. Reminiscent of the old steam machines for bodies, Japan now has washing machines for humans. Yes, machines that wash people! Here are stories of how they work:

> With an electronic whir, the machine released a dollop of "peach body shampoo," a kind of body wash. Then as the cleansing bubbling action kicked in, Toshiko Shibahara, 89, settled back to enjoy the wash and soak cycle of her nursing home's new human washing machine. "The temperature is just right—the bubbles are really comfortable," she said, happily sealed up to her neck inside Sanyo Electric Co.'s latest elder care product. Turning to an attendant hovering around the

pink, clamshell-shaped "assisted-care bath," she asked, "May I have a bit more water, please?"

"It automatically washes my body, so I am quite happy about it," said Kuni Kikichi, an 88-year-old in a wheelchair who is paralyzed on her left side after a stroke. "These bubbles are good for the massage effect."[145]

Yukiko Sato, the general manager of a large chain of nursing homes, tells why his company decided to purchase the machines:

"Residents say it is really good because they warm their whole body; they can take the bath on their own; they can protect their privacy. As for the staff, it means less burden on their backs. Also, they can save time because the whole procedure can be done in a very short time."[146]

In fact, the washer works like an MRI. "The person sits in a chair that is rolled backward into place. The sides of the machine then close like a clamshell, forming an instant tub with the person's head sticking out the top. Shampooing and drying off are done by hand."[147]

However, more recent studies have found major problems in the distribution and use of robots for elder care even in Japan. Author James Wright concludes in the *MIT Technology Review*: While care robots are technologically sophisticated and those promoting them are (usually) well intentioned, they may act as a shiny, expensive distraction from tough choices about how we value people and allocate resources in our societies, encouraging policy makers to defer difficult decisions in the hope that future technologies will "save" society from the problems of an aging population. And this is not even to mention the potentially toxic and exploitative processes of resource extraction, dumping of e-waste in the Global South, and other negative environmental impacts that massively scaling up robotic care would entail.

Alternative approaches are possible and, indeed, readily available. Most obviously, paying care workers more, improving working conditions, better supporting informal caregivers, providing more effective social support for older people, and educating people across society about the needs of this popu-lation could all help build more caring and equitable societies without resorting to techno-fixes. Technology clearly has a role to play, but a growing body of evidence points to the need for far more collaboration across disciplines and the importance of care-led approaches to developing and deploying technology, with the active involvement of the people being cared for as well as the people caring for them.[148]

ECHO Housing

For those who don't have the time, energy, or financial resources to remodel their existing home to accommodate a senior, another option to consider is Elder Cottage Housing Opportunity (ECHO)—for more details see Echo-fairhousing.org. An ECHO house (basically, an ADU) is a small, portable, self-contained house designed to enable older people to live on the property of relatives or close friends so they don't have to be placed in an institution. It is a low-cost alternative since the homes are factory-built and there is no land cost. Installation of an ECHO unit takes two to three days. The main benefit of an ECHO house is that it allows an older person to live independently and privately in their own home, while living near family caregivers who can keep their own privacy—a win-win for all.[149]

To find out if there is an ECHO program in your area, you can contact your local Housing and Urban Development office. Depending on where you live, ECHO units are owned and rented out either by the government or nonprofit organizations. You could also buy your own prefabricated cottage or trailer to put in the rear or side yard of your single-family home. However, be aware that zoning often limits ECHO housing or trailers to large lots and rural areas.

In New England and the Hudson Valley, the Home Store is the largest builder of custom modular homes and offers ECHO in-law apartments with over forty universal design features. One of their clients tells the following story on their website:

> "My parents have now been living in an ECHO in-law apart-ment with me for about two years. It has actually turned out

better than I ever expected it could, and that's why I'm telling the story, so that others who might be thinking about this can know how we did it and how we make it work, both financially and emotionally . . .

"The first step was to get estimates for the job. Originally, we were just going to have a conventionally built addition. Dad got a quote from a builder he knew and trusted for a 526 sq. ft. completely self-contained one bedroom apartment. The price was unbelievable! We were all shocked. My folks could never afford to go to Florida if the cost of the apartment was going to be so high, and I was, unfortunately, not in a position to help finance the apartment with my oldest son getting ready to start college. We agreed that we would always provide a home for my folks from this time forward and help with their care whenever they needed us.

"Fortunately, Mom and Dad came across an AARP publication titled 'ECHO Housing.' It described affordable free-standing modular homes and in-law apartments that were specifically designed to meet the needs of elders. Both are built with Universal Design features that make the homes accessible for people of all ages, sizes, and abilities. The publication described how the modular homes are built in a factory and trucked to their destination. The amazing thing is that they can easily be removed if the family is relocating or no longer needs the ECHO home. The idea seemed intriguing. Mom and Dad remembered seeing a modular home at a home show a few years back and inquired with that builder about his cost for the same size apartment. The Home Store, who built the home-show house, was able to beat the local builder's price by thousands of dollars. It helped a lot that The Home Store has a specialty in universal design and ECHO housing. We were also pleased they were able to do everything that needed to be done from start to finish.

"We then had to go before the Zoning Board of Appeals to get the OK to add a supplemental apartment. In addition, we had to inquire about any restrictions on the size of the apartment. We did not have any difficulty getting approval for our addition. Our neighbors and the town were supportive of the idea and are pleased with how seamlessly the ECHO blends with our home.

"Now that our ECHO apartment is here and lived in, we have found that the quality and sturdiness of the modular home is exceptional. I learned that the reason the modular addition feels so solid is that it has to be built to withstand the trip from the factory and being lifted by a crane and placed on its foundation. That apartment does not have one single spot that squeaks or creaks. My home, on the other hand, squeaks and creaks everywhere we walk."[150]

For more information, you can call The Home Store at (413) 665-1266, ext. 1, or see The-homestore.com.

CONCLUSIONS

This chapter provides you with multiple options for creating an elder-friendly home, using universal design features. Examples include grab bars, 36-inch doorways, lever handles on doors and faucets, hardwood floors, lower counters, and many more. All of these innovations can increase the accessibility of your home for people of all ages and abilities. Such design enhances the ability of people to limit obstacles and maximize independence for as long as possible. Planning ahead to include universal design features can make the changes more affordable, as well as make your home more functional and accessible now, and in the future. It pays to plan ahead!

PART FOUR

THE
CHALLENGES

OVERCOMING CULTURAL STIGMAS: FOUR CURSES AND A BLESSING

In the progress of personality, first comes a declaration of independence, then a recognition of interdependence.

—Henry van Dyke

We identify four kinds of barriers to getting together again with your extended family. First, we discuss the financial and legal ones in some detail in the next chapter. Second, we summarize the constraining building and zoning codes at the end of chapter 10. Next, we mention the psychological obstacles in many places in these pages—that is, extended family living will not work for everyone—some folks just cannot get along because of the mix of personalities. And, now we turn to the fourth kind of barrier: the cultural kind. The good news for Americans is that the cultural barriers are beginning to fade.

E arlier, we describe how almost all people have always lived in, and are still living in, multigenerational households. Moreover, in this country we also used to live in predominantly multigenerational households. How is it then that twentieth-century America became unique among societies? The answers to this question reveal much about taken-for-granted aspects of American thinking. The answers to this question also reveal the path to a new freedom that will allow us to live together again and enjoy doing so. Let's start the story with the latest symptom of the fluidity of American culture, the so-called boomerang kids.

Figure 12.1. Zits © 2005 Zits Partnership, Distributed by King Features Syndicate, Inc.

BOOMERS, BOOMERANGS, AND BARRIERS

The *Zits* cartoon says it all (see figure 12.1). You can bet that Jeremy's *fear-appeal* will yield tons of the sweet stuff. In fact, we know that what fear-appeals do best is get your attention. They may make you fearful or just plain mad, but they do get your attention—they elicit an emotional response. Indeed, look at today's politics. Republicans tell us we should be afraid our international neighbors will kill us. Democrats tell us we should be afraid our international neighbors will steal our jobs. But, what's really going on in all these cases is that journalists themselves also realize that fear-based headlines and disputes sell newspapers. Thus, we see a profusion of confusion about twentysomethings and thirtysomethings living at home (the boomerang kids). Take a look at a sampling of recent headlines and book and movie titles:

> *Adult Children Moving Back Home: Don't Let Them Derail Your Goals*
> *Returning College Kids Shake Things Up at Home*
> *Look Who's Back*
> *The Coddling Crisis: Why Americans Think Childhood Begins at Age 26*
> *The PermaParent Trap* [perhaps the scariest]
> *The American Dream Runout: The Cluttered Nest*
> *Home Sweet Home—Again*

Hi Folks, I'm Home! As College Grads Move In, Some Parents Are Put Out
Mom, Can I Move Back In with You? A Survival Guide for Parents of
  Twentysomethings
When Our Grown Kids Disappoint Us
Failure to Launch

The single worst case of this unfounded youth bashing we've run across is on page 5 of Senator Josh Hawley's disgraceful book, *Manhood*. He criticizes young men: "More and more young men are living at home with their parents."[151] We see this as just part of family members helping out and learning to live together again. The worst consequence of the popular media's negative interpretation of the boomerang kids phenomenon is the undeserved pain it delivers to our kids.

Yes, the negative headlines get everyone's attention. But, they cause angst for us all, particularly the kids. But, these headlines misrepresent reality. The reality? Perhaps it's not all that bad? Perhaps it's more of a mixed blessing? At least you'd gather such from some of the more recent headlines:

"Boomerang Kids Don't Have to Be a Financial Drain"
"Boomerang Kids: How Do Parents Deal with the Blessing of
  Children Who Move Back Home? Or, the Curse?"
"Is It a Happy Nest the Second Time Around?"

Moreover, recall the Del Webb survey mentioned in chapter 10 by the Standard Pacific executives—only about 25 percent of boomers expect to be happier when their kids leave. The survey goes on to report that happiness seems to decline with the length of time the nest is actually empty:

- Zero to five years since the children left: 27 percent feel happier
- Six to ten years: 11 percent
- Eleven or more years: 5 percent

Too bad the kids themselves haven't heard the news that they're missed.

Finally, we can even find a few headlines and associated articles and books that coincide with this reality:

Decorating for Boomerang Kids [our favorite]
Boomerang Joy
When a Child Returns Home: At Times, Freedom and Privacy
Can't Hold a Candle to the Fullness of Family Life

So, despite the media, the American population seems to recognize that boomerang kids are actually a good thing. Most folks writing in the area agree that things work out better if: the kid pays rent or contributes to the household in tangible ways, it's a temporary and one-time situation, the parents are in a long-term marriage, it helps the kids with some sort of transition,[152] and the kid is good company.

Most folks also agree on the causes of the return home: economics/safety net, the kid's divorce, graduate school or other extended education, drug/alcohol problems, and temporary transitions. We actually don't agree with either list, particularly the notion of a "temporary transition" embedded in both.

When you step back and look at the big picture, it's clear that boomerang kids are just another symptom of the cultural change affecting American society as we prepare to enter the year 2024. Indeed, based on a 2011 study of more than 700 so-called boomerang kids, researchers at the University of Minnesota reported: "The fact that young people depend so heavily upon their parents well beyond the age when most people from earlier generations had already started families and had dependable jobs has triggered a great deal of public anxiety over whether these trends signal young adult immaturity and stunted development. The larger social trends in delaying family formation may be one reason for the extended dependence upon parents. Today, the road to adulthood is much longer and more arduous than it was thirty years ago."[153]

The last sentence above clearly describes a cultural shift. And, as we mention in chapter 2, we see the current boomerang kid/baby boomer interaction as a very useful preparation for the fast-approaching years of the boomers' retirement. We as a society are relearning how adult parents and children can live and work together cooperatively in extended family arrangements.

Grandparents moving back is another symptom of the same cultural shift. The failing pension and health care systems are also symptoms. The fundamental point is that people are moving back together again because the grand experiment of the World War II generation hasn't worked. Three-generation households may indeed belong together, and not just for financial or psychological reasons. Fundamentally and by nature, humans are built this way and have evolved this way. We've survived the millennia by living in such extended family arrangements. We are happiest in such groups. And, we are now quickly learning that other institutions (companies, unions, governments, religious organizations, etc.) ultimately cannot take care of us; only our families can and will.

The growing numbers of boomerang kids bear this out. Estimates vary, but the numbers are huge. As we mention in chapter 2, more than one third of all Americans ages eighteen to thirty-four are now living with their parents, according to the latest U.S. Bureau of the Census figures. For those aged eighteen to twenty-five, the numbers were even higher: more than half live with one or both parents. Such living arrangements exist only because they work. Most recently, the COVID-19 pandemic has boosted these numbers.

So given the natural tendency of humans to live in extended family groups, why did this strange experiment with separation occur in America during the latter half of the twentieth century? The explanations are several, intertwined, and crucial to understand if they are to be overcome. Indeed, the faster we "get over" the odd culture of relative familial isolation we have inherited from the World War II generation, the sooner we can begin to enjoy the benefits of extended family living, of being together again.

Boomerang kids? What seems to be a curse is actually a societal blessing, albeit one disguised by the media. Indeed, it's often easy to confuse blessings and curses. This is particularly so when abundance is involved. Think food, cars, oil, kids, and so on. You can be too thin, and some say you can be too rich.

We now turn to the four curses of American culture affecting multigenerational family living. All four have deep roots in American culture. Moreover, most Americans consider them blessings. And, certainly these curses do have their positive attributes. But, all four act to constrain the freedom of Americans to be inventive in designing appropriate households and living arrangements. The point is that we are victims of our own culture. Recognition of these constraints will give us freedom to think and act differently than the previous generation. And, as the problems facing our generations are different from the past, we *really* need this new freedom.

1. THE CURSE OF THE MISSING "TER"

America started with the Declaration of Independence. On July 4, 1776, the
Founding Fathers formally broke from Great Britain to form a new country.
That document and the idea of independence represent the essence of being
American. Independence is literally the most celebrated notion of the nation.
Indeed, the goal of mainstream American parenting is to inculcate this notion
into the noggins of our kids. We make them make their own beds, make their
own lunches, wash their own clothes, do their own homework, drive their own
cars. How else can they be independent adults?

There are at least three problems with this approach: First, it stigmatizes
both the boomerang kids and the grandparents living with their kids. Second,
it doesn't work. Third, there is no such thing as independence. There is only
*inter*dependence, and thus the missing "ter" in the heading.

The Declaration of Independence was about politics and had little to do
with interpersonal relationships. King George III of Great Britain was a tyrant:
denying our human rights, taxing us without representation, and perhaps worst
of all, "cutting off trade with all parts of the world." That is, we had to pay more
for tea from China and rum from Jamaica because they were shipped through
British ports. So the Founding Fathers declared "that as free and independent
states, they have the full power to levy war, conclude peace, contract alliances,
establish commerce, and to do all other acts and things which independent
states may of right do." Indeed, after we won the Revolutionary War some
eleven years later, our ships started sailing directly to Canton and Kingston,
rather than only to Britain. The Declaration of Independence was and is a wonderful and pathbreaking document. But, it says nothing about teaching your
kids to wash their own clothes or to do their own homework. And, even after
we won the war, we still traded with Britain. Indeed, the United States is by
any measure still interdependent with Great Britain. Today's United Kingdom
remains one of our most important partners in both trade and defense. And
so it goes. One can make a good argument that political independence doesn't
really exist either, given the new globalization.

And this foolish (even by some accounts dangerous[154]) notion of independence, originally applied only to politics, makes Americans feel incorrectly
guilty about the clear interdependence that has always and will always exist

across generations of family members. This American overemphasis on independence is now being recognized among the most independent-minded of all Americans, CEOs. In Bill George's wonderful book *Authentic Leadership*, he argues that the job of chief executive officers depends on six constituencies. Without surprise, George, the former CEO of Medtronic, lists shareholders, employees, customers, vendors, and the larger community. What is unique, even revolutionary, in his list is his own family. He recognizes that his own success as a CEO in part depends on the quality of his family life. Thus, he organized his executive team and responsibilities such that he had time to attend his kids' soccer matches and such. Remarkable![155]

There's also a final irony about the notion of American independence. We made a lot of tanks during World War II. Right after the war, the extra industrial capacity created during the war made cars cheap in this country. As indicated in table 12.1, we have more cars per family than any other nation. And cheap cars created freeways and suburbia and shopping centers. With our cars we could load up at the grocery store and become independent of the daily shopping routine still facing households all around the world. Indeed, a car for every person in the family and everyone is independent. "See the USA in a Chevrolet" made road trips attractive and promised a new freedom and independence

TABLE 12.1. PASSENGER CARS PER 1,000 PEOPLE IN SELECTED COUNTRIES

United States	890
Germany	628
Mexico	391
Canada	790
Japan	624
France	668
Brazil	366
Italy	755
United Kingdom	594
South Korea	485
China	221
India	62

Source: A series of country-level agencies summarized by Wikipedia, accessed 2023.

from public transportation. The latest incarnation of the "car = independence" argument has been the billions of dollars spent selling Americans SUVs. "Go anywhere, anytime in your Hummer. Your Hummer even gives you independence from roads (and traffic)." So now, while we are independent of our local grocery store, as a nation we Americans are completely dependent on our cars, big refrigerators, the continuous construction of new highways (for our sanity), and oil from foreign countries. The fuel burned in our cars is polluting the planet, changing global weather patterns, and reducing the amount of land to live on. Perhaps the greatest irony of all is that the space taken up by all our cars is limiting our freedom to build sensible housing. Granny flats are often built above garages, yielding the extra steps that will plague the coming elder generation. And, worst of all, providing the parking for our metal monsters subtracts living space for American families, as noted in our discussion of the constraining building and zoning codes in chapter 10.

Independence isn't just overrated. Most simply stated, *independence is a myth*. Human beings are social animals and are by our deepest nature interdependent on one another. Shouldn't the design of our homes, households, and communities recognize this fundamental fact? Perhaps the Founding Fathers should have held this truth to be self-evident, as well.[156] Had they done so, getting together again in multigenerational family arrangements would be much easier for all of us.

Both elders living with their kids and the young living with their parents suffer from this cultural stigma of "dependence." Their own words testify to the lack of recognition of their actual state of interdependence. They are missing what they are delivering in the interpersonal exchange of living together:

> *Stacie*: I think the thing that affects me the most living here with my parents is it makes me be more dependent on them, when I should be establishing my independence. That's hard for me because it's right there for me to grab. My parents want to give it to me, but they don't. Sometimes I grab it and sometimes I don't. Like, I depend on my parents for transportation, and I'm working for them for food. So I'm paying that back. I

just sometimes feel like I take advantage of the things that are there for me, if I need them. They also want me to be independent. But, at the same time, it's hard to establish that line.

Greg: There is an ego issue where you think that your peers might look down upon it or think that you are not out on your own or that you're strange for living with your in-laws. Once we had Ryan, all of those concerns disappeared because we could see how beneficial our living arrangement is to the whole family. When it's just yourself and a set of parents, you are all adults, and it might look a little strange. But, as soon as you throw a child into the mix, the benefits are just so amazing. I talk to so many people and I'm almost embarrassed to tell them our situation, if they have a similarly aged child. They just can't believe how lucky we are and how much help we have. I know so many people who have moved out here for a job and don't have any family in California. They have no support system and it's just incredibly hard to raise a child without having that support system, especially with both parents working.

So, at least Greg is now seeing past the dependency stigma. Betsy also recognizes the reality of interdependence in her family's relationship with her mother:

Betsy: When my mom left San Diego, she was going to move in with my sister who is single. She owns a home in Valencia. My husband and I had been augmenting my mom's rent. So she was putting in $1,100 and we were doing the balance of it for her to live in San Diego. Bringing her here brought us something, the companionship and the family that my daughter needed and support that I needed, because all of my siblings are at a distance. She was a constant support that was missing for us. So that was how we justified the financial cost for us.

Therefore, my siblings did not help us with the San Diego residence because they said, "We didn't tell her to go over there." I think that's fair. Now they are saying that if she moves in with my sister, and my sister is going to be driving her to the doctors and all of those things and possibly having to upgrade her house to accommodate my mom, we should all help out. "Let's set up a Mom's fund," where all of us contribute $500 a month. Then, at the end of this year, maybe our sister can take that money and redo her house with it. My sister protested, "Well, nobody helped you guys." We said, "Well hang on, the value we got was different. What you are doing will require you to make some changes, since you are single and working. Maybe Mom can contribute what she might be paying if she lived in an apartment." So, as it worked out for the year, we decided to have my mom in an apartment.

Accessory-apartment advocate and housing expert Patrick Hare clearly sees the American independence stigma as a major problem:

Pat: Here is one of the things that seems to be really important. Somehow through the single-family house, we have projected independence as a value. It has come to mean, I think without anybody intending it, "isolation." Because, after the kids leave, statistically half of all the people live as couples. So what it means is that you are going to have two people at least living in a household by themselves. One of them is going to end up alone. But psychologically, the status of having that house is so important. The irony is that it is not really independence. What it means is that, when there is any crisis, you are going to be dependent on strangers. You're going to be dependent on home health aides, EMTs, all these strangers. And, strangers that don't know how to deal with taking care of you. A person has to be there if you are going to the hospital. If your relatives live two hours away, they won't be able to help you there. In terms of quality of life, this whole independence in a single-family world is a disaster.

2. THE CURSE OF "I"

America is a strange place among nations. Americans generally don't notice this because we assume people everywhere think just like we do. Well, they don't. And, the American difference is most prominent on the dimension of individualism/collectivism. Look at the numbers in table 12.2. We're at the top of the list, the end of the scale. Americans place higher values on individualism than folks from any other country. These numbers are based on the research of a Dutch international management scholar, Geert Hofstede. In 1970 he surveyed IBM employees around the world about their work-related values. From those data he developed four dimensions of cultural differences, the most salient of which is his "Individualism/Collectivism Index."

TABLE 12.2. INDIVIDUALISM/COLLECTIVISM INDEX*

United States	91	Slovakia	52	Hong Kong	25
Australia	90	Spain	51	Serbia	25
Great Britain	89	India	48	Chile	23
Hungary	80	Suriname	47	Bangladesh	20
Netherlands	80	Argentina	46	China	20
New Zealand	79	Japan	46	Singapore	20
Italy	76	Morocco	46	Thailand	20
Belgium	75	Iran	41	Vietnam	20
Denmark	74	Jamaica	39	West Africa	20
France	71	Russia	39	El Salvador	19
Sweden	71	Brazil	38	South Korea	18
Ireland	70	Arab countries	38	Taiwan	17
Norway	69	Turkey	37	Peru	16
Germany	67	Uruguay	36	Trinidad	16
South Africa	65	Greece	35	Costa Rica	15
Finland	63	Croatia	33	Indonesia	14
Estonia	60	Philippines	32	Pakistan	14
Luxembourg	60	Bulgaria	30	Colombia	13
Poland	60	Mexico	30	Venezuela	12
Malta	59	Romania	30	Panama	11
Czech Republic	58	Portugal	27	Ecuador	8
Switzerland	58	Slovenia	27	Guatemala	6
Austria	55	East Africa	27		
Israel	54	Malaysia	26		

Source: Geert Hofstede, *Cultural Consequences*,
2nd ed. (Thousand Oaks, CA: Sage, 2001).

*Higher numbers = more individualistic cultural values.

John reports in his textbook:

> **Individualism/Collectivism Index**. The Individualism/
> Collectivism Index refers to the preference for behavior that
> promotes one's self-interest. Cultures that score high in IDV
> reflect an "I" mentality and tend to reward and accept indi-
> vidual initiative, whereas those low in individualism reflect a
> "we" mentality and generally subjugate the individual to the
> group. This does not mean that individuals fail to identify
> with groups when a culture scores high on IDV, but rather
> that personal initiative and independence are accepted and
> endorsed. Individualism pertains to societies in which the
> ties between individuals are loose; everyone is expected to
> look after himself or herself and his or her immediate fam-
> ily. Collectivism, as its opposite, pertains to societies in which
> people from birth onward are integrated into strong, cohesive
> groups, which throughout people's lifetimes continue to pro-
> tect them in exchange for unquestioning loyalty.[157]

Individualism is, of course, directly related to and reinforces the notion
of independence discussed above. But, while independence is a myth, individualism is not. Moreover, individualism leads directly to competitiveness.
Competitiveness can be a good thing. Our hugely successful American economic system is based upon the principle that competitiveness breeds efficiency.
But, competitiveness is not always a good thing. Think sibling rivalry as just the
problem most pertinent to the topic of this book. In order to avoid suffering
the negative consequences of our often-wonderful American individualism, it
is important to understand its origins. Why are Americans the most individualistic people on the planet?

Reference to two books, one new and one old, provides us the answer. In the
first, *The Geography of Thought*, University of Michigan psychologist Richard
Nisbett tells us that the fundamental difference between Western (American
and European) and Eastern (Asian) thinking is rooted in the geography of

ancient Greece and China, respectively.[158] Simply summarized, 2,500 years ago, Greek culture grew up in an island geography where people weren't much affected by their neighbors. If you live on an island you don't have to worry so much about your neighbors attacking you and you cannot so much depend on them helping you either. In contrast, 2,500 years ago, if you lived in the crucible of Eastern culture, between the great rivers of China, you were literally surrounded by people. You had to pay attention to your neighbors because they could easily harm or help you. John Donne's 1624 poem "No Man Is an Island" would never have come up in China or Japan, then or now, because folks from collectivistic cultures take the poem's central notion for granted:

> No man is an island, entire of itself every man is a piece of the continent, a part of the main if a clod be washed away by the sea, Europe is the less, as well as if a promontory were, as well as if a manor of thy friends or of thine own were any man's death diminishes me, because I am involved in mankind and therefore never send to know for whom the bell tolls it tolls for thee.

We also understand the individualism embedded in Northern European culture, including our own Anglo culture, with reference to the cold climate there and the Protestant Reformation. Harsh winters and snowdrifts prevent your neighbors from helping or hurting you, so folks from northern climes tend toward cultural values for individualism and independence. Indeed, the cold climes kept out the Romans and ultimately led to the Protestant Reformation. That is, it was tough to be dependent on a priest through which to talk with God when a blizzard was blowing outside your door. Bad weather makes a direct, individual relationship with God more practical. It's no accident that Geert Hofstede noticed these differences. As a kid he grew up living on the northern/southern border of Europe demarcated by the three great rivers of the region. The western flowing Rhine, Waal, and Maas once cut Europe in half, north to south, cold to warm, barbarian to Roman, Protestant to Catholic, and individualistic to collectivistic. These geographic influences can roughly be seen with reference to table 12.2.

But, what puts Americans on the top of the individualism list? The answer lies in a question we have for you. Before reading on, we want you to sit back and ask yourself, *What is the most influential sentence first written in English?* Really, stop reading here, sit back, and contemplate our query.

Give up? Good guesses include something from the Magna Carta, John Locke, William Shakespeare, or perhaps our own Declaration of Independence. But, we think the best answer is: "By pursuing his own interest he frequently promotes that of society more effectually than when he really intended to promote it."

This is Adam Smith's "invisible hand" statement from his *Wealth of Nations*, published in 1776.[159] We paraphrase: individualism (and the often-associated selfishness, even greed) actually promotes competition, which, when healthy, promotes society by boosting overall productivity. The words of this Scottish philosopher were fundamental in the design of the American social, economic, and political system that so greatly influenced the rest of the world in the last half of the twentieth century. The date is important. All of our Founding Fathers would have read and been deeply influenced at the time by his book. Perhaps even more important is the identity of his coauthor. Smith's arguments are in large part based on copious data about the American colonies, supplied by none other than our own Benjamin Franklin. The sage among the authors of our Constitution was intimately connected with Adam Smith.

And, Smith's epiphany so stated above solved the human conundrum of the ages. That is, "Do I worry about me or my group?" Smith advises folks, at least in the context of economic behavior, to simply worry about themselves and that will take care of your group. Individualism, even competition, are not just justified, they're elevated as almost righteous. And, Smith's philosophy writ large upon the blank slate of our new country. In Smith's own Great Britain, social hierarchy prevailed, thus limiting the impact of his ideas at home. So, we Americans value individualism higher than even the United Kingdom, consistent with Hofstede's numbers in table 12.2.

Finally, it is important to note that embedded in Smith's epiphany is Smith's hedge. You may have gotten a glimpse of it in the Academy Award–winning movie, *A Beautiful Mind*. Mathematician John Nash (well played by Russell Crowe) proved mathematically that it can be in one's self-interest to cooperate. But, this would not have been news for Smith. Notice the latter's strategic use of the term "frequently." Smith is clearly saying that there's room for cooperation in human society and economy. This is a notion often lost on Wall Street these days (think Gordon Gekko's "greed is good" diatribe in the movie *Wall Street*) and in our MBA programs around the country, where individualism, competition, even selfishness and greed are often exalted.

Long-winded perhaps we are. Our point here? We believe it's important for you to understand the depth of influence our culture of individualism has on our thinking. That knowledge frees you to consider the negative consequences of those cultural values. Indeed, even Adam Smith, the father of the philosophy of individualism, argued for cooperation. And, there's no more sensible context for cooperation than your own extended family.

3. THE CURSE OF SAMENESS

> Little boxes on the hillside,
> Little boxes made of ticky-tacky,
> Little boxes on the hillside,
> Little boxes all the same,
> There's a green one and a pink one
> And a blue one and a yellow one
> And they're all made of ticky-tacky
> And they all look the same.[160]

No one would argue about the importance of equality to American society. That's one topic on which we even agree with the French! However, the high value we place on egalitarianism does cause problems when it comes to the design of communities. Edward T. Hall, anthropologist and father of the study of proxemics, or spaces, well describes the differences in community design he has observed:

> The American pattern emphasizes equality and standard-
> ization of the segments which are used for measuring space
> or into which space is divided, be it a ruler or a suburban

subdivision . . . whereas towns in many other parts of the world are laid out with unequal blocks. This suggests that it was no accident that mass production, made possible by the standardization of parts, had its origins in the United States.[161]

Our American value of equality serves us well when it comes to human relations but not when it comes to community design. New-home builders, consumers, and zoning officials tend to favor houses of equal value and size without mixing. Mixed neighborhoods of size, value, and use are disfavored. The current hue and cry against the so-called McMansions is the latest symptom of this downside to equality, and in this case sameness. Or, consider the report that PeopleSoft's billionaire founder, David Duffield, downsized his planned 72,000-square-foot "castle" to only 17,000 square feet because his Alamo, California, neighbors protested its girth. His neighbors circulated a petition to limit houses to 10,000 square feet in the development where Duffield purchased a twenty-two-acre site. There is some humor here! Somehow, we Americans have confused equality with sameness, and this has mightily deterred creativity in housing and community design.

Before we close this topic, we do want to make clear that egalitarianism and equality are important and pertinent in the discussion of multigenerational households in other respects. That is, egalitarianism promotes creativity by allowing all members of a group to table ideas—the more ideas the better. Moreover, egalitarianism is also important in negotiations. In chapter 6 we present the decision to live together as a negotiation among adults. Once kids are eighteen, they are *legally independent*. According to the law, no one owes anyone anything across the parent-child relationship at that point. And, the negotiation about living together proceeds most efficiently recognizing this fundamental equality, the fairest question being, "What resources do you have to offer in this relationship?"

4. THE CURSE OF THE WIDE-OPEN SPACES

The original colonizers of America came for the wide-open spaces. The appeal of the road trip goes back some 500 years. Seeing new things and getting away from the crowds attracted our ancestors and still attracts people today. And, this fundamental yearning for being in and particularly owning the wide-open spaces has a dramatic, if somewhat hidden, influence on our daily lives. Edward T. Hall puts it best when he explains how space speaks:

> Man has developed his territoriality to an almost unbelievable extent. Yet we treat space somewhat as we treat sex. It is there but we don't talk about it. And if we do, we certainly are not expected to get technical or serious about it . . . The man of the house is always somewhat apologetic about "his chair." How many people have had the experience of coming into a room, seeing a big comfortable chair and heading for it, only to pull up short, or pause and turn to the man and say, "Oh, was I about to sit in your chair?" The reply, of course, is usually polite. Imagine the effect if the host were to give vent to his true feelings and say, "Hell, yes, you're sitting in my chair, and I don't like anybody sitting in my chair." For some unknown reason, our culture has tended to play down or cause us to repress and dissociate the feelings we have about space. We relegate it to the informal and are likely to feel guilty whenever we find ourselves getting angry because someone has taken our place . . .
>
> Once while talking on this subject to a group of Americans who were going overseas, one very nice, exceedingly mild-mannered woman raised her hand and said, "You mean it's natural for me to feel irritated when another woman takes over my kitchen?" Answer: "Not only is it natural, but most American women have very strong feelings about their kitchens. Even a mother can't come in and wash the dishes in her daughter's kitchen without annoying her. The kitchen is the place where 'who will dominate' is settled. All women know this, and some can even talk about it. Daughters who can't keep control of their kitchen will be forever under the thumb of any women who can move into this area."

The questioner continued: "You know that makes me feel so relieved. I have three older sisters and a mother, and every time they come to visit, they march right into the kitchen and take over. I want to tell them to stay out of my kitchen, that they have their own kitchens, and this is my kitchen, but I always thought I was having unkind thoughts about my mother and sisters, thoughts I wasn't supposed to have. This relieves me so much, because now I know I was right."[162]

The territoriality so well elucidated by Hall is of course related to the individualistic competitiveness described earlier. Indeed, individualism + territoriality = privacy. And, privacy needs are the bane of most extended family arrangements.

A related aspect of our wide-open spaces values is the value we Americans place on size. Supersizing meals at restaurants is making Americans fat. How about our housing? It's clear that for mainstream Americans in the twenty-first century, size is equated with status. This has been so for some time—note Hall's comments on this topic:

> Our pattern calls for the president or the chairman of the board to have the biggest office. The executive vice-president will have the next largest, and so on down the line until you end up in the "bull pen." More important offices are usually located at the corners of and on the upper floors of the building. Executive suites will be on the top floor. The relative rank of the vice-presidents will be reflected in where they are placed along "executive row." The French, on the other hand, are much more likely to lay out space as a network of connecting points of influence, activity, or interest. The French supervisor will ordinarily be found in the middle of his subordinates where he can control them.
>
> Americans who are crowded will often feel that their status in the organization is suffering. As one would expect in the Arab world, the location of an office and its size constitute a poor index of the importance of the man who occupies it.

What we experience as crowded, the Arab will often regard as spacious. The same is true in Spanish culture . . . .

The American will look at a Japanese room and remark how bare it is. Similarly, the Japanese will look at our rooms and comment, "How bare!" Furniture in the American home tends to be placed along the walls (around the edge). Japanese have their charcoal pit where the family gathers in the middle of the room. The top floor of Japanese department stores is not reserved for the chief executive—it is the bargain roof![163]

Like American offices, our housing reflects the value we place on view, elevation, and, of course, size. This is actually good news because the girth of our houses allows for creativity in how we use the space inside. That is, if we can just suppress some of our values for individual privacy. Although the growth in size of new single-family homes abated some since the Great Recession, overall the trend has been steady increases in size in this century to about 2,500 square feet. This is still very large compared to house sizes in other countries.

Further, our houses remain among the most sparsely populated among nations around the world. See table 12.3 below, based on a study reported by environmental news organization Shrink That Footprint.

TABLE 12.3. OCCUPANTS AND SQUARE FEET PER HOUSEHOLD

Germany	2.05	1173
Sweden	2.17	893
The Netherlands	2.23	1261
United Kingdom	2.27	818
France	2.22	1206
Italy	2.40	957
Japan	2.28	1023
Canada	2.45	1948
Spain	2.69	1044
United States	2.49	2164*
China	2.70	646

Sources: Shrink That Footprint and United Nations and U.S. Census data, accessed 2022. Estimates vary depending on the source.

Folks from all around the world are astonished by how much room we Americans take up, how big our houses are. When a Dutch friend said about his first visit to an American home, "Your refrigerator is bigger than my closet," he was not only commenting on the size of the appliance. He was also commenting on the size of his closet back in The Netherlands! Yes, Europeans stop by the grocery store more often because the typical home only has one relatively small refrigerator, while many American homes have two big ones. Similarly, Europeans do own nice clothing; they just don't own as much as comparable Americans. They don't have walk-in closets, let alone ones with furniture in them, as some new homes do now.

While American closets have been expanding, so have American garages. And, while we are all making our closets and garages bigger to store the fruits of our consumerism, we are shrinking the space and time for our family interactions.

Recall the comments from Patrick Hare from the beginning of chapter 7: 32 percent of American homes have the potential for accommodating ADUs. Since he made his original calculations almost twenty years ago, American homes have become even larger with fewer people under any one roof. All these figures suggest there is housing capacity available in the United States, if we can just be creative in our building and usage practices and adjust our basic values to allow for extended family living. The curse of the wide-open spaces can be transformed into a blessing of space for more generations as we progress into the twenty-first century.

THE BLESSING OF IMMIGRATION

Many in the country today decry immigration as a major social problem for America—the curse of the unwashed knocking on our doors. We don't see it that way. Immigrants to the United States have always brought with them a bounty of new ideas. Now, they are showing us new ways to live, or actually old ways, depending on how you look at multigenerational families and housing.[164] As indicated in exhibit 12.1, most of the recent immigrants to the United States are from countries where multigenerational households have always worked and are still working well. Indeed, we get the term *casita* from Spanish.

Exhibit 12.1. Immigrants to the United States,
Top Ten Sending Nations, 2015–2020
(by 1000s of Immigrants)

Mexico 919
India 348
China 395
Dominican Republic 330
Vietnam 210
Philippines 295
El Salvador 156
Cuba 318
South Korea 114
Colombia 102

Source: Data from the United States Department of Homeland Security, accessed 2022.

We close this chapter with excerpts from two of our interviews with immigrants to the United States who are thriving in three-generation households. You will notice they do not suffer from any of the four curses: the need for independence, individualism, sameness, or wide-open spaces. We can and should learn from them. We will need the blessings of their good ideas to help us manage the changing circumstances of twenty-first-century America.

As you may recall in chapter 5, Lan, a first-generation immigrant from China, told us how she's imported the psychological advantages of three-generation living here to the United States. Her husband, their two children, and she live in a town house right next door to her parents. Lan said this housing arrangement works so well for all of them. Her parents can enjoy being with the grandkids every day whenever they want. Likewise, the children love having the grandparents nearby. Her parents also help with babysitting, and, since they don't drive or speak English very well, she is happy to take them shopping or to doctors' appointments. And recall, having her parents live nearby was her idea.

Ironically, the worst of Western values seem to be seeping back in the direction of Lan's original home, aided by the new affluence delivered by the changing business system. At least as reported in the *Wall Street Journal* in 2005:

For thousands of years, Chinese have made the family para-
mount, with generations often living together, and younger
members deferring to their elders. But opportunities born of
China's move to a market-based economy over the past two-
dozen years are creating new wealth, new hierarchies and
new strains . . . . Younger Chinese are opting for privacy over
extended-family living. Over the past decade, the number of
nursing-home residents has increased 40 percent to more than
one million.[165]

Let's hope for the sake of the Chinese that this is another case of journal-
istic overstatement similar to the pejorative descriptions of the boomerang
generation described at the beginning of this chapter. Indeed, twenty years
of the new economy will change things for some, but we don't imagine most
Chinese will give up on exchanging support across the generations as they've
done across the millennia.

Finally, let's examine cultures in Polynesia. Margaret Mead first learned, on
some of these islands, about the power of culture and about how families work
in other places. We've heard about Hawaiian *ohanas*. Now, Paula comments
here about the three-generation glue that traveled with her from the Pacific
Islands that Mead first visited so long ago:

Paula: Well, we have Pacific Islanders, and that's a really close
network. There are two different types of Pacific Islanders.
There are Samoans and then there are Tongans. They both
have very close networks where the family lives together—the
mother and the father and the children. Once the children
get married, they come back into the family, preferably the
father's family. It's a closer network. When the daughters get
married, they come back with their husbands. They pool their
money together and they purchase a home for the oldest sibling. That's how they get their homes. So then they start their
own trickle-off, and then they get cousins and nephews and all
come in together . . . pooling their funds together, resources

together. You have the grandparents raising the children, while the daughters and sons are out working.

For some fifty years now, Americans have drifted away from family structures that have always before delivered happy and successful lives for most. Ignoring the importance of interdependence in favor of a mythical independence has hurt our interpersonal and familial relationships. While individualism and competitiveness often work well in the marketplace, they have no place in the context of a cooperative three-generation family arrangement. The sameness, often mistaken for equality, has led to homogeneous neighborhoods that suffer from a lack of multigenerational participation. A culture of yearning for the wide-open spaces has yielded a neglect of those close by. Luckily new Americans are reminding us of the old ways that can work again now and in the coming years. Please pay attention to your culture. Recognize its many strengths but at the same time resist its constraints.

CHAPTER 13

FINANCIAL AND
LEGAL CONSIDERATIONS

Since the dawn of history, the family has been humankind's
most efficient economic unit.[166]

—Ralph Warner

W hat's the worst thing that could happen? That's what an attorney
is paid to think about—the worst things that could happen.
Indeed, for this chapter (and book) we have to include our own
disclaimer for fear of litigation. That is, the laws and tax codes vary substantially
across the fifty states and the District of Columbia. We are neither attorneys
nor tax experts. We have talked to some of those.[167] But, what works in one
state may not in another. What works for one family may not for another. So
we are not giving you specific advice here. We are only trying to demonstrate
how some folks in different places around the country have handled the financial and legal aspects of living together again in extended family arrangements.
At the end of this chapter, you should know the right set of questions to ask
financial and legal professionals, should you decide to consult them.

What's the worst thing that could happen? Family disagreements about
money and such can often destroy families. Good intentions are important.
But, planning, anticipating, and writing things down can mitigate the potential
conflicts that do erupt among family members. Talking to legal and financial

experts ahead of time can go a long way toward easing the friction, particularly when family agreements don't work out or when key family members die suddenly, or when economic circumstances deliver unpleasant surprises.

So, you will still want to talk with a local attorney and tax consultant, particularly if you are planning to combine resources by living together with your adult kids or parents. Below we try to cover some of the more important issues, but, of course, it will be your job to make your bed before you sleep in it, so to speak. We can only tell you where the sheets are. See table 13.1 for the issues demanding your consideration and that you may wish to consult experts about. Heads up on these as you read this chapter and as you begin to think about and plan your multigenerational living arrangements.

Now, let's get to the good stuff. The folks we've interviewed have told us about all kinds of creative ways to conclude negotiated agreements with sons, daughters, sisters, brothers, mothers, and fathers that help make living together again a comfortable experience.

TABLE 13.1. ISSUES TO CONSIDER

FINANCIAL ISSUES	LEGAL ISSUES
Down payments and mortgage(s)	Ownership/control
Rent	Inheritance (trusts and wills)
Property taxes	Nonperformance
Transfer of wealth (estate/gift) taxes	Health crisis
Insurance (property, liability, health, life)	Employment crisis
Utilities	Pension crisis
Maintenance/repairs	Contracts
Remodeling	Legal relationships
Goodwill of the siblings	Caregiving contracts

HOUSEHOLD FINANCES

When living together again, how do you manage household finances? Simply put, who pays for what? In most cases, individuals living together pay for their own separate cell phones and groceries. Making agreements up front regarding rent, utility bills, mortgage, and taxes is an important step in keeping the peace.

Down Payments and Mortgages

As you see below, a variety of approaches have been reported by the folks we've interviewed in arranging for the financing of their three-generation housing. Most of these substantial financial arrangements depend on the continuing goodwill of the family members, at least as described in the interviews. Here are people's comments about down payments and mortgages:

> *Nancy*: Since we owned our previous house, we had a great deal of money to put into the new place that we were buying with our daughter and her husband. But they had the money coming in monthly to take care of a great many of the expenses of the house. That part has worked out very, very well. Naturally, we don't make the kind of money that our son-in-law is making. So, financially from that standpoint, it has worked out beautifully, freeing us up. When you think about it, it makes a lot of sense. We do share in the mortgage. We both pay equally the mortgage. Our son-in-law and my husband got together and figured out what should be done.
>
> *Roger*: We have all three of our kids living in separate quarters on our property now. One of them built his own house and is buying a fraction of our property. We have an arrangement where they are paying us what will amount to one-quarter of the appraised value. The downside is that the other two siblings aren't able to participate—they don't have the money. So we thought that we'll just do this because otherwise it just goes into our estate.
>
> *Leslie*: A Realtor suggested I take the money from selling my house and build an apartment onto my daughter's home. She and her husband agreed to the idea but then ended up having to buy another house with enough property to do it. So they sold their house and moved into a bigger home with a lot. I helped them a little bit financially. Then after they were there for about a year I put an addition on it. My apartment is

about 1,200 square feet. I have my own private entrance and it just works out very well.

Sharon: And financially, after you sold your house, you helped pay for the remodel yourself?

Leslie: Yes, I did. Also, they're paying me back the money I initially gave them to help with the down payment for their new house.

Sharon: So that's a form of income for you.

Leslie: They haven't started yet, but that is what they plan on doing. So I am on the title right now.

Sharon: So will that be a form of retirement income for you?

Leslie: It could be. But eventually, they would like for me to get off the title, which I would want to do. My unit I paid for. They said that if they ever sold the house, they would give me back the money I put into it. So that would include the money for the down payment to their house, as well as what I put into my addition. That was written in. I did agree that they would only have to pay back half of what I put into their house. The other half I'm giving to them as a gift because if ever I get old and feeble, they are going to have the brunt of taking care of me. So it was sort of a reward to them for taking this responsibility.

Sharon: You were saying that the Pacific Islander families will pool resources. Do they leave initially and then come back when they marry? Do they ever leave home?

Paula: They don't leave home until their resources are all together. I guess they have a situation where the older sibling is the first one to leave the house.

Sharon: So the family, including brothers, sisters, and parents, will come up with a little stash of cash to help the older kids get the down payment for a house and then leave home.

And, recall the story told in chapter 8 by Judy Richter of the *San Francisco Chronicle* about the creation of a family compound in Fairfield, California.

Finally, as we mention in previous chapters, in the Hawaiian Islands there is a cultural history favoring *ohanas* (ADUs). Mike told us he plans to take advantage of these options in continuing to expand a family compound on the Big Island (Hawai'i):

> *Mike*: It was designed so there would be a central sort of communal area surrounded by the other houses. Most of the houses would have *ohanas*, actually just as places for visiting family and friends. Obviously, family members are invited to stay or participate in ownership. But, one person would buy all the property and as other people came in, he would basically sell the property to them at cost.
>
> *Sharon*: So it would be maybe your older brother assuming the responsibility of buying the land and selling you a portion of it?
>
> *Mike*: Right. And you could buy into it. It's mostly family, but they were also talking about having close friends, especially for the *ohanas*. Just having close friends come in for an extended stay. So we would have a mix of individual houses and *ohanas*.

Rent

We talked with Mark, a young college student living in Southern California, who shares an ADU in his parents' home with his friend. A part of the written agreement he has with his parents includes a nominal charge for rent to help with household finances. Other families we talked with do the same thing. In one case, the parents told us that they are quietly banking the so-called rent to later give to their child as a surprise down payment for a future home. In another instance, the son-in-law of a couple we know lived at home with his parents rent-free for twenty years before he married their daughter. In doing so, he saved a lot of money himself and was able to put a very large down payment on his first home. Most parents know whether their children are the type who will save money or spend it. Accordingly, unless it's a financial necessity for themselves, they can decide whether or not to charge rent.

So, a rental agreement is a part of many three-generation households where the property ownership is not split. Sometimes the kids and sometimes the parents are paying the rent. We start with Carol, a young woman, who lives with her husband and two small children in a duplex next door to her parents, who told us about their rental agreement:

> *Carol*: At this point, we pay my parents $500 a month rent. When we first moved in, I was in law school and we were rent-free. At some point, they offered to pay off all my law school loans. Then they said, "Well, how about, if you don't have that burden anymore, then you guys can start paying us rent." Obviously, $500 a month is below the market for anything around here. So, that's something that we are contributing to them. Of course, by paying so little we are also saving money for our future home.
>
> *Lan*: I own only my town house. The other one next door, my father-in-law owns. So for that one, where my parents live, I have to pay half the rent and my brother, who lives with them, the other half.
>
> *Mark*: We wrote up a little lease. The rules I can remember are: no smoking, we have to park on the street, no one else is allowed to move in with us. We normally have my parents call when they want to come. And, it includes the rent. That's about it.
>
> *Frank*: Even though our son owns his own home, he saves money by renting it out. He lives rent-free with his grandmother and by doing so is better able to afford the mortgage on his place. When he gets married next year, he and his bride will move into his home. With both of them working and living together, their two incomes will make it easier for them to pay the mortgage.
>
> *Patrick Hare*: Here is a story I use a lot in lectures. A woman sold her house to her daughter on the condition that the woman's mother (her daughter's grandmother) had a permanent

lease for the rest of her life of the ADU in the basement for a dollar a year. So things are fine. Both the parents worked, and the grandmother played a major role raising the kids. Then the grandmother suffered a stroke. She came back somewhat lethargic for a long time, and it seemed she didn't want to continue living. Both the daughter and her husband had a crisis in their work and asked the grandmother to take back over at least some of the work she had been doing in taking care of the kids. That is when the grandmother came back to life!

Property Taxes

Most folks we talked to were just splitting the property taxes one way or another. The following is exemplary:

> *Norma*: I get a copy of the tax bill on the lots here including this house. Being a mortgage broker, he [my son] calculates the amounts we both owe. So he figures out what he owes and he pays me or I pay him my portion. So the tax bill gets paid.

Transfer of Wealth (Estate/Gift) Taxes

Many of the families we have talked to around the country see two primary purposes of three-generation household arrangements. The one we discuss in great detail is the exchange of care services across the generations. Another important consideration is the transfer of wealth to the younger generations. The form of many of the agreements we've heard about reflect this latter purpose:

> *Eleanor*: I think one of the greatest benefits, beyond the fact that you have your family close, is the financial benefit gained by making arrangements to reduce or eliminate many aspects of inheritance and estate taxes. The fact that the parent can come and say, "Look, we got this much out of our house and

we want to do an addition on your house for us to live in. Then we can form a partnership or other type of legal arrangement." It's a wonderful way in which to give to your children this gift from you, without having to pay a lot of tax on it. It's something that you need to be aware of and that you can do. For example, I now have a 5,500-square-foot house because I've added 500 square feet of garage and 1,000 square feet onto it for my mother to live in. As the years come and go and we sell this, we're going to reap the benefits of that. I can turn around perhaps at that point and say to my children, "Let's build an addition on your house." That way, they will inherit this money, and it will keep surviving for many years to come after I'm gone.

Susan: I think there are two really important things about living together. One is the personal relationships that people have and how that is related to the physical layout of the shared space. The management of the costs and inheritance of the home are also very significant. It is important to get professional help with the latter. Just assuming that if you die the kids will take over the house, it's not that easy. The taxes could be terrible with our kinds of housing values. The government is very confusing about the rules on all of this. It's not nearly as simple as a lot of people think it is.

For instance, I'm involved with a revocable family trust. It means that I can change my mind. There is a point when it has to be made irrevocable for them to use it in some ways, but I think that's after I die, at which point maybe it becomes irrevocable. And I gift them $12,000 a year as part of the house equity. We have an attorney who does it. It is relatively complicated because they actually do something called fractiles, in which they say that a portion of a million-dollar house is not really worth much, so they take a greater proportion to get up to $12,000. That makes quite a difference in proportion that you're giving or getting. And, of course, the houses here are so expensive, you have to wait a long time to give them a great deal of it. I don't really understand it, but we do what the lawyers and tax people tell us to do. Definitely get professional advice on how to get it managed.

Sharon: You also have a second child, so how does that get worked out?

Susan: In fact, my domestic attorney gave me good advice about that. What I try to do is give my other daughter, Margie, $12,000 a year. She's in the will, so that when the house becomes available on my death, her sister, Julie, who lives here, may have to end up paying Margie an amount of money for some years to pay for her half of the house. They're not likely to have a lump sum to give her. That's something we should sit down and work out better. It's written down how it will be done, but the actual amounts have not been determined. Also, Julie and her husband should get some credit for the remodeling and house maintenance they're doing on the house. It's almost like they're beginning to pay part of the mortgage. By the way, if I were to die and they were living here, they could rent out this apartment where I'm now living. If they just paid the rent on this place to Margie, that would be a nice way to handle it.

Insurance (Property, Liability, Health, and Life)

The viability of the family partnership that we are recommending depends on hedging the risks of potential disasters related to both the property and the people living there. Fire, flood, accidents, and so on must be anticipated and insured against. Obviously, health and life insurance is associated with the individuals in the family, and the expenses are thus easy to assign. But, property and the associated liability insurance will require thoughtful rules of division similar to property taxes and such. The key here is that all potential beneficiaries should be informed and consulted, given the intimate involvement and financial interdependence of the extended family unit.

Utilities

As for parents living in their adult children's home, we also found instances where rent is charged to help with household expenses. Caroline, a Northern California widow, will soon be living with her daughter, son-in-law, and two grandchildren in an apartment in their house. When asked how they plan to handle household expenses, such as utilities, she replied:

> *Caroline*: Well we talked about that and came to the conclusion that rather than doing a percentage of what gas and electricity I use, I would pay them a flat rate for monthly expenses. Also, I would have my own cell phone. It's just too complicated to figure out who uses what percent of what on the bills that come in.

Another couple we talked to in Washington take a different approach. They have a large lot with two accessory units where two sets of adult children are now living. In one case, a single daughter lives with her child in the unit attached to their home. Because of economic necessity, the parents pay the utilities for her and the grandchild. It's a different story for the other daughter. Using their own money, she and her husband built a small house on the property for themselves and their three children. Here's what Roger, the father of the two daughters, had to say about how they handle the utility bills:

> *Roger*: We have a single lot, but they have a separate meter. So when I get the bill, I give a copy of it to my son-in-law, Charlie. He reads his meter, knows how much he has used, and makes that adjustment. We do the same with the water; we each pay our own share.

Of course, those who live in duplexes, houses, town houses, or condos in the same building have entirely separate meters for utilities and receive separate bills. This separation certainly makes their lives a lot easier, in most cases eliminating the need to make agreements about utilities. However, in many other cases, we found that families pay all the utility expenses for either parents or adult children who live with them in attached apartments or cottages in the backyard. They also tend to pay the mortgage, insurance, and property taxes themselves.

Maintenance and Repairs

Depending on circumstances of home ownership and financial capabilities and personal preferences, there are a number of ways that families can handle property maintenance. Susan lives in a converted garage in the backyard, while her daughter, son-in-law, and three grandchildren live in the main house on the property. Although Susan owns the house, she has made provisions for her daughter to eventually inherit it. Here's what she told us about how they pay for household repairs:

> *Susan*: So far, I pay for every major repair on the house. I do have a home equity loan, which, of course, will be deducted from the value of the house when they take it over. And that, at least, reduces the taxes. Of course, they may inherit a loan that they'll have to pay. But, for them to live here is a lot less than they would ever have to pay for a house anywhere around here. Meanwhile, I have this great advantage of having a son-in-law who will do most of the fix-it work. Before they came, when I was here by myself, I used to have to hire someone to come in to do things.

Gardening and other maintenance issues also came up with another family we talked to. Elena shares a duplex with her daughter, her son-in-law, and grandchildren. Here's what she had to say:

> *Elena*: At first, I didn't always agree with what their yard should look like. I would offer to go in and help. On my way in or out of their house, I would pull weeds along the way in and just dump them. They were both working and they didn't have time to do that. Now we both have gardeners and

things look a lot better. Also, even though I have the smaller of the two units, I own 50 percent of the whole property. So whenever we put a new roof on, we will share half-and-half in the costs.

Remodeling

Remodeling can also be a source of angst, particularly when long-term and short-term views collide:

Paula: My mother had about two more years before she retired. She decided to sell her home. My sister and her three children were living with her at the time. My mom decided, "I've got to make a move. I've got to go on." She realized that staying in Silicon Valley with the high cost of living wouldn't work for her as a retired person. So she decided to put the house up for sale and it sold within thirty days. Since she had to stay at her job to get the full benefits of retirement, she thought she would purchase a mobile home, which was a couple of blocks away. At the last minute, she said, "Well, you have a garage and it's detached with a bathroom in it. Why don't I fix it up, and I'll stay there until I retire?" My husband and I were already thinking about doing that anyway, so we agreed. We wanted a little hideaway place for us away from our three kids.

The only problem that I saw was with my husband and my mom. Since Mom's paying for it, I thought we should let her make all of the decisions on the remodel. But my husband, as the head of the house, had his own way of thinking of how he wanted it done. I had to pull his coattail and say, "Did we put any money in this?" There were times he said, "I want this type of toilet." I'd say, "Well, then, pay for it." That happened a lot. He knew that my mom had money but also wanted to let her know that he could pay for some things, too.

Contracts

Several of the folks we talked with provided their insights into the importance of writing things down in signed contracts, particularly when arrangements are complicated. A bit later in the chapter we include an interview with a legal expert on several of the topics mentioned here. But, the fundamental point is best made by Tony:

> *Tony*: You really have to treat it like a business deal, like a business transaction. Because if you do it on a personal level, it is easier to hurt up front than it is down the road.

And Helen, a knowledgeable real estate agent, told us about how complex things can get:

> *Helen*: It depends on how you hold title on a property when one party dies, if parts need to be sold or it can be deeded to the other person. So you want to make sure that doesn't put your children in jeopardy financially or force them to move out of their housing situation. Who gets the tax benefits for the property and what is the percentage? What happens if one party decides to leave? There needs to be a mechanism on how that part can be sold or if both parties decide to sell. When two parties own a property and one party chooses to sell, the value of that parcel is devalued perhaps 20 to 30 percent because no one in the market wants to buy into a family situation.
>
> *Sharon*: I am just wondering if what you are talking about is a shared piece of property? With your situation with the house next door to your daughter, there is no concern about that because you own it outright. I guess what we have been talking about is really the idea of the guest cottage or two families investing together in the same property. Do you have a recommendation if you were going in on a piece of property with your children—how would you set it up for yourself?
>
> *Helen*: I would make sure that it was a big enough piece of

dirt that we could subdivide and put it in separate ownership. My experience is that when you mix money and emotions and family, it can get really messy.

Sharon: What is happening these days are situations where families just can't make it unless they combine resources. So if parents offer to buy a house and tell their adult children they can live in it, while they will live in the cottage in the backyard, is there a way that you would suggest structuring that?

Helen: I guess you have to have a good understanding of who your kids are and how they work. It is probably cleaner if you own the property, and you might want to sublet. There are a lot of ways to do it. If your children rent, a lot of parents would put that money in an account for the children later on and not even tell them about it. You need to talk to a very sophisticated accountant. This is particularly so because the pertinent tax laws are complex and they change substantially from year to year.

Sharon: What happens if you want to loan your kids money for a down payment on a house?

Helen: One option is to make the loan and then gift it back to them over time. If you do choose to forgive the loan by gifting it to them, you can gift up to $16,000 per year. What I do is gift my children a portion of the loan I gave them for their house every year in January; it is on paper. I send them a letter stating that I've done this; they sign and return it to me. That way I have a paper trail that I've lent them this money, but in reality, I gifted it to them.

Many folks also have questions about contracts and legal and financial options. Here are some of those:

Dan: When it comes to financial matters and combining resources, are advantages gone and flexibility reduced because you are intermingling? What will that look like? What have other people done? What would the lawyer say? That would be helpful. We are going to have to find information ourselves, so if you could give us examples of what other people are getting into, that would be great. Because regardless of the specifics, if there is any intermingling going on, what are the dos and don'ts?

Mary: I guess you also have to consider the other siblings involved.

Dan: That is a tough one, too because my daughter has a family and she is so very much on the outside, not included in this. She sees us doing things for them that she would like to be involved in and stuff like that. We haven't worked that out yet, but we will.

Here, Todd and Lynne ponder the issues associated with building a *casita* on their property for her mother, and Eleanor talks about what she did:

Todd: For the utilities and cell phone, we will probably be able to run separate lines. We will be able to get two services for the power so that it can be completely separate. We will run into problems when it comes to the mortgage. If there are two separate mortgages, then we run into subdivision restrictions. So we will be kind of playing with that. Technically it will be our house. Either she is listed on our property title as a tenant or she gets to gift us the money for x number of years for the house, and we make the payments. We can get it to the point where we both own the mortgage, are paying a percentage, and can take the deductions. Essentially, we've talked about this being our inheritance up front.

Lynne: I think it would be nice to have a section in the book regarding tax and estate planning and what ways to get around issues . . . But just the whole idea of how to prepare your estate and how to prepare yourself financially is complicated, especially when there are other siblings involved that are not involved in this housing situation. So how do we do it clean and fair? Those are questions that we still don't have answered. *Eleanor*: I think there are a lot of questions that people don't think to ask. I have consulted with some families who are considering doing this. There are a lot of issues that come up about "Mom or Dad has their own home and we need to sell that and we're going to use the funds from that to build this addition." That's all well and good; however, there are tax situations to be dealt with. There are inheritance situations. If Mom or Dad is in a nursing home, there are other situations to get into there. If they have certain types of problems, you have to think ahead when you are going to do the construction. Are they ill? Do they have a special situation? What are the tax problems? What are the inheritance problems? How are you going to handle the money issue? What are you going to cover? Also, if there are health considerations, it's much less expensive to prepare the house for that when you build than it is to go back and retrofit. Retrofitting is very difficult sometimes.

A MODEL OF HOW TO DO THINGS

One of our families has been particularly conscientious in organizing the financial and legal affairs associated with their special three-generation household. Their case touches on many of the questions just set out. They live in a big home in a nice neighborhood, with three kids and the mom and dad in the main house, and the grandparents in the spacious pool house out back. It's a perfect setting, but it took a while for them to get settled. Let's let them describe it in their own words:

> *Janet*: When we first moved in here, it was crazy. We didn't know whose responsibility was what. Four adults managing a home is hard. The gardener would come. We didn't know who would instruct the gardener. The pool guy would come. Who was in charge of that? Something would break down. I felt like

with four adults someone should be in charge. It took a while to delineate responsibility.

Craig: We did set up ground rules for household finances and bills. We just kind of sat down and figured out who pays what. It probably only took us forty-five minutes. Certain things were split 50/50 like the gardener. Initially, the property taxes were also 50/50 because when we started, we had equal shares of the whole place. Other things we use more of, so we should pay more. Since we have three-quarters of the total square footage of the house and cottage combined, we pay three-quarters of the power bill. We each have our own cell phone. We don't get too detailed; we either say it's 50/50 or 75/25. Then whatever the bill is that month, we'll each pay our respective percentage.

Sharon: So you had a democratic meeting, it sounds like?

Craig: Right. When we bought this place together, it worked out perfectly. It worked out because an older generation usually has either equity in a property already or they have cash savings. But they don't have a lot of income if they're retired. Whereas the younger generation doesn't have the savings and equity, but they are at or entering a peak earning capacity. So when you look at a normal mortgage, you have typically 20 percent down and a high monthly payment. In our circumstances, Janet's parents didn't even have a mortgage on their previous home. They owned a nice piece of property outright. We were kind of a typical younger family with young kids, doing fine in our second or third home. But we were outgrowing our house. Although to find a bigger one to buy (we could afford a larger monthly payment), it would have been difficult to scrape together a down payment large enough to keep the monthly payment reasonable.

So the way we approached this is 50/50. They actually were able to spend less than they would have if they had found another house. Fifty percent of this property at the time was less expensive than a smaller property would have been for them. We put our home equity in, too, but we took roughly the 80/20 rule. We contributed 20 percent of the down payment, and we pay about 80 percent of the monthly mortgage. They were responsible for 80 percent of the down payment, and they pay 20 percent of the monthly mortgage. So it solves both things because they didn't want to have a large mortgage payment, and they shouldn't. And we're completely comfortable with it because we wouldn't have been able to come up with such a large down payment by ourselves.

Sharon: So in terms of ownership, are you 50/50?

Craig: Exactly. We have agreed that it is a 50/50 ownership. At the present time, they actually have contributed more than we have because their down payment was so large. Since our monthly payments are so much greater than their payments, the ratio of cash each of us has in the home reduces each month. At a certain point in time, the sum of our monthly payments will equal their total cash contribution. From that time on, we'll have put more cash in the house than them. Nevertheless, we agreed on a 50/50 ownership, regardless of the amount of time we'll live here together.

Sharon: Ultimately, then, say they should pass away—how would you work that out with your siblings?

Craig: Their 50 percent interest would go into a family trust and be divided up between the beneficiaries. After they pass away, and when that equity is requested by other siblings, we would refinance the house. We would convert their interest into cash to pay them off, so we could still remain in the house. It has to be fair for everybody.

GOODWILL OF THE SIBLINGS

Consideration of their siblings was mentioned by several of the folks we interviewed. We are not really surprised by such consideration expressed by our sample because they are all cooperative family members, in a sense defined as such by their extended family living circumstances. Our point here is that the best care for elders is delivered by all their kids' combined efforts. Obviously, in most cases only one child will carry the burden of cohabitation, that is, if and when it becomes a burden. But, all the kids should pitch in as they can. And, the goodwill of one's siblings becomes an important family asset in both the interpersonal and financial senses. It is an asset that should be invested in, particularly in the context of any extended family agreement.

PERSPECTIVES FROM A LEGAL EXPERT

As you know, we've interviewed more than one hundred Americans involved in extended family living arrangements, and with the exception of this chapter, we have primarily focused on the interpersonal aspects of this wonderful institution. The interpersonal aspects are our area of expertise. When it comes to the combination of legal and financial issues described above, we've called in a relief pitcher, so to speak. Tom Peterson, a partner at O'Brien & Peterson, a law firm in Orange County, California, specialized in general business, real estate, and estate planning for thirty-two years. John's interview with him, on what Mr. Peterson calls a "new area" of law, is both interesting and informative. So, we've included it here in its entirety:

> *John*: What I tried to do is make up this case and talk about a specific example. Let's take the example of our "model" family as just described in the previous section. Recall that a daughter and her husband decided to move in with the daughter's parents. They decided to buy one home that has a large pool house. So the parents are living in the pool house and the daughter, son-in-law, and three kids are living in the main house. The younger folks are paying 80 percent of the mortgage and they put up 20 percent of the down payment on this piece of property. The older folks put up 80 percent of the down payment and are paying 20 percent of the mortgage. They share the ownership of the property 50/50. So

the question is, What are the different legal instruments that might be applied in such a case? Let's also assume that the daughter (and parents) is worried about how her brother will react to this substantial blending of his sister's and his parents' resources? One of the things I would like to do is make a list of the concerns and a list of the instruments. By instruments, I mean things like a living trust and a will. Are there family partnerships and prenuptial or cohabitation agreements? What other legal instruments might be pertinent to this?

Tom: Well, another one would just be the method of holding title to the property. So we just refer to title holding documents. Another could be just a straight contractual agreement. That's a pretty good list because otherwise, you get pretty exotic. I don't think you need to be talking about corporations or LLCs. They are just forms of business entities. But the latter two are still possibilities. I would just lump them all together.

John: Would there be specialists that would handle these different things?

Tom: Yes. The living trust and the will would be done by an estate-planning attorney. The family partnership would be done by either an estate-planning attorney or a family law attorney. The title holding documents would be a real estate attorney primarily. The contractual agreements would be the business attorney. If you find somebody who does all of that, just let me know. I'm probably one of the closest. The only ones I don't do are the nuptial agreements—you need a family law attorney for these.

John: So if we go back to my example, I'm moving in with one of my kids and we're co-buying a house, one of my questions is, How complicated do we want to make this? The purpose would be to give our readers an example saying, "See how complicated this actually is? You need to seek professional advice."

Tom: Well, I'm just shooting off ideas. There is sort of the simple way and the complex way. Just on your example of you and your wife moving in with one of your children or another relative, a simple approach would be to adjust how you hold the title to the property. So you could just say, assuming your daughter or son is married, that each of the four of you now hold the title one-quarter each as tenants in common or as joint tenants, however you want to do it. That's so simple. It's just one title document and it's recorded. That's the ultimate simplicity. But the trade-off for that ultimate simplicity is that all of your rights, including determinations and survivorship, are all set according to law by how you set it up. So if you set it up as a joint tenancy among the four of you, then whoever is last standing gets the whole thing. If your son and his wife get killed in an automobile accident, the whole thing goes to you if you are the last standing, and their kids don't get anything. So it's a very simple thing to set up, but it probably doesn't meet your intentions because it's all done by rules of law that you don't control. It's the same if you do it as a tenancy in common. That means it's not the last standing. But it means that each quarter interest goes, by law, to whoever your heirs are. So, if you have a will and direct who your heirs are going to be, you can do it that way. So that would take two documents: a tenancy-in-common deed and wills. If you didn't have wills or any estate-planning documents, the tenancy in common would just say it goes to whoever your heirs are by the succession law. So again it's very simple, but you may not accomplish what you wanted to accomplish.

John: So the other issues that need to be considered are 1. Inheritance and 2. Tax laws. We haven't even talked about tax implications. I wonder what else there is to worry about. Inheritance, I realize, is a very complex issue by itself. But what would be the tax implications of all of that? If we are thinking about the middle of the country—let's say it is a $500,000 piece of property—does the size of the property make a difference?

Tom: Sure, because there are currently a $2 million estate tax and a $1 million gift tax lifetime exemptions. So, let's say this piece of property were worth $2 million and there was a tenancy in common. Then if something happens to you, you are going to be now dividing one-quarter of that $2 million, so $500,000. So you would have been using $500,000 of your exemptions based on this one piece of property. If you did it by joint tenancy, it automatically goes to the survivor; so you don't have to worry about doing any court probate, but the decedent's portion would still be included in his/her exemption. So there are all sorts of tax consequences that are going on there. On each one of these—the trust, will, partnerships, nuptial agreements, title contract, or business entity—the tax implications are very important and very tricky.

John: Do you think most folks do this by some kind of verbal agreement?

Tom: Without knowing them, that would be my guess. There are a lot of people that do these things just verbally. It's just not mothers and fathers and children and grandchildren. I've had a lot of cases of the father being the surviving parent and the mother passing away. The surviving parent is getting older and lonely, so he has somebody move in with him. So they have an agreement orally that they'll do this and do that if something happens to him. That gets to be real messy. Nine times out of ten it's just some oral agreement. People always say "Well, it's just my family or it's just my girlfriend. I trust them." It's not really a question of trust; it becomes a question of proof. How do you prove this was their agreement? And if you don't prove it, then it's going to go under inheritance law or some other state-mandated method. And especially having to prove it to the IRS. They are not going to say, "Well, that was your father, so we trust that you did it that way." The IRS doesn't care. They will say, "Well, prove that was the agreement that you had with your father or girlfriend."

John: Then what do you suggest?

Tom: Well, for the example you gave initially, about the 80/20 down payment/mortgage split, I guess I would most recommend a family partnership. That's literally what they are doing, setting up a partnership among the four of them setting out who has what responsibility getting what share of what. It really is a family partnership. You could do it by all the other different kinds of instruments, but boiling it down, it really is a family partnership. The problem with calling it a family partnership is that, from the IRS point of view, this implies that there is a business, a partnership business that's being conducted. In this case it's really not a business; it's really a method of dividing property and dividing the benefits or the burdens of that property, as opposed to running a business. So, either a family partnership or just a straight contractual agreement would be the simplest way for them to do that.

John: Then you would have a separate will for each person or a living trust to handle the inheritance issues?

Tom: Yes.

John: The tax implications would be managed through the living trust?

Tom: Yes, the living trust or in the will, that's pretty straightforward. The contractual agreement would need to be set up based on how it's being operated while they are all alive and . . . I'm trying to think of a way . . . you couldn't really control it upon death because the contract wouldn't be an estate-planning document. It wouldn't qualify as a will. It wouldn't qualify as a trust, although you could modify it to make it do those kinds of things, at least the trust part of it. So you have more of the contract governing how they deal with their property while they are alive, and you have an estate-planning document to take care of what happens if they pass. You could do very exotic things and have a contract that says, "We are all in this, but if something happens to one of us . . . we have a buy/sell agreement, so my share gets bought by the other three." For purposes of this, the purchase price is x, y, or z. So in effect, you can keep that piece of property in the survivor's control, but you get a little more exotic at that point.

John: Now let's say I'm the father in this model arrangement described above. My wife and I are moving in with my daughter and her family, but at the same time I'm worried about the goodwill of my son. My son would have no legal recourse. But, from my point of view, I want all my kids to feel like they are being treated fairly. So I need to specify for them what the kid that I'm living with is providing to me and my wife. One way to handle that would be do an annual report of this family partnership agreement. I don't know if you ever heard of such a thing?

Tom: Yes. It is a good idea even without worrying about non-participating siblings. It would also be useful for tax purposes as well.

John: So, that's something you would recommend? It does two things: it's recording what's happening, and also it is informing the other family members who have an inheritance stake.

Tom: I would recommend it. I guess the question is, Who should get it or what is the purpose of doing it? One purpose is just to inform the participants so you, your daughter, her husband, and your wife—everybody—knows the tax implications. You would almost have to do it for your housemates, but do you want to inform your son or other children so they know what's going on? That's not necessary, and they don't have any tax interest in this, so that would sort of be a bonus to them.

John: It's hard to avoid the problem that you were talking about . . . I think that you said that very often, the first time you hear from potential clients is when they are trying to figure out what to do about some cohabitation deal their parents and siblings are cooking up. So the idea would be to avoid that and to keep peace in the family. Sharon talked with a woman in San Diego whose mother moved close to them, and they paid her housing costs for a five-year period. Now their youngest kid is going off to college. So an elder mother is going to move next to the home of another sibling with another financial arrangement. So, the question is, "How do you allocate credit for the help that everybody is giving?" The main thing would be just to inform everybody. If somebody has a complaint, then let them voice it.

Tom: But what is it that you are concerned about if they have a complaint? Let's say the brother who isn't part of this deal . . . I'm just talking from strictly a legal point of view. He doesn't have any legal complaint or any legal right or any legal say-so to this deal. But from a family point of view, just to know what's going on is different. Nonlegal issues are more significant in that situation. So let's assume that the nonparticipant son says, "Well how come Dad is only getting half of this even though he is putting up 80 percent of the money?" Suppose he gets upset about this? There is nothing legally he can do about it. Should he have some family right to say, "You guys need to modify this"? I suppose that is what you are looking at.

John: I'm actually more worried about this arrangement: let's say after five years or for whatever reason it dissolves and then the parents want to move in with another kid, you want their goodwill. You want to keep goodwill in the family. So it's not so much what recourse they might have, it's maintaining the goodwill so everybody continues pitching in.

Tom: Trusts are required to have an annual report. So this partnership or this family arrangement could have an annual accounting in the same way.

John: Okay. And then that would also document . . . as you said, it would keep the tax implications updated.

Tom: Right.

John: How lengthy is a family partnership document? Are we talking about five pages, twenty-five pages?

Tom: It could be anywhere from two pages to thirty pages; it just depends on what you want covered in it. If all you are intending to cover is something like, "It's our intention to buy this piece of property together, and this is how we are going to do it, and this is who is contributing what," you could probably do it in two pages. If you are saying, "Well, this is what we are buying and this is when we are going to do it; and if something happens to one of us, this is what happens; and if something happens to somebody else, this is what happens," you can go on for thirty pages.

John: You must be amazed, sometimes, at what people have done to themselves by not planning and documenting their agreements. We are talking big amounts of money.

Tom: Big amounts of money and people who should know better.

John: Those are the cases that end up in court?

Tom: Yes, they are the ones that end up in court. A mess gets left behind because legal documents were not prepared. Thus, the whole family ends up coming apart at the seams because everybody is at cross-purposes at that point. The person who set it up, who everybody could look to and say, "Well Dad wanted it this way," but then you get, "Dad didn't want it this way; we're going to do it this way." They are all doing it in Dad's name. But, Dad is not around. So, everybody starts arguing about what Dad wanted and nobody knows.

Please see exhibit 13.1 for an example of a very simple family partnership agreement that captures the essence of the model arrangement described earlier. For such a simple two-page document you will need to invest about $500 in legal fees. The thirty-page document will require an investment of about $1,000. The return on these investments will be invaluable.

Exhibit 13.1. Example of Family Partnership Contract

This Partnership Agreement ("Agreement") is entered into by and between John L. Smith, _____ and _____, ("Smith Children") on one hand; Jack Smith, _____ and _____ ("Smith _____ Grandparents") on the other hand; and Becky Smith, _____ and _____ and _____ ("Smith Grandchildren") on the final hand, effective the day of June 2023 regarding the following interests:

Recitals

a. The Smith Children currently own an interest in real property identified as (address) ("Real Property"), which they desire to share with the Smith Grandparents on an equitable sharing arrangement and pass on thereafter to the Smith Grandchildren.

b. The Smith Grandparents desire to contribute to the shared living arrangements in exchange for a life estate and certain tax benefits.

c. The Smith Grandchildren agree to share their family residence in exchange for a remainder interest, love, comfort, and support.

Agreement

Now therefore, the parties each agree to form this Smith Family Partnership on the following terms and conditions:

1. The Smith Children agree to contribute the Real Property to this Partnership at its current fair market value of $ _____ together with all mortgages, liens, and other encumbrances against said Real Property in the amount of $ _____. The Smith Children further agree to manage, supervise, and direct this Family Partnership, including the responsibility for preparing all income tax returns, real estate tax returns, gift tax returns, estate tax returns, and other documentation related hereto. In return for this consideration the Smith Children will receive a 50% interest in the Family Partnership and a share life estate in the Real Property.

2. The Smith Grandparents agree to pay to the Partnership $ _____ total cash and/or $ _____ monthly toward their uses, repairs, support, taxes, and maintenance obligations. In return for this consideration the Smith Grandparents do hereby receive a shared life estate in the Real Property and 50% of the Partnership tax benefits therefrom

for as long as said financial contributions continue or are hereafter waived. The Smith Grandparents will receive their Real Property interests and 50% Family Partnership interests by means of a Partnership Deed and/or Life Estate Deed as the parties shall determine.

3. The Smith Grandchildren agree to share the Real Property with the Smith Grandparents and fully participate in all Family Partnership activities. In return for this consideration the Smith Grandchildren will receive a remainder interest in the Real Property to be disbursed upon conclusion of the life estates and this Partnership.

4. The Partners each agree that all tax benefits and burdens of this Partnership will fall solely upon the Smith Children and the Smith Grandparents in proportion to their financial interests as determined from time to time by their tax accountant and/or attorney, but intended to be 50% each. Partnership deeds, life estate deeds, and other real property recording documents will be prepared as required. A Partnership bank account will be established to collect all payments received hereunder and disburse all funds required hereunder, including Partnership mortgages, taxes, maintenance, repairs, reserves, and otherwise as determined by the Partners. It is *specifically* agreed that the Real Property can be sold, exchanged, or otherwise disbursed solely as determined by the Smith Children as Managing Partners and upon such disbursement the Partners will each receive reimbursements according to their financial investments hereunder.

5. This partnership will terminate upon the death of the last partner, bankruptcy, assignment to creditors, attachment, move-away, termination of payments or other breach of this Agreement by any Partner as determined by a majority of the other non-breaching Partners.

IN WITNESS WHEREOF, all of the Partners of the "Smith" Family Partnership Agreement, have executed the Agreement, effective on the date set forth.

"Smith Children"

(signature)

(signature)

"Smith Grandparents"

(signature)

(signature)

"Smith Grandchildren"

(signature)

(signature)

(signature)

QUESTIONS TO ASK YOUR OWN EXPERTS

You will need to talk with your own local legal and financial experts. Recall that the pertinent laws vary substantially around the country and over time. You will want to ask which of these legal instruments apply to your specific situation, which do not, and why:

- Title holding documents
- Joint titles
- Tenancies-in-common
- Shared equity mortgages (a relative, etc. provides the down payment as a coinvestor)
- Sale of house to child (at a deep discount)
- Reverse mortgages (the bank provides a stream of tax-free cash subtracting from your home equity)
- Private mortgages (you pay tax-deductible interest on a loan from a relative, etc.)
- Trusts (revocable/irrevocable)
- Living trusts
- Wills (including living wills)
- Corporations
- Limited liability company (LLC)
- Contractual agreements
- Nuptial agreements (pre- and post-)
- Cohabitation agreements
- Local government subsidies for provision of low-cost housing–low-cost mortgages for the creation of *casitas* (Boston is an example)
- Tax deductions and other government assistance for elder care and dependence. Find more information at Irs.gov or by calling (800) 829-1040.
- Family partnership agreements (including an annual accounting)

Family Partnerships, Defined

Because the best answer to most of these questions will be a family partner-ship agreement, we have defined that instrument: Family partnerships (FPs) reduce estate taxes and protect assets from creditors' claims. They allow a person to retain control over assets without having them eroded by estate taxes. FPs are structured as either limited partnerships (Georgia being the most favorable state) or LLCs (Virginia being the most favorable state).

Parents can establish an FP by transferring assets such as real estate, marketable securities, or an interest in a family business without adverse tax consequences. The parents retain exclusive control over the partnership, such as the power to make management decisions, to sell assets, and to determine the time and amount of distribution to the partners. The FP has the following features:

- The parents may receive compensation for the reasonable value of their services.

- The parents can give interests to their children, either outright or in trust, over a period of time at discounted values of 20 to 40 percent.

- The children are taxed on their proportionate share of the income, which provides an effective income tax–shifting device.

- The assets owned by the FP are not generally subject to an individual partner's creditors' claims.

- After the interests are transferred to the children, any appreciation in the FP's assets attributable to those interests will escape taxation in the parents' estates, and the parents' retained interests are entitled to valuation discounts.

- The business can be passed to the younger generation without losing it to a forced tax sale or liquidity crisis.[168]

Caregiving Contracts

Finally, we are happy to report a new form of family contract that seems to be growing in popularity and is completely consistent with our advice in this book. The *Wall Street Journal* well summarizes this innovative and timely option:

A small but growing number of families are setting up caregiver contracts, in which adult children or other relatives are hired, for modest salaries, to take care of elder or disabled family members. These arrangements can help reduce the size of a parent's estate and thereby improve their chances of becoming eligible for long-term care coverage under Medicaid. They can also minimize battles between siblings and other family members.[169]

For more information on caregiving contracts please see the websites listed in the resources section of our book beginning after chapter 14.

LOOKING INTO THE BABY BOOMERS' (AND THEIR KIDS') FUTURE

The agreement that makes sense this year may look pretty silly five or ten years from now, depending on the economy and, in particular, your own extended family's economy. The latter is hard to predict, but the former is not. Quite common in 2024 are a variety of plans for transferring wealth from the World War II generation to their kids—instruments such as living trusts, shared equity mortgages, discounted sales of real estate, investments in *casitas*, and so on. However, by 2030 all this may change dramatically with the potential demise of Social Security, Medicare, and most private pension funds. Prominent in any long-term family partnership agreement should be consideration of this darkness on the far horizon. That is, what happens when your elder family partners can't produce the current or expected income stream they've promised? Planning for it now will reduce its impact a decade from now.

At the beginning of this chapter, the family is described as "humankind's most efficient economic unit." Prudence, planning, and communication across the generations will keep it so!

CHAPTER 14

MAKING AGREEMENTS FOR LIVING TOGETHER

Peace, like charity, begins at home.
—Franklin D. Roosevelt

How do you keep the peace when you're living together again? That's the bottom-line question. The answer lies in one key word—communication. When creating an extended family living arrangement, it is advisable to set up democratically determined ground rules that are fair for all and allow for both communication and privacy. As we mention in chapter 6, we recommend an egalitarian family meeting among adults to talk about expectations up front. It helps to have a formal chat to make some agreements. That way, you are all clear about what's what—what they expect from you and also, what you expect from them. One young man we spoke to did just that. Mark is a young college student living in Southern California, who shares an ADU in his parents' home with his friend. Here's what he had to say about the ground rules that he and his parents have established to facilitate positive relations:

> *Mark*: For making up ground rules, I think the most important thing is to get everyone together and see what bothers people and what doesn't. Just common courtesy. We had a meeting and wrote up a little lease; my mom typed it up. The

rules I can remember are no smoking, we have to park on the street, no one else is allowed to move in with us. We normally have my parents call when they want to come over or if they need help with anything. That's about it. It's a pretty laid-back situation. If I'm not happy with something, I will just talk to them about it.

Sharon: How do you handle expenses, such as heat, gas and water, and cell phones?

Mark: We have separate electricity and pay our own bills. Also, we are responsible for our own phone and cable bills. We share the utility bill for gas and the hot-water heater. We pay a tiny little rent that goes toward those expenses—I pay $100 and my roommate pays $200. It's still dirt cheap; you can't find anything cheaper than that around here.

FAMILY MEETINGS

One way to encourage positive relations within extended family living arrangements is to conduct family meetings on a regular basis. A friend of ours told us how worthwhile her weekly family meetings are. She said that they conduct what is called "family home evening" on Monday nights. It is an evening dedicated to the family where group decisions are made and responsibilities are assigned. It also provides a forum for sharing positive feelings and choosing activities for family fun. To keep order and be productive, she said these gatherings often include a printed agenda and someone designated as the facilitator to run the meeting.

In another case, a couple told us about their current and future plans for family meetings. Mary and Dan moved to Colorado to help babysit their two grandchildren. They've been living in their own separate house nearby but are planning to move into a cottage in the backyard of their son and daughter-in-law's property. They look forward to the convenience of being closer to the grandchildren and having the ability to just pitch in and help out when needed. Also, both families have good communication skills and like being together. Here's what they had to say about the possibility of ground rules being established with their new living arrangement:

Dan: I am sure there will be some. I feel very flexible right now because I have felt so very comfortable with them. I trust them and I am not worried about boundaries. However, we will, as we see a need for them, create clear boundaries.

Mary: What we do is have family meetings. Dan and I have marriage meetings; they have their own family meetings every week. Sometimes we will just mix the meetings. We talk about everything—chores, responsibilities, and also fun things. We plan our dates and look at our calendars, that kind of thing. When we live on the same property with them, I'm sure we will continue having joint family meetings there.

Meeting Guidelines

In the *Parenting Toolbox* report, Ron Huxley lists these steps for a family meeting:

1. Meet on a regular basis.
2. Everyone gets a chance to talk.
3. Everyone gets treated with respect and has an equal say.
4. Stay with the real issues and don't get sidetracked.
5. Keep the meetings short and stick to a schedule.
6. Focus on members' strengths and not their weaknesses.
7. Keep a record of the family meeting and post it where everyone can see it.
8. Remember to plan to have fun.[170]

When establishing households in close proximity, it is important to talk both before and shortly after the move takes place to make agreements on how to live together. Regular follow-up meetings to see how things are going are also recommended. Step one for your own family would be to sit down and decide who is going to act as the meeting organizer and facilitator. That role could be alternated among family members, depending on your preferences. Then you need to determine when, where, how often, and how long to meet. If a time cannot be found that works for everyone, try rotating the meetings to accommodate other members' schedules.

The meeting organizer can prepare an agenda for the meeting. If someone can't make it, then ask for their input on any known agenda items. Also, invite people to bring topics to discuss. If an agenda is not copied ahead of time, those topics could be listed on a large sheet of paper (a flip chart) for all to see. You could even make the list at the beginning of the meeting.

When meeting, it is helpful to sit around a table or in a circle. Then the facilitator can go around and give everyone an equal chance to speak. Family members can be encouraged to listen to others, not interrupt, and be supportive, not critical. They should try to keep their comments to the topic at hand and not dominate the conversation space. They can use humor, when appropriate, to keep it light. Above all, they need to respect and listen to each other.

At the start of a meeting, it is a good idea to agree on an ending time. Then, if someone needs to leave early, his or her business can be addressed beforehand. One way to begin on a positive note is to ask each individual what he or she thinks is working well in the living arrangement. Next, you could switch to what issues need to be worked out. The facilitator can ask questions to clarify what the problems are, then brainstorm solutions with the family. During the negotiations, it may become necessary for people to compromise. Ultimately, try to make decisions by consensus, where most agree. At some point, make your plans for family fun. At the end of a meeting, establish the next meeting date, time, and place, as well as who will be in charge.

You may want to have someone take notes to recap what was said. A good follow-up to any family meeting is to distribute a written summary of what was discussed, including who has agreed to do what by when. These notes could be sent out by email. Also, the report can include information about the next meeting.

The Casual Approach

For those who prefer a more casual approach to family meetings, certainly issues, along with outings and vacations, could be discussed informally around a dinner table either at home or in a restaurant. One family we know has a tradition of getting together on Saturday mornings for coffee and doughnuts, so if there is a problem, it can be aired at that time. Other families prefer less structure and like to call meetings on an as-needed basis, sometimes incorporating them into driving time. On the other hand, if the extended family living arrangement includes only two or three adults, a walk-and-talk approach could be used for family meetings. That way, you get a two-for-one. You're getting family business accomplished and exercising—at the same time. Regardless of how they are set up, family meetings are an essential step in enabling families to help themselves to create unity and love in the home, heal resentments, and avoid serious problems.[171]

Discussion Topics

A number of topics lend themselves to discussion at family meetings. All of these broad subjects came up with the people we interviewed:

- Length of stay
- Communication preferences
- Relationship issues
- Privacy issues
- Household finances
- Shared responsibilities
- Personal preferences
- Childcare
- Family fun

Specific examples within these general topics follow, as we tell the stories of how families have made agreements for living together that work.

LENGTH OF STAY

In making agreements for living together, we suggest you also talk beforehand about when *not* to live together. In the case of adult children moving home, you may want to set up time lines for them to move out. Sharon and her husband told each of their five children that after they graduated from college, they were welcome to live at home rent-free for six months until they could find a job and save enough money to rent an apartment. That was during the 1990s, when the economy in California was more robust and housing was not as expensive. Today, they would probably extend that time period to one year or longer, if need be. So many of their friends with younger children are doing that now. As we state earlier, more than half of eighteen- to twenty-five-year-olds nationwide are currently living at home.

Likewise, another friend has a daughter in her early thirties who has just moved back home with her. Although the daughter, who is single, is employed, she had run into financial difficulties. Her mother agreed to let her live at home rent-free for a year so she could pay off her credit card debt. As we say earlier, 30 percent of adult children between the ages of eighteen and thirty-four are now living at home in the United States. Certainly, this statistic represents further evidence of the growing trend for more Americans to live together again.

Moreover, there can be other benefits with this type of arrangement. In fact, many young people are living at home to save money for a down payment on a place of their own. One young couple we spoke with in Utah said just that. Brenda and Joe have an agreement to live rent-free with her parents in a separate apartment above their garage for six months to a year. Here is their story:

> *Brenda*: We're looking at houses right now. In the next couple of months, we think we'll be into a home of our own. Although we considered other living choices, in the end we realized we wanted to buy a home sooner without having to rent a place first. Renting would have prolonged our inability to buy a house.
>
> *Joe*: We had to take care of some financial issues and living here allows us to do that. We did look at other apartments, but it just seemed like Brenda's parents were very open and willing to let us use their apartment. In the end, we realized it's a better situation not only for financial reasons but also to

have them nearby to help or to just spend time with. She has a large family and it's very enjoyable. We have Sunday dinners over there and also get together on special occasions. It's really nice to have them close by.

In the case of elder parents who live near their children, a question that often comes up is, *When is it appropriate to move them into a caregiving facility?* At some point, it may simply become too much work and responsibility for the family caregivers to continue to have an elder parent or disabled relative live with them and have any kind of decent life for themselves. When mobility, safety, and incontinence become major issues, then it may be necessary to seek alternative housing for the family member. It helps to talk this over ahead of time, particularly to see if the individual has any special preferences as to where he or she would like to be. Eleanor, whose in-laws used to live in an apartment in their backyard, told us how she and her husband handled the predicament that developed with her disabled mother-in-law:

> *Eleanor:* The biggest problem we had was when my mother-in-law got to the point where she was not able to bathe or feed herself. Even though my father-in-law was a very large man and strong, she was dead weight and he could not lift her. We did try having a nurse there on eight-hour shifts for a short time but found that did not work. We ended up having to place her in a nursing home. Explaining it to them was so difficult. Even though we had agreed when they came to live with us that when it became necessary, she would have to go to a nursing home, they still didn't get it. They couldn't accept that we were not a nursing home, that I could not lift her and do those things. She begged to stay home. She also got to a point where she didn't think anybody was doing anything for her, when in fact everything was being done for her. Her husband was just turning himself inside out for her and she was starting to treat him very badly. Finally, we did have to put my mother-in-law into a skilled-nursing facility.

Even though Eleanor and her husband had a tough time moving his mother to a nursing home, at least they had the comfort of knowing they had communicated ahead of time what would need to be done. Indeed, making agreements up front for when not to live together can give all family members peace of mind in the long run.

COMMUNICATION PREFERENCES

Daily interaction with family members can involve a myriad of different ways to communicate with one another. From making contact to giving advice to handling disputes, it's up to you to let family members know your communication preferences. And nowadays there are so many new options. We won't list them here, but the intergenerational communications may involve some training and patience. For example, John has a level of discomfort with texting. He has two issues. First, because of his vision problems, he often has trouble locating things even on a small cell phone screen, let alone a large computer screen. Second, his self-described "fat fingers" make typing a chore on the cell phone. Better to call him or email him. To his credit, back in the olden days in the Navy he used both hand signals and semaphore flag waving. But even as a young man he was bad at cursive!

Making Contact

When living so close to each other, how do you want family members to contact you? Most of the people we talked to prefer a "call first" means of communication. Instead of dropping by, they want people to call them first to see if it's a good time for a visit. That way, they would not be interrupted if they were doing something. Certainly, that method would allow for more privacy for both sides, as well. In other words, treat your family with the same respect and consideration you would show your friends.

Caroline, a Northern California widow, would agree. She will soon be living with her daughter, son-in-law, and two grandchildren in an apartment in their house. When asked about what type of ground rules might be established in her new living arrangement, she replied:

Caroline: We've always maintained a certain respect for each other's privacy. So we decided that we are not just going to drop in whenever we feel like it. We are going to call first and say, "Is it convenient?" I think it is a very good rule because, you know, they could be having a family argument or something, and I could burst right into the middle of it. And the same way in reverse. I may be having a nap, and not only that, I do have friends who come and stay with me, too.

In another case, Tracy told us that when she wants to see her mother-in-law, who lives in a cottage in their backyard, she will call first most of the time. She also said that they will occasionally use an intercom to communicate with her. In fact, several other families mentioned using intercoms as a way to make contact with extended family members. Still others use email instead of the phone to make plans or put in requests for help on certain dates. That way, there are no interruptions.

One family told us about the "no-fly" buffer zone they installed in their home when they built an attached apartment for his elder parents. It is a 15-foot-long hallway with doors on each end "to separate them from us." The door on his parents' end has a mail slot, so they don't have to interrupt each other to deliver mail. They use a whiteboard that hangs on one of the walls to leave messages for each other. Importantly, when one or the other of them wants privacy, the door is shut: an open door says, "Come on in."

So far, we've talked about making contact between adult members of a family. What about young grandchildren making contact with their grandparents? Here's what Helen had to say about her preferences when she stayed at her daughter's place in her RV:

Helen: One of the most important ground rules was that the grandchildren could not come over without permission. At first there were no ground rules with the RV, and then I felt my grandchildren needed ground rules. I needed to be present in the RV when they came. The other understanding I had with my daughter was that when I was tired I would excuse myself and return in two hours. The other strategic thing I figured out was to start the day by saying, "This is what I can do to help you today." That makes it so much easier.

On the other hand, some individuals prefer a more casual, free-flow approach. A woman who lives with her husband and four children in the house next door to her in-laws told us how both she and her children make contact with their grandparents:

> *Linda*: If the kids want to go over to Nanny's house, I'll say, "Why don't you give her a call and see if she's there." But oftentimes, we'll be out in our yard and Nanny and Papa will be in their yard, and we'll have this over-the-fence communication. "Mom, could I go over to Nanny's house?" There is that verbal invitation. So, I would say it's fairly loose. We've never sat down and established firm ground rules; we haven't had to. It's interesting, my father-in-law is a very private person. My mother-in-law is much more casual. She will knock on the door and say, "Hello, I'm here. I need to ask you a question." I don't necessarily call when I go over there either. I will just knock on the door and say, "Are you there? I need to talk to you about something." I think it's just comfortable for both of us. We probably interact with each other this way about four times a week.

An adult grandchild, whose grandmother lives next door to her, her husband, and three children, said that she and her grandmother do not have a "call first" rule. When asked why she didn't, Dana replied:

> *Dana*: Because I think her having to call me to say, "I'm coming over," would make her feel like a guest and she's not. She is part of our family.

As it is, Dana receives more than enough calls every day from her grandmother. She told us how she has handled that communication dilemma:

Dana: She calls constantly. I mean, my cell phone rings twenty times a day. So I now have caller ID so that I can see when she is calling. The times that I won't answer the phone are the times when I've just dropped her off after lunch. If the weather is bad, and I've just dropped her off, she'll call. I know it's over nothing. I know it's over, "Did you watch the news? There is an epidemic in China, so don't let the children out."

Karen, who lives in a family compound of four houses with her mother and six siblings with families, told us about her family's different styles of making contact:

Karen: If I want to go over to my mom's house, I just show up. Like I said, everybody is different. I have a sister-in-law who is from the South, and she is very formal. At her house, you know, you respond differently or behave differently. Whereas at my house, the doors are never locked. Cousins come and go all the time. Everybody has their own rules, but there's no specific code of conduct. Everybody just respects everybody else.

However, as this next story shows, failure to talk about ground rules for making contact ahead of time can also produce negative results. One woman spoke about a communication pitfall that occurred when her parents moved into an apartment attached to their house. Gail and her husband had decided to build this addition as separate living quarters, so they would have to walk outside if they wanted to visit each other. As they were to find out, this helped with the privacy issue but didn't entirely take care of it. They had not discussed ground rules ahead of time for making contact with each other. As a consequence, here's what she said happened:

Gail: Dad had a copy machine in his condo that he wanted to keep, but there really wasn't room for it in the apartment. We had room for it in our house. We were, of course, thrilled with the idea of having use of the copier in our house, but it made for a sticky privacy issue. It's their copier, and they should be able to use it whenever they need to, but it's our home, and we cherish our privacy just like everyone else.

In addition, Mom enjoyed just popping over for a visit. Sometimes this was great because the timing was perfect. At other times it was an inconvenience and I or my husband were kept from something we needed to be doing. As the months went by, my husband and I both found a bit of resentment building up yet were at a loss as to how to handle this. My folks were, after all, being incredibly helpful with childcare, errands, and countless other things. I felt guilty being resentful of the frequency of the drop-in visits, but I knew it had to be dealt with because we were all in this for the long haul.

Luckily, I didn't have to be the one to bring this up. My father, bless his soul, was commenting to someone else about our new living situation, and then, as an aside, said to me, "By the way, we're not stopping in too often, are we? I've been meaning to ask you about that. We don't want to intrude."

That was my opening, and we ended up having a very good, frank discussion about the problem. We decided that Mom and Dad could come into the downstairs area anytime they needed to use the copier but that they would just make their copies and leave. If they wanted to visit or needed help with something, they would call first (as we would), and we could arrange a time that was good for everyone. Having this discussion was such a relief. Now I thoroughly enjoy my visits with my parents because I don't have other things demanding my attention at the same time. Also, my husband can arrange helping Dad with a project when it's convenient for him, rather than feeling that he has to drop everything because Dad is standing right there in the kitchen waiting for him.[172]

Giving Advice

How tempting it is to offer unsolicited advice on raising children, especially when you see a situation where you think you know the right way! Gail talked about yet another example of a communication problem with her parents:

> *Gail*: One day, I was out raking some piles of grass from the previous afternoon's mowing. While I was out there, I overheard Mom in the apartment saying to Dad, "What is she doing that for? She has boys who can do that for her. Do you think I should say something?" I was glad to have warning of what was to come because after a moment or two, out came Mom, who asked me why I was doing the raking. "Because I want to," I replied. "But, you have enough to do," she said. "You have boys who could do that for you." I took a deep breath, put on my best "Mom, I love you" smile, and said, "Mom, I'm going to say this as nicely as I possibly can. It's none of your business." With a look of surprise (because I had probably not spoken to my mother this way since I was an argumentative 13-year-old), she went back into the apartment and complained to Dad about what I had said. Then Dad came out and made a peace offering of some freshly sautéed Portobello mushrooms. While I was munching, he said, "Just for the record, I don't think you should be doing the raking either." "Well, it's none of your business either," I said, with that same endearing smile on my face. When I told this story to a friend, she said, "Wow, it just strikes me how much worse this would be if your parents were actually living in the same house with you. This kind of loving interference could be happening on a daily basis." She definitely had a point.[173]

Later, while on a walk-and-talk with her dad, Gail continued the discussion about the unwanted advice on parenting. She explains how she was able to clarify her position and indicate her communication preferences:

Gail: Dad and I take exercise walks together, and on one of these walks, the raking incident came up. I was able to say, "You have to trust that whenever I do something, it's because it's something that I really want to do, or I've decided that it's most efficient for me to do it. My children are not wanting for chores. They help out a lot around the house and are very good about doing what is asked of them. I know you don't see everything that goes on, but please trust me on this. If I have to explain or justify every decision I make to you and Mom, I will grow to resent it very quickly." Although I am not sure Dad and Mom really believe that my kids have enough chores, they have respected my request not to interfere in these matters. I, in turn, do not make a fuss when they tell the kids, "We're the grandparents, and we can spoil you if we want. You can stay up late and have extra cookies when we're in charge."

The most important thing we have all done is to take the risk to speak about things that might hurt the other's feelings. We have grown closer because of it. I think that keeping silent on the difficult issues would have pushed us apart.[174]

Handling Disputes

With any family, occasionally disagreements will surface that need to be attended to on the spot. It's important to come up with ways to fight fairly. Registered nurse Susan Miller suggests that you:

> Agree to fight constructively. This means setting out ground rules for fair fighting, such as taking turns to say what you want to say, agreeing to follow up on issues raised, and finishing the fight so that bad feelings do not go on forever.
>
> Honesty in communication is generally good but sometimes too much honesty can really hurt and damage a

relationship. Remember that you want to nurture the relationship and some things are better left unsaid.

One difficulty of living with elders can be dealing with their negative attitudes. George, whose wife's grandmother lives next door, told us how he feels about having daily contact with her. He uses a "stone wall" approach to handling the grandmother's complaints:

> *George*: [laughter] It's difficult living with an older person because I get home from work, open the door, and want to relax. The first thing I see is Grandma sitting there because she's always over for dinner every night. So the first person I see when I walk in the door is Grandma. Instead of, "Hey, George, how are you doing?" it's "The TV is not working." From my experience, if you ask someone who is elder how they feel, the glass is always half empty. "Oh, I don't feel good." I've even said to her, "The day I walk in the door and ask you how you feel and you say, 'Great!' or 'I had a nice day,' I'm going to think I'm in the wrong house." My own grandmother is 97 and she is ten years older than Gram, yet she's got more of a positive perspective. Things are always bright and shiny, whereas with Grandma things are "my aches and pains." It can get tiring.
>
> *Sharon*: Some of that is just how the family dynamic is and what they are used to. Good for you, though. I like to emphasize the positive myself.
>
> *George*: Yes. It makes life a lot better if you come from the positive side. We had a choice when Gram wanted to move in with us—move into our house or move in next door. When we bought the place next door, there was a stone wall between the two houses. I took the stone wall out and made it all into one big yard. So I told Grandma when she moved in, "I took the stone wall down, but every time you complain, I'm going

to put one stone back on the wall." The wall should be about twenty feet high by now. But, so far, we haven't put any stones back in there. [laughter]

George has a great sense of humor, which undoubtedly helps him get through a not-so-perfect lifestyle. Indeed, we've found that using humor and looking at the positives in life can be helpful in most relationships.

RELATIONSHIP ISSUES

Sometimes relationship issues can be associated with generational differences or the position of someone in a family, that is, a parent or in-law versus an adult child. Problems can also arise out of personality conflicts between individuals. In all these instances, it is advisable to establish ground rules for communication.

In-Law Issues

In some cases, we found the in-law factor did not seem to make a difference in how people got along. In others, it did. Leslie lives in an apartment attached to the main house of her daughter, her son-in-law, and two grandchildren. She talked about the easy relationship she has with her daughter:

> *Leslie*: I think it's easier to live with a daughter, and I love my other daughters-in-law completely, but it's just a lot different. My daughter, if she doesn't like something, she can say it to me; I can say it to her. But you would be a little bit more hesitant to say something to a daughter-in-law and vice versa. I think it would be harder.

Another mother, Jean, who lives across the street from her daughter, issued a warning about potential problems with a son-in-law, stemming from the close relationship she has with her daughter:

Jean: I think the only thing that you might be careful about is the other partner. My daughter and I are very close, but how does her husband feel about that? The spouse needs to be truthful about how he really feels about living across the street from his mother-in-law. How is that relationship? It could be difficult. My daughter and I, we don't overdo it. If you are really close and spend all of your time communicating with your mom, that might be hard on your husband. There could be some jealousy.

A young woman, Paula, told us about difficulties she encountered with her husband when her mom helped pay for their garage to be remodeled into an apartment, where her mother now lives:

Paula: The problem that came up was between my husband and my mom. My idea was, since Mom's paying for it, let her make all of the decisions on the remodel thing. But my husband had his own way of thinking of how he wanted it structured. There were times when he said, "I want this type of toilet." I said, "Well, then, pay for it." That happened a lot. He knew that my mom had money but also wanted to let her know that he could pay for some things, too. Of course, my mom felt she was being helpful. She is not expecting us to pay her back because in the long run, she knows it will help us. Later, if we wanted to rent it out, we could. If we wanted to live there ourselves and fix the other portion of the house up just for the kids, we could. We could even have that as a second house if we wanted to for the kids when they get older.

On the other hand, some people told us they get along fine with their in-laws but couldn't live with their own parents. Individual personalities and lifestyle preferences can make a huge difference in the ease of making agreements to live together. Marge, a young woman we spoke with, will soon be living in a cottage on the same property with her in-laws. When asked whether she would recommend this type of living arrangement to others, she responded:

> *Marge*: I don't think it is for everybody. I think you need to have the same kind of values and priorities in life, pretty much the same lifestyle or close, and really open communication. It would be very difficult for people who are closed-minded or someone who was brought up in an authoritarian household. I couldn't do this with my parents, as much as I absolutely adore them. There is no way that I could live with them or even move this close to them. The other issue would be the whole wife/mother-in-law or husband/mother-in-law situation. My mother-in-law and I have bonded uniquely, but there are some people who would not be able to live with their mother-in-law.

Personality Differences

Along with in-law issues that need to be worked out, personality differences can also lead to problems with living together. When such problems do occur, it is worthwhile to make agreements on how to deal with them. Vicky, whose parents live in a guesthouse in the backyard, told us how she and her "controlling" mother have learned how to compromise with each other:

> *Vicky*: In terms of ground rules, my husband and I feel honesty is the best policy. If something is bugging you, you need to speak up because if you shelve it, that can lead to a problem. But there are differences in communication styles between generations and also people. My family used to be really closed about most stuff. We couldn't say, "Hey this is bugging me." It's really more the communication between my mother and me. That has changed over the years. My mom is very controlling, but she is also very, very sensitive. If I say stuff that hurts her feelings, she just crumbles. I tend to

be more direct than she is. She's always been upset with me for being that way; she wants me to be softer. But over time, she's realized the importance of being a little tougher, and I've understood that I need to couch things in different terms to really get my point across.

Overall, close relationships do play a key role in successful extended family living arrangements. A family in Utah with whom we spoke, Paul and Charlotte's, splits the house up. Paul and Charlotte live on the ground level of their home, while their daughter Stacie and two of her friends share a basement apartment right below.

Here's what they had to say about recommending their living arrangement to others:

> *Paul*: I think people whose relationships are very close and open would stand a much greater chance of making it work than people who may be more distant or not tolerate one another as well.
>
> *Stacie*: I would definitely recommend it to other people. I get to be close to my family. If I need the privacy, I get it. That closeness does need to be there because, although there is a locked door, we are very close in proximity.
>
> *Charlotte*: I think it's important to have family counsel often. That's where you get together and you talk out problems. Rather than waiting for conflicts to get into crisis-like states, we deal with them right away so they don't get run up the flagpole and become major issues. No matter what, I think that active communication is really essential for sustaining positive relationships.

PRIVACY ISSUES

Privacy is another important topic that comes up at family meetings of those who live together. How do people get away from each other and have time to themselves? Certainly, we all need to have seclusion, solitude, or emotional space in our lives. Earlier in this chapter, we discuss making agreements on how and when to make contact with family members. Other privacy issues include shutting or locking doors and rules for accessing each other's cupboards.

Giving Space

One woman we spoke with made reference to knowing when to "give space." Nancy and her husband live in a guesthouse in the backyard of their daughter and son-in-law's home. She talked about how they manage privacy:

> *Nancy*: We haven't had any friction. It's been absolutely amazing. I think we know when not to get too involved over there. We just give them their space.

How much easier it is when the grandmother lives full-time in the self-contained house in the garden with its own separate entrance, kitchen, and bathroom. Then, there is little call for either party to have to move somewhere when the other needs more psychological space. Each person is able to live an independent life without intruding on other members of the family. Certainly, their lives can flow more smoothly with this luxury of more privacy.

A family we talked to in Oregon has already tested this idea. A young couple live in the larger house on their property with their six-year-old daughter. Since they both worked at jobs that required travel, his mother was invited to come from Florida to live with them and help babysit. Initially, Madeline lived with them in a wing of their house, with the understanding that a cottage would be built in the backyard as soon as possible. She now lives in that cottage and had this to say about her new-found privacy:

> *Madeline*: Well, I finally have my privacy. Before coming here, I had lived alone for so many years and gotten used to that. I don't think we ever had any issues while I lived with them. But, when they had guests over, I was always concerned about how visible I should be. I didn't want to act like I was ignoring their guests, especially if it's people that I knew. But, on the

other hand, I didn't want to be in the middle of their conversations. So, this way, I think we each have been able to enjoy our guests more.

Madeline's son, Jim, also commented on their mutual need for privacy:

Jim: We put a lot of thought into what we did, before we did it. The cottage has enabled us to give Madeline her own space and privacy. We can enjoy our privacy as well and still have a family between us. I think the key thing is to give the women in the family some privacy. Even though we may not see each other every day, we are only seventy-five feet apart and know that we're there for each other.

In another case, a woman's mother lives in a guesthouse attached to the main house. Joan told us why and how she established ground rules for privacy during the dinner hour:

Joan: Our friend who does marriage counseling said, "I think it's important that you do establish some ground rules." One is, "Whose turf is where? When do you cross that turf, and when is it appropriate?" We didn't come up with any written ground rules. But we did discuss some issues in terms of privacy. In particular, we talked about when we could all come together as a family. My husband and I had not been married that long before we did this addition to the house for my mother. We both got married later in life and then had our daughter. The dinner hour for us, especially since we are both working, is really the main time that we can come together as a couple. So, we don't invite my mother over for dinner during the week. She is also on a schedule. My mother likes to have her dinner at noontime or go out with friends for lunch and have a heavy meal. She would just prefer a sandwich and soup or something like that for dinner.

So that is one of our understandings, that we as a family need time-out together. Especially when my daughter was young, it was the "bewitching hour" or another friend of mine called it the "arsenic hour." It was that period between 4:30 and 6:00 or 5:30 and 6:30 where children are getting maxed out, and they are not on their best behavior. They want their food as quickly as possible. They want to eat it as quickly as possible. Having a parent there, even though she's like a close friend of yours, is not the best idea.

A young couple live with their two small children in a duplex next door to her parents. Greg and Carol told us about what they have encountered with privacy. As you'll see, they actually benefited from a negative experience Carol's mother had previously had with Carol's grandmother:

> *Greg*: Carol's parents were in a similar situation as we are in now with them. Her grandmother lived next door to them in this same house. I think Carol's grandmother was not as respectful of their privacy. She would barge in on them unannounced. So, they've had a lot of experience with what that's like. That's why I think they've been so respectful of our privacy, and I'd love to think that we have done the same for them.
>
> *Carol*: For us, from the beginning, my parents really left us alone unless we wanted to be with them. I'm sure that comes from their experience with my grandmother imposing on them so much. So we have our privacy. We don't have to see them if we don't want to. If we come home and we're tired . . . it's not like, "Hello, I made you cookies." But whenever we do want to be with them, they always seem just happy to see us.

Locking Doors

In contrast to the informal arrangement regarding privacy just discussed, Charlotte and Paul use a locked door as a formal vehicle for privacy. Again, Paul and Charlotte are the couple from Utah, who live on the ground level of their home, while their daughter Stacie and two of her college friends share a basement apartment right below. Here's what they had to say about their ground rules for privacy, including how they handle all women living with one man in the house:

> *Stacie*: One of our ground rules is they don't come down without notifying us first. I think it has to do with the tenant situation, where they have two people renting from them. Most of the time they will just knock and call down the stairs to say that they are coming. Also, the door is locked and I'm the only one from downstairs who has the key. Normally, I'll just come up and knock and use the key.
>
> *Paul*: I like having the run of the entire house, and I do when it's just our children that are here. But, when we have other people here that are formally renting, then there are courtesies that we extend to them for us to be able to access our food storage room downstairs. The other thing is that there is a gender difference. They are all females that are here and I'm the only male. So my wife might ask me to get five potatoes out of the food storage and bring them up. I know one particular girl is a little bit more sensitive to me being down there than the other, so I will ask my wife, "No, I think this girl is home. Would you go down and get it or can you wait, and then I'll go down and get it later?" So there are those kinds of contingencies you have to think through in order to make the thing work.
>
> *Charlotte*: The locked door does give us a sense of privacy, both entities—the children downstairs and Paul and myself up here. It's very important we have that privacy.
>
> *Stacie*: I like the fact that I can be close to my family, but also I can have some privacy when I need it, too. I can just go downstairs and be with my roommates.

Accessing Cupboards

Charlotte: Another thing I need to say is that we did set a limit on Stacie's ability to be able to take whatever she wants. We feel when they graduate from high school, they need to be responsible for themselves. We've raised them like that. We don't go out and buy our children cars. We don't buy them their clothes; they buy their own clothes. They get a job; they support themselves. Since Stacie has been living in this house downstairs, if she uses food out of our kitchen cupboards in our part of the house, she is expected to ask us first. The very fact that she has to ask for it makes her feel responsible. I think that's really important.

SHARED RESPONSIBILITIES

When living together, there are numerous responsibilities that need to be shared. General responsibilities include household chores, along with safety and security questions. Also, issues around pet care, the mail, and parking need to be figured out.

Household Chores

The basic questions are, Who does what household chores, and when and how do they do them? The subjects that came up in our interviews were the garbage, ironing, and mail. Most families living in separate households took care of their own laundry and housecleaning.

Only one family we spoke with talked specifically about taking out the garbage. Madeline lives in a cottage in the backyard of her son and daughter-in-law's home in a small town in Oregon. She helps babysit their daughter when both of them travel. Taking out the heavy garbage cans to the street would be difficult for either Madeline or her young granddaughter, Katie. She told us about the unique way they handle taking out the garbage at their house:

Madeline: Jim works as a volunteer with the local fire department. When he and Christine go away for work or are on vacation, the fire department guys always tell Jim, "Leave Madeline our list of names and phone numbers. If she needs anything, have her call." If Jim and Christine are out of town, they will come by, take the trash cans out, and bring them back in. They're just wonderful.

Her granddaughter, Katie, told us how her grandmother helps them out by living so close:

Katie: Neither one of my parents know how to iron, so Grandma does the ironing for us.

And recall from chapter 3 that Madeline's daughter-in-law told us how they handle the mail:

Christine: It is important to me for Katie to have easy access to Madeline because she is the only grandparent that lives nearby. I want their relationship to grow and develop. The mail sits on our counter until Katie comes home from school every day. I have Katie take it out to Madeline so that they can visit with each other, even if it is only a two-minute exchange.

We found that picking up the mail can present all sorts of challenges, especially if families share the same mailbox. Roger, who lives with his wife in Washington on a large rural lot with two accessory units and two sets of adult children, told us how they came up with a process for mail delivery with only one box for so many people:

Roger: The mail is in a lockbox up there with another group of boxes. So whoever drives up the hill first in the afternoon can stop for it. The person who picks up the mail will put the flag up. So when the next guy comes by and sees the flag up, he won't stop. If the flag isn't up and it's late in the afternoon, they know the mail is still in the box and will stop and get it. Here at home, Charlie's mail goes in the top box and ours goes in the yellow box right outside our front door. Whoever gets the mail sorts it and puts it in the appropriate boxes.

In another case, a family with a guest cottage in the backyard spoke about the difficulty they have had with mail delivery. It seems that their cottage has become like a revolving door, with different family members and friends living there for several months at a time. Tony gave us suggestions on how to handle the mail for long-term guests:

> *Tony*: Instead of letting them use your address, have the guest get a P.O. Box. That way you won't get all their junk mail later that you can't get rid of. Also, after they've left, you won't have the challenge of arranging for their mail to be redelivered to them.

How much easier it is to live in close proximity in completely separate residences. Linda, a young woman who lives with her husband and four children in a house next door to her in-laws, talked to us about the mutually beneficial system they've worked out for mail pickup:

> *Linda*: When they're gone, we pick up their mail and water the plants. And they do the same for us. That's a real plus. We go to Hawaii for one week out of the year together as a family. Then, there is one week in the summer when we piggyback with them to the cabin. But, other than that, our vacations typically don't overlap. So there is that "neighborhood watch," close-up and personal, that goes on.

And Elena, who shares a duplex with her daughter, son-in-law, and grandchildren, told us the benefits of living so close when it comes to the mail:

Elena: We do have separate mailboxes—"A" and "B." If she has a delivery, I go over and get it and vice versa. It's fun because we can trade magazines, and, if I am not home or vice versa, we can easily pick up each other's mail.

As well, Nancy, who lives in a cottage in the backyard of her daughter's home, talked about how she will pitch in and help with household chores when needed:

Nancy: I will go over when Janet is busy and unload the dishwasher and pick things up. She is always so grateful. I love being able to do that.

Sharon: So it sounds like a pitch-in family. That is what I did raising my daughters. Everybody pitched in. It wasn't so much that I had to make a list for them. If something needed to be done, we all worked together.

Pets

We heard a number of stories about the benefits of living nearby when it came to sharing responsibilities for pet care, especially when people are away on vacations. One man, who lives with his wife in a cottage in the backyard of their daughter, son-in-law, and grandchildren's home, helps out by walking the dog every day. An invalid woman, who lives with her son and daughter-in-law, feels good about assisting with their dogs. She lets them sit in her room at her feet while she watches television. Another woman, who lives with her daughter and son-in-law, feels useful by looking after their cats while they're away. In other cases, family pets both keep people company and also provide security. Madeline, who lives in a cottage in the backyard of her son and daughter-in-law's home, had this to say about how they share the family dog:

Madeline: The dog stays between both houses. So I can watch it, like I watch my granddaughter. If they're away for the weekend, the dog spends the weekend with me. I take care of the dog and the dog takes care of me. It's the best of both worlds.

And Jane, whose mother lives in a house nearby on a family compound, had a similar story:

> *Jane*: We realized as the years went by that this really was the best situation because when we were gone on vacation, my mother would keep an eye on the house and our animals. We've always had dogs. They knew when we were gone, they would be able to go down to my mother's house and stay there. It was good for her because she had a dog there and she felt safer, rather than being all alone in the house.

We will add that it helps to make agreements for acquiring pets, too. Leslie, who lives in an apartment attached to her daughter's house, now babysits the family dog when her daughter and grandchildren are out of town. She also told us about wanting to get her own dog when she retires. She has talked to her daughter about this, and they've set up ground rules already for the future dog.

Parking

Parking cars can be a huge issue in neighborhoods with limited parking. Tony, who has the revolving-door guest cottage in the backyard where family members and friends stay for months at a time, spoke about the importance of determining how many cars will accompany your house guests. From his own experience, he warned:

> *Tony*: At first, it is cars. Then all of a sudden, it is motorcycles and RVs and all sorts of things that show up. The problem is where do you put them all?

Then Mark, a college student who lives with his parents in an apartment attached to the main house, talked about his problems with not enough places for parking. When asked what he disliked about his living arrangement, he said:

Mark: Parking. In our neighborhood there are a lot of situations like this. Everybody has at least two cars; there is never any parking. That's the only downside of this whole situation. There is a family on the other side of us that has their grandparents and brother-in-law living with them. Across the street, they rent out the garage. They just put a triplex in there. Nobody has extra parking; you have to park on the street.

The other thing that came up in talking with people is the inconvenience of having to park outside a garage. It's much harder to bring in groceries in the rain with no garage to park in. Also, what can be done about excess cars when entertaining? Leslie, who lives with her daughter, son-in-law, and grandchildren in an apartment attached to their house, had this to say:

Leslie: I like to entertain. I like to cook. The street is wide, so there is no problem with parking on the street. My guests can't park in the driveway because my son-in-law can't get out. So that has worked out well.

In another case, Joe, who lives with his wife in an apartment over the garage of his in-laws, told us how he handles parking there with such a large family and so many cars. Fortunately, the home site is a large one. He said that he just always parks outside on the street to be considerate.

Safety and Security

We heard several stories regarding safety and security issues with living together in close proximity. Many families told us how nice it was to have family nearby to look after things if they were away and to help out in emergencies related to health issues. Also, the personal security of having someone else around (even if just the shared dog) made many folks feel more at ease. Additionally, we discuss in some detail safety issues for seniors in chapter 11, "Making Your Home Accessible to Seniors." Of course, avoiding stairs altogether by using ground-level housing or installing an elevator, along with putting grab bars and stall showers with seats in bathrooms, are key safety issues for seniors.

In addition, a number of people told us stories about safety issues for children. In one case, Jean, who lives across the street from her daughter, son-in-law, and two grandchildren, explained how they have handled their proximity problem:

> *Jean*: It is a very busy street, which is a concern because of the children. I have two little ones. I have a 7-year-old grandchild and a 3-year-old. So, of course, we had to be careful of them crossing the street to come and see me. What they decided to do is put a lock on their front door way up high, where neither boy could reach it. They keep that door locked at all times.

A swimming pool was a concern for another family with young children. Susan, the grandmother who lives in an apartment in the backyard, told us how they manage that situation and still allow the grandkids to come by when they want to:

> *Susan*: The swimming pool is between the house and the front of my apartment. We fenced it off so the little kids can't get to it. Also, one of my doors was childproofed. We did that not so much for my privacy but mostly so they couldn't be wandering around my place when I wasn't there.

PERSONAL PREFERENCES

When living together, it is important to consider and discuss at family meetings how to accommodate personal preferences. Lifestyle differences between people and generations can and do come up. In particular, we heard numerous stories about issues around neatness, decor, noise, house temperature, laundry, pets, and smoking. Once again, it helps to bring things up and try to resolve differences.

Lifestyle Differences

In chapter 6 we tell you about Helen, a Northern California Realtor, and her quest for privacy when visiting her daughter and three grandchildren in Arizona. She has tried a number of housing arrangements, including staying at a hotel, in their house, and renting an RV. Here's what she had to say about those experiences:

> *Helen*: When I stayed at their home, the two boys were in a bunker across the hall, and I had the other guest bedroom next to the bath. But, our lifestyles are different. The kids are active in the middle of the night, crying from nightmares and things like that. I would be awakened and then have to try to go back to sleep. For me, it was hard to live in their house, meet my own physical rhythms, and have some privacy.

On the other hand, lifestyle similarities were what led one woman we spoke with to decide to build a house together with her adult daughter that would include her own separate two-room wing. Carla is a retired widow, and her daughter needed help with babysitting her ten-year-old daughter. Originally, Carla had planned to live by herself in a home in Monterey, California. However, she changed her mind about living so far away from her children and decided to move to Southern California to be with her daughter instead. Here's her story:

> *Carla*: Since I was not going to move to Monterey, I thought that maybe I should move in with one of the children. The question was, Which one? Well, with the three of us having such different lifestyles, I thought perhaps I was far more compatible with my daughter. Plus, she had just gone through a difficult divorce and has a 10-year-old. So she said to me, "Well, with my work at the college and having to be gone, and since you are going to be writing and consulting, maybe we can build you an office. We could buy a house together." It was her idea to purchase this property in Southern California and decorate it together. It's a new house in a subdivision, so

we've had a chance to select the flooring, walls, and carpeting. We have similar tastes and it's been a good experience.

Neatness Issues

In our interviews with people about personal preferences, the one topic that came up the most often was neatness. Of course there are lifestyle differences when it comes to being neat and tidy. In many cases, we also found generational differences, with the older generations being more concerned with neatness. The question is, How do you make agreements regarding this issue? Caroline, who plans to live-with her daughter and son-in-law in an apartment in their house, told us how they have already handled this issue:

> *Caroline*: They are very laid-back, and that could be a problem in the house. In being very laid-back, they don't care if there is stuff lying around. They clean up once in a while, but they don't clean up every day. On the other hand, I like to have everything straight and neat all the time. That's not the way they live. So, she said, "Mom, the only thing that you have to promise us is that you won't come and clean up after us." Before, I had always thought that since they're so busy all the time, I could help them. In fact, as I found out, they don't want the help; they want to do it themselves. I'm so glad they thought to tell me that up front.

The next story illustrates what happens when families don't communicate about lifestyle preferences. Dan lived with his wife for a time in the home of her parents in order to save money to buy their own place. They did not have a separate apartment with their own entrance and kitchen. He told us how privacy and boundaries related to neatness became an issue for him:

> *Dan*: My mother-in-law is very neat and tidy and doesn't do well with untidy places. At one point, my wife and I had separate closets. In my closet above the hanging clothes were

shelves of sweaters. It was just not that important to me to keep them neat and organized. At one point, she went in and pulled out all of my sweaters, folded them, rearranged them, and put them back up there neatly. After that, I wondered, "If she feels comfortable going into my closet and rearranging my clothing, does she feel comfortable going in and looking at other things like finances, just out of curiosity?" I have no reason to believe that she did, but it still was a concern. I couldn't say, "Stop doing that," because then it would seem like I wasn't grateful to them for giving us a place to live.

That would be a concern if we did move close together again. If for some reason they moved into the guesthouse that we have on our new property, what are the boundaries going to be? Is Grandma going to be coming over and cleaning our house because it's not vacuumed to her standards? Those sorts of things. From that experience, we would now set up ahead of time what the expectations would be for living together with other people. That's the most important thing.

So, Dan has learned from experience the importance of making agreements up front about living together. He is also in the sometimes difficult position of being the in-law. He needs to learn ways to overcome his hesitancy to communicate his preferences to his wife's parents.

In yet another case where two families share the same house, neatness has become a major problem. Tim and his wife invited his daughter and her three children to come and live with them after the daughter was divorced. Even though they have their own separate kitchens, they do share a common entrance. The daughter's apartment is downstairs and they live upstairs. Here's what Tim said about the problem they have with neatness and how they've managed it:

> *Tim*: Our greatest area of conflict is that of neatness. It's gotten so bad that we don't go downstairs to their place because our standards are so different from theirs. We just can't stand

the mess and the chaos. Fortunately, they are more in our space than we need to be in theirs. We eat together a lot at night up here.

When given a choice of whether to live together or not, neatness can be a criteria for making that decision. Although Paul and Charlotte are happy to share their home with their daughter Stacie and her college friends, Charlotte told us why they would not do so again with one of their sons:

> *Charlotte*: Paul and I have high expectations about keeping the house nice. Most of our children do that, but we have one child that does not. He is a catastrophe. He is living in an apartment now because we don't want him to live in our house anymore. He's just horrendously messy. I think it's really important that you talk before you do this with people and find out what kind of expectations they have about keeping the place nice. Since Paul and I have high expectations, and Robert didn't, that caused a problem for us. Stacie does. We like our home taken care of. Even though we don't go down there, we know that it's okay, that there is not grease on the floor.

And in another example, over time, Vicky and her mother have worked things out regarding their neatness differences. Even though they have separate living quarters, with her mother and father living in the guest cottage in the backyard, her parents are often in their home. Vicky explained to us how they've come to terms with the tidiness issue:

> *Vicky*: When we first moved in here, I remember it was hard because my mom had a real high standard for how this place should look. Even in our house, she used to come in and freak out when the kids' rooms were a little bit disarrayed. Well, over time she mellowed because she realized we needed to live here, too. She had to back down from her expectations, and

we had to raise ours a little in terms of how everything looked. She used to come in here and say, "The windows need to be cleaned. Oh, your rug needs to be cleaned." Now she doesn't do that anymore.

Surely, learning to compromise has been a key to the successful merger of this extended family.

Decor Issues

Of course, there are personal preferences when it comes to decorating a home. Whether it be an attached or detached apartment on the same property, ideally the people living there should have their own choice of wall colors and placement of furniture. Several families we spoke with have done this. In one instance, Jim and Christine, who live in Oregon, gave his mother, Madeline, the freedom to make most such choices in the cottage they built for her in their backyard. However, Jim and Christine picked out the cabinets and other permanent fixtures, as all recognized that eventually, it would be turned into an office.

Joan would agree with the importance of utilizing an aging parent's belongings in planning housing for them. She told us that many friends have asked to see what she and her husband have done in creating an apartment attached to their home for her mother:

> *Joan*: They've come and they've looked. I've talked to them about how to care for an aging parent and how you plan for it. In terms of planning, since my mother had her own house, we tried to plan it so that some of her furniture would fit into her new surroundings. Since she wasn't completely selling everything and starting over, she was able to pull from her past. That has worked quite well.

In yet another situation, Leslie paid for the remodeling done to her daughter's house to create an apartment for her to live in. Although the house belongs to her daughter, Leslie was given free rein to design it and pick out all the wall colors and floor coverings.

House Temperature

The temperature of rooms in a house can become a problem for some, especially for older people. Jane, whose mother-in-law lives with her and her husband, told us how they have handled the room temperature issue:

> *Jane*: My mother-in-law likes it very warm because she does not have very good circulation. I like it very cold. Actually, having my office upstairs helps. I have control over my own heat up there. Downstairs, we've put an extra portable heater next to my mother-in-law.

In fact, when possible, we recommend separate thermostats for those living in two-story houses. That way, if there is a separate apartment downstairs, residents then have choices regarding room temperature. Of course, the advantage of people having separate, detached housing is that the heating problem doesn't come up.

Noise Issues

If you're considering making a move to live together, do think about the type of neighborhood where you'd like to be. Carla told us how her experience of living in a noisy condominium influenced where she and her daughter decided to build their home. When asked what criteria were used to make the decision, she replied:

> *Carla*: I wanted to know what kind of neighborhood it would be, whether there would be lots of children, lots of noise, and all of that. Would it be a place where I'd be comfortable? If you are in a planned community, the house shouldn't be next to the swimming pool, where everybody is there swimming all the time and making noise until late at night. That's how it is in our complex. My condo is right over the swimming pool.

I wanted to know the location and what kind of community it was. Were there a lot of teenagers with loud cars? I was very anxious to help my daughter select a place where we didn't have to live far out in the suburbs or have all the nuisances of the city, such as motorcycles and loud cars.

Fortunately, in this day and age, there are a number of ways you can get around noise issues. Using earplugs is an obvious solution. With all the electronics available to us, you can also find headsets for listening to radio or television. In Sharon's kitchen, she has a TV that she likes to watch while cooking dinner. So she doesn't bother her husband with the noise of the TV while he's reading the newspaper, she'll frequently put on a lightweight, cordless headset. He gets a quiet room, and she gets to hear the news on TV.

Hearing loss can cause all sorts of problems for multigenerational families. We often heard in our interviews about negotiations over the volume of the television. There is a voice-clarifying headset called TV Ears (now in version 5.0) available at online retailers like Amazon and Walmart.com. TV Ears lets people with hearing loss listen to a TV program at a higher volume without disturbing others who may want the volume turned down. People in the same room can be sleeping, reading, or studying, while someone else is enjoying television or music on the radio.

Folks living directly below and above each other is another common noise problem. Adding insulation between floors can help. Also, the Japanese approach of leaving the shoes at the door literally cuts down on the noise of walking.

The noise of crying kids also came up when we spoke with a grandmother. Susan initially lived with her daughter and son and their children together in the main house while her apartment in the backyard was being remodeled. She told us how difficult it was for her to sleep at night with the crying babies and how relieved she was when she was able to move into her own separate place. She can now play her own music loud at night and appreciates the separation, sound-wise.

In another case, a teenage granddaughter told us how she and her sisters try to be quiet for their grandparents who live in a cottage in their backyard. When they use the hot tub near the swimming pool, they know they can't be very loud, otherwise they would wake them up.

A friend told us the story about yet another noise issue for a family of six adult children all living at home with their parents in a large house. The problem is, with so many people who work, when can people do their laundry without disturbing others? One daughter's bedroom is right next to the laundry room. There are times when her sister, who works odd hours, will throw a load of wash in at midnight. The noise from the machine will wake up the sister sleeping in the room next to the laundry room. Certainly, the noise at that time of night would wake up others, as well. This family needs to meet and set up a plan for doing laundry that does not interfere with someone's sleep.

Laundry

We found that most families we spoke with prefer to have separate washers and dryers for doing their laundry. For example, if someone needs to walk through a family member's kitchen to use their laundry facilities, privacy can be an issue. One couple told us how they came up with a solution to this problem. Both of them work and her mother does not. The mother lives in an apartment in their home and only uses their washer and dryer when they are both at work.

Also, another family uses the laundry room in the main house as the connecting junction for both the separate apartment for their son above the garage, as well as the attached cottage for her in-laws. The laundry room serves as a hallway that goes from the garage to the kitchen of the main house. Through it, they also can go upstairs into the addition that is above the garage or into her in-law unit. This design feature allows all of them to share the laundry room without infringing on each other's privacy.

So, different families have different needs. If space is a problem, in this day and age, we have the benefit of stackable appliances. In the space the size of a small closet, one can have a washing machine on the bottom with a clothes dryer on top. Ultimately, it seems to work better for all parties to have separate laundry facilities.

As for who does the laundry, one individual we talked with learned from experience that it is important to talk that issue over ahead of time. Dan and his wife lived for a time with her parents. He told us about the problem he had with the way his mother-in-law did his laundry:

Dan: It was great that my laundry was done. Yet, my mother-in-law would fold my jeans, put them away in a drawer, and they came out all wrinkled. So I had to iron them, and it would drive me nuts. But I couldn't say, "Stop doing my laundry." Because then it would seem like I was not grateful to them for giving us a place to live.

Dan's story illustrates the problem that some families have with communication. How much easier it might have been for all concerned if family meetings were held in his household.

Smoking

Making agreements for where and when people smoke when living together can be a huge issue. One man shared the difficulties that he and his wife have had in establishing ground rules about smoking with his mother, who lives in the same house with them. Now, after years of debate, she has made the decision that, if she wants to smoke, she has to smoke in her own bedroom, not in their family room where everybody sits together. In another case, the mother-in-law agreed to smoke outside the house. An older woman who uses a wheelchair and has Alzheimer's, and who also smokes, required a different solution. She lives with her son and his wife in their home now. The only places she can smoke are in the kitchen corner or outside the house. They put a giant fan right over her chair in the kitchen so it can suck the smoke out of there.

CHILDCARE

In chapters 4 and 5, we talk about the many benefits of having grandparents and siblings around to help with childcare. For everyone's sake, it helps to have agreements about when, where, how often, and how long people are expected to look after the kids. Some families prefer a flexible, on-call system. Others like to have specific days of the week set aside for babysitting, so they can schedule around it. Still others don't want to babysit at all or will do so on a limited basis, especially if the grandparent is still working outside the home. The main thing we recommend is that you talk things over ahead of time so people don't feel encumbered by being expected to do what they hadn't planned for.

In addition, a marriage and family counselor offered some advice to us on the topic of childcare. Mary lives near her son, daughter-in-law, and two grand-children, and frequently babysits:

> *Mary*: I think it really helps if you agree on ways to raise children. I think that is part of the reason that we have gotten along so well. We are all on the same page regarding expectations and discipline. I think that is a big piece of it because it is about respecting other people and respecting yourself.

For those who don't mind being called on at the last minute to babysit, several people gave us examples of when this might be done. Joan, whose mother lives in an apartment attached to the main house, told us about her mother acting as a backup to day care:

> *Joan*: We decided to live together because, at that time, I was still working. My daughter was a very young baby. We had a nanny come in while I was at work. From my perspective, my mother provided an extra set of eyes around the home environment during the day. Even though we had a caregiver for my daughter, if that person wasn't able to come or was coming an hour late, there was just another person around. We did it for that reason, and also so my daughter could have a relationship with her grandmother.

Others told stories about their reasons for requesting or providing help with childcare on an as-needed basis:

> *Todd (whose parents live nearby)*: We can call up one of the grandparents and ask them to look after the kids while they take their nap, so we can go do something else.

Linda (whose in-laws live next door): Well, probably on a selfish note, it's so nice to have Nanna there if I need to park a kid somewhere and run out with another child. She is more than happy to do that for me.

Jean (who lives across the street from her daughter and son-in-law): Whenever they have to go out by themselves, my daughter will call and ask if I'm available to look after the grandkids. Of course, I always jump at the chance to babysit and be with them.

Jean's enthusiasm for being with her grandkids reminds us of hearing from people that one major advantage of such activities is "keeping people young." Craig, whose in-laws live in a cottage in the backyard, told us about the benefits to his in-laws for being flexible in helping him and his wife with their childcare needs:

Craig: I think it's great for them having us here because they have so much fun following the kids' basketball and water polo games. Our calendars get synced and they go to every single game. I think it takes the older generation and keeps them young longer. It plugs them into our day-to-day activities. "Can you pick up so-and-so from school?" or "Can you take them to the dentist?" We are so lucky they live so close to us. By staying engaged and active, they are bound to live longer, too.

Another man, whose daughter and three grandchildren live in an apartment in the same house with him and his wife, Dorrie, talked about ways they've agreed to help out with the grandchildren on a regular basis:

Tim: Right now between us we spend six hours a day in the car, driving three children around to school and after-school activities such as ballet, gymnastics, and baseball. We really devote a lot of our time to just being chauffeurs. In fact, we don't know how a single, working mother does it. It is unbelievable the amount of time necessary just to take them around to their various activities. That, to me, was a huge revelation, in terms of generational shifts. When I was a child, my parents took me nowhere. I went on my own; I biked or did not go. So this whole concept of chauffeuring and taking children somewhere has been an extraordinary learning experience about different generations doing things differently.

Living so far out in the country leaves Dorrie and Tim little choice other than to drive their grandchildren everywhere. These days with so many youngsters being chauffeured and with the problem of obese children nationwide, we were especially glad to hear the following story about a grandmother who has a schedule of walking with her grandchild to school. Jean, who lives in her own home across the street from her daughter, described how she does it:

> *Jean*: I run across the street about 8:05 in the morning, and we walk up to school, which is a short walk. In September, my daughter went back to school. She wants to be a nursery school teacher. So she goes to class and also takes her little one to nursery school on Tuesdays and Thursdays. My oldest grandchild didn't really have a way of getting to school safely, so I walk with him to school two days a week, which is wonderful because it gives us a little quality time to be together. It's a win-win situation.

Perhaps one of the most favorite scheduled activities we heard about is that of grandparents giving their adult children a regular night off for what now is commonly called a date night. Kristi, whose parents live in a cottage in the backyard, told us how they set it up:

> *Kristi*: Yes, we will set it up in advance. When they moved in, I did ask if maybe Tony and I could take one night a week for a date night and they were perfectly happy with that. They are always willing to pitch in that way.

For those who prefer a more scheduled routine in caring for the grandkids, we heard about a number of options for families where both parents and grandparents work outside the home. Gail, who works part-time as an accountant and lives with her husband in a duplex next door to her daughter, son-in-law, and grandsons, told us about the babysitting schedule they've set up:

> *Gail:* I babysit all the time. They have no day care outside of us. Don watches them in the morning, and I only work half a day. So I come home at noon and I have them with me in the afternoon. They do have a sitter, but she only gets them once a week. So I do have a day off. I just love having that close relationship with my grandsons. I feel like I'm almost a second mother, rather than a distant grandmother.

Another working grandmother told us she plans to help babysit her grandson, who attends a year-round school, during his intercessions. Carla, who writes and works part-time as a consultant, has the flexibility to help out. She will soon be living in a house with her divorced daughter and ten-year-old grandson and will have her own separate wing with an office there.

For so many families with both parents working, the question of who will care for the children is a huge concern. In one case, a young woman gets collective help from a number of different sources, including her mother, her mother's housekeeper, siblings, and a nanny that she shares with her brother. She and her brother each have two children. Fortunately for her, her mother lives nearby and her brother lives next door. Kathleen's story is told in detail in chapter 4 under the section "Siblings Help Out."

FAMILY FUN

In the beginning of this chapter, we make reference to Ron Huxley's steps for a family meeting in the *Parenting Toolbox*. The last of the eight steps listed is "Remember to plan to have fun."[175] Consequently, we decided to end this chapter with a discussion about making agreements for family fun. Certainly, making arrangements for fun, both together and apart, is important. We already give an example of grandparents and siblings providing time off for adult children to have date nights, weekends, or vacations by themselves. In addition, we heard a number of stories about families taking joint vacations, sharing meals, attending kids' games, plays, and concerts, as well as going to movies, zoos, and parks. Playing board games such as Monopoly or dominoes is also mentioned, along with playing tennis, swimming, and walking. In other cases, families have fun cooking and gardening or even playing musical instruments together.

Actually, multigenerational family vacations (some folks call them "togethering") can be not only fun but also a useful way to experiment with living with your adult family members again. Indeed, a vacation with relatives, with the associated tight quarters and group schedules, can bring out the worst in some and the best in others. And, the travel industry is happy to help out in your experiments. Several cruise lines offer lower rates for large family groups, actively encouraging entire family reunions. Holiday Inn Resort Orlando Suites–Waterpark in Orlando, Florida, has extended-family suites that include four beds for children and two private rooms for adults with king-sized beds. Additionally, several travel websites promote multigenerational trips as a growing family-bonding trend.

Women typically are the key contacts for families. They set up kin gatherings, keep track of relatives, and promote intergenerational contact. We've found that women in the middle generation are the most involved with these relationships. The mother-daughter link is central for both maintaining family contacts and the flow of support across generations.[176] One woman we spoke with whose in-laws live next door had this to say about inviting them over for family fun:

> *Linda*: One worry I have is that I'm taking advantage or overstepping my bounds as far as the children go. If I lean on my mother-in-law too much, I would like to think that she would just say, "No." I brought it up with her, and she has assured me that she would. They end up doing a lot for me as far as watching the kids goes. Specifically, when my husband and I go on vacation, just the two of us, they have been able to actually live in our home and watch the kids. It's so much easier. One thing I like to do to show my thanks is have them over

here for dinner every couple of weeks. It's a way I can recipro-cate and show appreciation. By the way, my 12-year-old son is extremely sensitive. If a week or two goes by without Nanna and Papa coming over for dinner, he'll ask me, "When are they coming for dinner?" It's a special event for all of us.

Linda also told us about arrangements for her mother-in-law to give the children music lessons:

> *Linda*: The fact that my kids have such a close relationship with their grandparents is wonderful. Just as an example, my moth-er-in-law is instructing my 7-year-old on how to play the flute. He and my 12-year-old, who will be playing the ukulele that she taught him how to play, will both be in the school talent show. When it's time to rehearse, they go over to Nanna's. Also, my daughter has been playing piano since third grade. Before she had formal instruction from her piano teacher, my mother-in-law started her on the piano for a six-month period. Anna was able to walk right next door and get her beginning experi-ence on the piano. It's the older generation passing on skills and talent to the younger ones.

Next, she talked about the fun they have together in the communal garden between their houses:

> *Linda*: My in-laws had the foresight to buy the empty lot between their home and ours. Before we moved here, they knew that they just wanted a physical buffer between their neighbors and themselves. Papa has always gardened that patch of yard, but he's older now. I would say in the last two or three years, his interest in laying all the crops has dwindled. My hus-band is the main gardener now. When my father-in-law is out in the yard, that usually induces the kids to go out. "What are you doing? Can I help?" They have a lot of fun in the garden

together. They help clear the land and with weeding. We had a family day when all of us, including Nanna and Papa, got out and did a lot of clearing. The following week, we all planted seeds. Also, we have a huge snail problem. My sons will go out and bring me back a bucket of snails. I pay them 5 cents a snail.

Nancy, who lives with her husband in a cottage in the backyard, told us how she and her husband enjoy attending their three granddaughters' sports events. They end up going to most of their games and will often pick the girls up from school and take them to their basketball and water polo games. In turn, the three granddaughters were very enthusiastic when they told us how lucky they are to have their grandparents around to give them support at their games.

Sharon also had much to say on this topic in the previous editions of the book:

> *Sharon*: I have had a lot of experience in making agreements for family fun, including treasure hunts, shopping, and travel. One time I had my grandson John over for the weekend, while his mom, dad, and sisters went out of town. I was concerned about how I would keep him busy, since his sisters are usually over when he is, and they play with him. Fortunately, I planned ahead. His birthday was just a few weeks before he came. Instead of giving him all three gifts he had requested, I only gave him one and saved the other two for him to open during his stay with us. I knew he would receive so many presents on his actual birthday and wouldn't miss them. By the way, for all the grandkids' birthday and Christmas gifts, I give them toy catalogues and let them make their own selections. They have a budget to work with. That way they get what they want, and I'm not buying them something they already have.
>
> One of the gifts John opened at our house was a bug and butterfly collecting kit. It included bug-scooper forceps. Instead of collecting bugs with it, I sent John on a Tom Sawyer (paint-the-fence) treasure hunt to gather acorns for

me. He and a neighbor child took turns using it to fill their respective buckets with acorns. It was a win-win activity for them and me. They had fun playing together, and I didn't have to weed out so many little oak tree seedlings that spring!

Also, I had this idea that it would be fun to take the grandkids on a special trip with us by themselves when they turned 10. So I brought this up with my daughter before Tori's 10th birthday last July. She agreed to ask Tori where she would like to go. With no hesitation, her answer was "Paris!" Tori went on to tell her mom that she would have to learn French before she went. Was I ever surprised! I had no idea that 10-year-olds even knew where Paris was. On her actual birthday, we gave her a travel book on Paris along with forty French lessons on CDs. We ended up having a fantastic nine-day trip to Paris and the Brittany coast the following summer.

We found that traveling with a preteen can be a great experience, if you plan ahead. We made a number of agreements on how we would manage the trip. Tori loves to read, so she brought several books with her. We also let her select all the places she wanted to visit in Paris. We made sure that our museum visits were no more than two hours long, and that she had plenty of free time to run around to work off excess energy at parks. Whenever possible, we walked from our hotel to visit places like the Eiffel Tower. During the trip she did endure one three-hour meal at a restaurant in Paris with our French friends. Afterwards, when we met up with them at their home in Brittany, she asked ahead if she could be excused from the table to go and read when she was finished with her dinner. Then, at the end of each day, Tori helped me edit photos I had taken of our activities on my digital camera. After we returned home, I let her select the prints she wanted for her own travel photo album.

In addition, I keep a history of family fun through photos and I do an annual biographical letter for each of the grandkids. I love to take pictures at family gatherings. What I do is make copies not only for us and our adult children but also for the grandchildren. My daughters have memento boxes for each of their children, so that's where they go for now.

Also, when each grandchild turns 3, I give them a First Reader book with him or her in it as a birthday gift. I work with their mother to produce this special biographical book. What we do is take pictures of the child between 2½ and 3 years old while engaged in his or her favorite activities. Then, we make up a list of questions that relate to the photographs. Some of the fifteen questions we used for Christopher's book were:

1. Do you want to build a planter box with Dad?

2. Do you want to ride your bike at Vasona Park?

3. Do you want to play in the sand at Pajaro Dunes?

4. Do you want to read the *Bob the Builder* book?

5. Do you want to sleep with your teddy bear?

Next, I make up a separate page on the computer, in large print. Where each question is used, Mom asks: "Do you want to sleep with your teddy bear?" Christopher says, "Yes!" These pages are placed in a 5x7-inch album on the left side, with the corresponding 4x6-inch photos to the right of each page. In Christopher's case, the title of his book is *Christopher Says "Yes!"* The title of Tori's book is *Tori Says "I Do!"* The title of Miranda's book is *Randi Says "Sure!"* The title of John's book is *John Says "Yes!"* Each indicator of agreement—yes, I do, and sure—was the child's favorite way of expressing the affirmative at age 3.

Finally, I include with each child's birthday card a letter to them outlining their activities for the year, including family fun. It's an annual biographical letter I do for them, which my daughters place in each of their memento boxes. I plan to continue that until they turn 18, when they're old enough to write up their own memoirs.

CONCLUSIONS

As we say throughout this chapter, communication is the key to success in making agreements for living together. Whether or not you have a happy and satisfying family life is determined by how well you communicate with each other. Certainly, the use of compromise, affection, and respect are all key ingredients essential for keeping the peace. Also, it is very important for all participants in the housing arrangement to meet on a regular basis to talk about what's working, what's not working, and how to fix things. General topics of discussion that come up during family meetings are length of stay, communication preferences, relationship issues, privacy issues, shared responsibilities, personal preferences, childcare, and family fun. As for length of stay, it helps to talk ahead about what events might precipitate a change in your arrangement. Regarding communication preferences, most families prefer a "call ahead" policy for interaction. As for relationship issues, try to determine compatibility before living together. When it comes to privacy issues, giving each other space is mentioned frequently. Regarding household finances, shared responsibilities, and childcare, talk ahead about needs and expectations. As for personal preferences, be aware that lifestyle differences, decor, neatness, noise, house temperature, pets, and smoking may all need to be addressed. Finally, be sure to take the time to make agreements for family fun. Having fun together can help nurture positive relationships. Indeed, living together again with good communication can add balance to your life, giving you more contentment, peace, and freedom.

Finally, we want to close the chapter with our favorite quote of all, reprised here from chapter 5:

> *Bill:* My wife and I enjoyed a few short years of three-generation living in a two-flat house in Chicago. We occupied the first floor. Our daughter and husband and our two grandchildren lived above us. We sat around the same dinner table every night. Those were the happiest, richest, and most rewarding years of our lives.

We wish such days for you!

CHAPTER 15

THE NEW CARE AT HOME

I n the previous two editions of this book, we ended with Bill's happy comments. Now, here we add two chapters on what is perhaps the extended family's most important and difficult role—managing the care of those members experiencing the challenges of poor or declining health. Angel Vargas's family history as he described in the preface is a wonderful example of how families have collaborated throughout human history. This chapter focuses on home health care. Chapter 16 covers the end-of-life stage.

CARE AT HOME, DEFINED

The institutional definitions of care at home are pretty clear but still vary. For example, MedlinePlus—a service of the National Library of Medicine, which is part of the National Institutes of Health—defines home care as "care that allows a person with special needs to stay in their home. It might be for people who are getting older (aging in place). It could also be for people who are chronically ill, recovering from surgery, or have a disability." See the Home Care page at Medlineplus.gov for details. Medicare defines home care more specifically as home health, which is "a wide range of health care services that can be given in your home for an illness or injury." (See Medicare.gov for more information.)

Generally, people call it home health, hospice, or personal care, and some think of it as emotional support. From a patient's perspective, as well as a multigenerational family perspective, care at home is the delivery of support and health services in the comfort of a patient's home, wherever and however "home" is defined for them.

So, asking "What is care at home?" is not the right question. The right question is "What *should* care at home be?" The best answer is more complicated—involving for whom, with what services, and when, as well as by whom and how. These are the important topics to explore that we hope to provide some answers for.

First, who should receive care at home? Quick instinct suggests "everyone," and most rational people will agree. In theory, that is the "who" of tomorrow, but in reality and practical terms, that is very difficult to achieve for the "who" of today, multigenerational family or not. With staffing shortages, lack of advanced technology, deeply rooted regulatory constraints, and a lack of full buy-in from patients used to going to the doctor or hospital, convincing them of the benefits of home health care will be difficult for "everyone" to be served via care at home.

That said, in the United States, the "who" of today are usually people age sixty-five and older, according to Medicare statistics. As you can see in figure 15.1 below, it is clear that a national crisis is facing families in the years to come: an aging population with high and growing demand for medical care.

Figure 15.1.
Hospital Beds/1000 Persons vs.
Percentage of 65+ Year-Old Persons in the U.S.

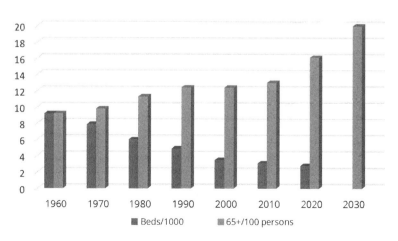

Source: www.medicare.gov

Figure 15.2.
Population over Age 65 by County

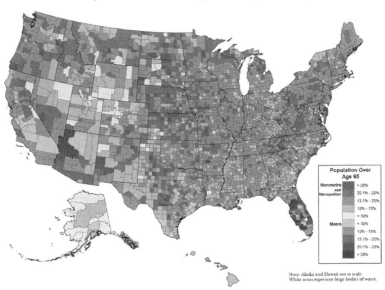

Source: Rural Health Information Hub,
"Demographic Changes and Aging Population."

Currently, the population in the United States over the age of sixty-five is 58 million. In figure 15.2, you can see the geographic breakdown of the density of elders. Take a look at your county. For we authors, in coastal Southern California, the density is around 20 percent.

This is today, but by 2050 the population of elders will be some 90 million. This burgeoning demand will significantly impact society and the workforce for years to come. And the problem confronting us is not just a shortage of beds. We are all now suffering from a national shortage of health care workers, and the shortages will increase each year as the number of elders explodes.[177]

Therefore, we feel that support from the extended family will be crucial both for elders and our oldest old. From a practical viewpoint, when a person can no longer care for themselves and do their daily activities, they need support from family, friends, or external caregivers. Unfortunately, caregiving services can be quite expensive, with round-the-clock care being anywhere from $5,000 to $10,000 a month, depending on intensity and frequency. That is just for the low-end costs of caregiving. Very few Americans can afford that level of care with housing, food, fuel, and other costs skyrocketing.

So, what then? This is where people need to get creative and where the extended family or extended community comes in. If someone needs round-the-clock care, families or a community member could be tasked with providing it: Someone who can help the person with personal hygiene, meal preparation, medication management, paying bills, keeping the house clean, and feeding animals or children. Home care helpers also may have to help a person with very limited mobility who spends most of their time in a bed by rotating them every few hours to prevent pressure sores. This is a big job and best managed by a team of loved ones.

The challenge society faces is, not everyone has a family, or, not everyone has a supportive family. This is where community comes in: utilizing networks, friendships, social welfare groups, and any other organization committed to serving others. Oftentimes, this will help offset the daunting expenses of paid, professional caregiving, as well as the fear of uncertainty of being left without support.

Adding to this challenge is the placement of patients into long-term care facilities. As noted with at-home caregiving, due to the costs or the type of medical problems involved, sometimes it may be better for placement in a fixed facility (although placement has costs too, and not all placements are created or charged equally). Exhibit 15.1 provides the latest statistics on care facilities in the United States:

EXHIBIT 15.1. REGULATED LONG-TERM CARE FACILITIES IN THE UNITED STATES

	NUMBER	PATIENTS SERVED
Adult day services centers	4,600	286,200
Home health agencies (discharged)	12,200	4,455,700
Hospices	4,300	1,426,000
Nursing homes	15,600	1,347,600
Residential care communities*	28,900	811,500

Source: National Center for Health Statistics, accessed 2023.
*includes assisted-living facilities

As mentioned, there are numerous options outside of the home; however, if a patient lives in a care facility . . . is that not home, temporary or not? The answer is yes, so care at home also applies in this care delivery setting. There are four major types of placement facilities: assisted living, board and care, skilled-nursing facilities, and hospice facilities or separate, home-based hospice care.

Assisted Living: These are living situations that are larger in scale, almost like a hotel. They usually have levels of personal care assistance, dining facilities, and other amenities. And costs associated are based on levels of care identified and needed by the family of the person they are trying to place. The environments often offer programs and activities promoting a sense of community.

Board and Care: These living environments are much smaller in scale, like a house. They tend to accommodate around ten to twelve tenants (depending on the size) and have caregivers there to support tenants' daily living activities. These settings are a bit more intimate.

Skilled-Nursing Facilities: Skilled-nursing facilities are meant to be temporary and geared toward those recovering from surgery, a stroke, broken bone, or injury. Usually, they are meant for people in occupational therapy or physical therapy or recovering from procedures or accidents. Usually, people share a room with two or three other people, there is very little privacy, and it feels much more like an institution than a home.

Hospice Facilities and Home-Based Hospice Care: Traditionally, "putting someone in hospice" meant getting a very ill or dying person admitted into a hospice care facility. Today, hospice care can still be delivered that way, but also now, typically, hospice teams come to the patient's residence. Hospice is discussed in detail in chapter 16.

THE CURRENT REALITIES OF CARE AT HOME

As we look at these national statistics, we must bear in mind that each case, patient, geographic, demographic, and value system is different. Thus, the statistics represent opportunities or challenges that have short-, medium-, and long-term requirements, as well as impacts. In a 2022 *Los Angeles Times* article, the reporter, Emily Alpert Reyes, did a great job describing the state of home care circa 2023:

The following personal story can highlight the experience impacting millions of families. In the mornings, Rosa Andresen showers hurriedly before her daughter wakes up, worried the 24-year-old might suffer a seizure or tumble out of the bed while she is still shampooing her hair. Her daughter Amanda Andresen, who does not speak, was born with a condition affecting the part of the brain that bridges its left and right sides. Her walking is unsteady, and she needs to be assisted from the moment she gets up.

In the front room of their South Gate home, Rosa guided Amanda gently from a cushy sofa to the dining table, where she had prepared a mixture of Malt-O-Meal and crumbled bits of toast smeared with peanut butter, stirring them until they grew mushy enough to swallow.

"I've been doing everything since birth for my daughter," Rosa said, feeding Amanda the Malt-O-Meal one spoonful at a time until her daughter pushed the bowl away.

When her husband died nearly a decade ago, Rosa worried about how she would pay their bills, since she couldn't leave Amanda daily to work. That was when someone told her about the In-Home Supportive Services (IHSS) program. It pays assistants to help people who are elderly or disabled stay safely in their own homes.

Rosa became a paid caregiver to her daughter through the program. However, Rosa earned only $16 an hour, straining her budget as prices tick upward for groceries and gas. Her landlord has notified her that she needs to move out of her South Gate unit so that the landlord can move in, she said. Finding another home that she can afford and putting down a deposit feels "almost impossible" on her current wages, she said.

For more than a year, workers like her have been pushing for higher wages in Los Angeles County. Each county has its own hourly rates for workers in the program, which range from $15 to $18.75 across the state. In Los Angeles County, the $16-an-hour rate is just four cents above the minimum wage for unincorporated areas.

Across the state, experts and advocates argue that paltry wages and a painfully complicated funding system have hampered a program that can prevent people from having to leave their homes and move into more costly facilities.

Without the IHSS program, Rosa said, Amanda would probably have to move into a nursing home or some other facility at government expense. Instead, Amanda has been able to stay in her longtime home filled with her Blue's Clues toys and family photos, attended by a parent who can read her unspoken signals, knows her love for long baths and heavy metal music, and is attuned to the signs of her seizures.

In October, a crowd of caregivers in purple shirts brought a meeting of the L.A. County Board of Supervisors to a halt, chanting, "Time for twenty!" after workers testified. SEIU Local 2015, the union that represents the caregivers, has been calling to bring them up to $20 hourly within a few years and bemoaning the slow pace of negotiations since their last agreement expired over a year ago.

"If we go on earning what we're earning, we'll end up on the streets," Blanca Carías said in Spanish. Carías cares for her elderly mother through the program, allowing the 90-year-old cancer patient to stay in her home. She said she has had to choose, at times, between paying for groceries or rent in Los Angeles.

"I'd like for [the county supervisors] to spend one week in our shoes to understand," she said.

Across the state, the program has grown dramatically over the past decade, and demand is only expected to keep rising with an aging population. More than 245,000 people in L.A. County are authorized to get assistance through the IHSS program, aided by more than 200,000 providers, according to data from the Department of Social Services.

Arnulfo De La Cruz, president-elect of SEIU Local 2015, called them "the largest public workforce in Los Angeles County" and said the majority are women of color. More than two-thirds are caring for a family member, state data show. Among those pushing for higher pay for the IHSS workers are people with disabilities who rely on their labor.

"A huge issue, within our community, is the sheer shortage of people who are willing to do it because of the wages," said Lara Minges, 47, a Sierra Madre resident who relies on an attendant to assist her with daily needs, including getting out of bed, going to appointments, preparing meals, and staying hydrated. The program is "really a matter of survival . . . Without my attendant I could die, and I would die."

Minges said she had struggled to find someone to assist her after her mother died.

"As soon as they hear that I need that much physical assistance, nobody is willing to do it for $16 an hour," said Minges, who uses a wheelchair. Her nephew ended up coming out from New Hampshire to help her and it took months to get him approved under the program, she said.

As disabled people, "we worry that if we lose it, or if the wages don't go up, we'll be without care and we'll be institutionalized," losing independence, said Minges, who is a social worker.

Last year, the California State Auditor released an audit that faulted low wages for making it hard to recruit needed caregivers, lamenting that tens of thousands of Californians were not getting the care that they needed each month. (In L.A. County, SEIU Local 2015 has estimated that 750,000 authorized hours go unused every month, which it attributed to a shortage of providers.) In many counties across the state, wages were so low that IHSS caregivers without any other income would qualify for public assistance, the audit found . . .

In the last budget year, the county said it spent nearly $640 million of its funds on the program, with the federal and state government covering the bulk of its $5.6 billion cost. Increasing hourly wages to $20 has been projected to cost the county more than $364 million annually if it took effect in or after January 2023, based on the way costs are split with the state, the executive office said . . .

One analysis, performed more than a decade ago when California was considering cuts to the program, concluded that if IHSS were eliminated and even a fourth of IHSS recipients had to go into nursing homes instead, the state would end up spending more to care for fewer people . . .

In South Gate, Rosa Andresen has been pitching into the union effort by making phone calls, for which SEIU 2015 pays her a small stipend. L.A. County leaders "tell us they appreciate everything we've done," she said. "Yet we're being forced to come, week by week, to express our needs" at the board meetings. "I almost feel like they're ignoring us."

After Amanda pushed away her breakfast bowl, Rosa helped her up to the bathroom. "Come here, let's go brush your teeth," she said as they maneuvered down the hall. In the bathroom, she tucked a towel into the neckline of Amanda's shirt, steadied her head, then gently cleaned her teeth with the brush. She cupped her hands to scoop up water for Amanda to rinse her mouth.

"One more," she coaxed her. "All done."

For Amanda, the program has kept her home with the family she loves. Her Sundays are spent with relatives at the grave of her grandmother, where they spread out a blanket, play music, and pray the rosary. When Rosa mentions her younger brother will visit soon from UC Berkeley, Amanda goes incandescent with joy.

It was the job that made it possible, for years, for Amanda to have this home. Rosa hopes the paycheck won't make it impossible for them to find another.[178]

Room for Thought 15.1.

We really appreciated Rebecca Parker's thoughtful note about a very young family member helping out:

Hi,

My name is Rebecca and I volunteer with an after-school learning program for students. We have been learning about health programs for seniors. We came across your web page, All in the Family Book, while discussing issues affecting seniors! We want to say thank-you!

I encouraged the students to search for more information online while at home. One of my boys, Joey, found this page that he sent for me to see about how to access free/low-cost adult diapers. I was proud of him for going above and beyond to find it—Parentgiving.com.

He also suggested that we share this with you because it has some great information and compliments [sic] the other resources on your site. If you agree, Joey would get a real kick out of seeing his suggestion added to that page. It would also be a teachable moment for the rest of the class, showing that you can make things happen—if you just ask!

Rebecca Parker

TEACHER | ADVISER

Of course, there are countless more stories of home care workers than just Reyes's *Los Angeles Times* piece highlighting the woman caring for Amanda. These stories make the case of higher pay for home care workers from around the country.[179] Furthermore, it's not just the money—paid home care workers, as well as family members or close friends doing the caregiving at home, need different kinds of support. Indeed, the *Wall Street Journal* reported on the serious cases of burnout (mentioning three kinds of challenges—mental, physical, and financial) facing home caregivers and home care workers.[180]

Training for Families Delivering Care at Home

Home caregiving is stressful—that's clear. A professional needs assessment will be indispensable. One major HMO advises family home caregivers quite explicitly:

1. Take care of yourself;

2. Don't help too much—target a high level of independence for your family member; and

3. Ask for help, particularly from other family members. A team approach works best.

We add that home caregiving training will be crucial. Private and public institutions provide a variety of training programs, including online and videos. You should ask your physician about referrals and resources. Training programs are available on key topics and managing specific conditions such as cancer, Parkinson's, heart and kidney conditions, diabetes, and Alzheimer's. Just one example is the "Family Caregiver Training Programs" listing at Meetcaregivers.com.

But please remember our key point—caregiving is a team sport!

Care at Home: A General Description

Going back to the original ask . . . What is care at home, and what should it be? Information in this section is provided to help you and your loved ones stay together at home. The array of services and associated workers is broad, from doctors, nurses, and licensed clinical social workers to professional caregivers who provide daily assistance to ensure the activities of daily living are met. For patients recovering from surgery or illness, home care may include rehabilitative therapies. For terminally ill patients, home care may include palliative and hospice care. Medicare-certified services may include short-term nursing or rehabilitative, therapeutic, and assistive home health care. This care is provided by registered nurses, licensed practical nurses, physical therapists, occupational therapists, speech language pathologists, unlicensed assistive personnel, home health aides, home care agencies, and medical social workers. Paid individual providers can also provide health services through programs, such as California's In-Home Supportive Services. The largest segment of home care consists of licensed and unlicensed nonmedical personnel, who assist with daily tasks such as bathing, cleaning the home, preparing meals, and offering the recipient support and companionship.

These traditional differences in home care services are changing regularly as the average age of the population continues to rise and as the needs of individual patients changes over time. Another disrupter is new technology creating a supply-induced demand; individuals typically desire to remain independent and use home care services to maintain their existing lifestyle. Government and insurance providers are beginning to fund this level of care as an alternative to facility care. And care at home is often a lower-cost solution to long-term care facilities.

Patients who received care at home after being discharged from the hospital are associated with decreases in use of the health care system, hospital readmission, and death. Care at home may include some combination of professional health care services and life assistance services.

It is important to note that there may be cultural differences in home care due to different familial structures—multigenerational households, multiple households, same-sex parents, and single-parent families can compose networks of culturally diverse individuals who require home care. Decisions may be made by one dominant authority in the structure or through the collective group.

Estimates for the U.S. indicate that most home care is informal, with families and friends providing a substantial amount of care. In most cases, when ordered by a physician, Medicare will pay for short-term, medically necessary services provided in a home setting. But a senior who requires only nonmedical care will not qualify for Medicare coverage of these services.

Home health care software falls under the broad category of health care information technology (HIT). HIT is the application of information processing involving both computer hardware and software that deals with the storage, retrieval, sharing, and use of health care information, data, and knowledge for communication and decision-making.

Care at Home by Health Care Organizations

The COVID-19 pandemic accelerated the possibility and necessity of acute-level care at home. Several health systems provide a useful example of the evolving services increasingly available as technologies improve and costs of hospitalization and institutional placement continue to accelerate. At the same time, studies have shown that most Americans prefer receiving care in the familiar surroundings of their homes, where they feel dignity, comfort, and respect. Expanded care at home programs, referred to by some people as "hospital at home," offer certain patients who qualify for hospital admission the opportunity to have their acute care needs met in the safety and comfort of their own homes, close to family and friends.

Advanced care at home demonstrates person-centered care by treating patients at the right time and right place, based on their choice. Several prominent health care organizations, including Kaiser Permanente, have provided this model of patient-centered care over the last decade.

Enabled by processes, some health organizations do provide 24/7 patient care through home visits, telehealth appointments, and remote monitoring. This is a clear enabler for the multigenerational family; more specifically, care is managed through specialized command centers overseen by physician-led teams that virtually direct patient care, supported by in-home visits. The program brings hospital-equivalent services and supplies into the home and seamlessly coordinates care with transitions and follow-up by the patient's primary care team.

An analysis by one health system found that the highest percentage of patients enrolled in the care at home program are also the most socioeconomically disadvantaged, demonstrating how this model of care may reach underserved groups and can help reduce health care disparities.

Advanced Care at Home Coalition
& Local and Federal Legislation

In 2021, the Advanced Care at Home Coalition was formed, which brings together industry leaders in home and hospital care to advocate for all patients treated in U.S. hospitals who could safely receive care in their homes. See

Achcoalition.org for more details, including a series of useful patient stories from around the country.

The current membership of ACHC includes Kaiser Permanente, Mayo Clinic, Medically Home, and, in 2024, more than twenty major hospitals including university institutions, such as the University of California, Irvine Medical Center near John's home. The coalition's stated strategy is, "We bring together like-minded stakeholders to advocate in Congress and to the Administration for policies that foster and support advance care at home services."

In early 2024, multiple bills are pending in Congress that, if passed, would provide additional support and incentives for care at home. Perhaps the most prominent is the Choose Home Care Act, H.R. 5514.[181] As of late 2023, it had forty-five bipartisan cosponsors. The bill specifies:

> This bill provides for coverage of home-based extended care services under Medicare. Specifically, the bill provides for coverage of services that are furnished to Medicare beneficiaries in their homes by home health agencies, including nursing care, meals and nutritional support, home medical supplies, nonemergency medical transportation, and care coordination. Coverage includes thirty days of post-hospital care and other periods of extended illness, as determined by the Centers for Medicare & Medicaid Services (CMS). Home health agencies that provide such services may receive additional payments in accordance with a specified methodology. The CMS may make payments for covered services furnished before 2022 during any period in which there is a public health emergency.

Local laws provide varying support for care at home at both the county and state levels. It will be worthwhile to consult with service providers in your specific areas.

The elders' unprecedented crush of the coming decade will demand *changes* more substantial than can be anticipated by the current authorities in Congress and state houses around the country. At least in California, we are beginning to see the direction health care in the United States is heading; that is, a single-payer system we see as inevitable.[182] Another positive sign is a recent study demonstrating the profitability of allowing consumers to bundle themselves in [extended] family plans.[183]

Indeed, the rather simple changes described in H.R. 5514 above, while recognized by many, remain stuck in Congressional committee. For us, the most ominous bellwether for things to come in health care for elders is a 2022 article from *Future Market Insights*, "Adult Diapers Market is Poised to Expand at over 6.9% (compound annual growth rate) through 2032." While the diaper manufacturers will be able to expand production, whose hands will *change* those diapers, including those of the current elder legislators around the country?

CONCLUSIONS

The story in this chapter is an unpleasant one. Demand for care at home is exploding. The shortages in medical care facilities and health care workers demand creativity. Health care firms and public institutions are providing some answers and defining some problems. Government actions will be needed, but partisan politics works against the societal and institutional collaboration needed. These circumstances are certain to worsen and place the primary burden for care at home on family and community members. According to the most recent AARP report, American families already supply some $600 billion worth of care at home services.[184] This system is unsustainable. Get ready for major changes!

THE FINAL CHAPTER: A DEATH IN THE FAMILY

The only certainty in life is death. The key question is, "And?"

B y one government estimate, there were some 2,300 centenarians living in the U.S. in 1950. Today there are more than 97,000, according to the Census Bureau. Three-quarters of them are women.[185] On the other hand, as we write this book during the COVID-19 global pandemic, we have the unpleasant reality of deaths and their causes, most recently reported by the U.S. Centers for Disease Control and Prevention:

Exhibit 16.1. Number of Deaths for Leading Causes of Death

- **Heart disease:** 696,962
- **Cancer:** 602,350
- **COVID-19:** 350,831
- **Accidents (unintentional injuries):** 200,955
- **Stroke (cerebrovascular diseases):** 160,264
- **Chronic lower respiratory diseases:** 152,657
- **Alzheimer's disease:** 134,242
- **Diabetes:** 102,188
- **Influenza and pneumonia:** 53,544
- **Nephritis, nephrotic syndrome, and nephrosis (kidney problems):** 52,547

Source: Data from the United States Centers for Disease Control and Prevention, 2020.

ARE YOU READY?

Most people don't want to even think about death—let alone to plan for it. Many people even believe planning for something will make it happen. However, it is the most responsible thing you can do for yourself and your family. In this chapter we first talk about the business of dying, then the social impacts, and finally we include spiritual aspects of death.

THE BUSINESS OF DYING

There's much best to be considered ahead of time. Emily has worked with hundreds of families and dying individuals over the years that really have found it disheartening to think of death and end-of-life matters. She worked in the hospice/palliative-care field for nearly a decade and facilitated grief support groups for about five of those years. She has witnessed positive stories, tougher ones, and many really sad ones, too. Our hope would be to impart to you the information you need to get what you must have in place so frustration, anger, and guilt don't interfere with the passing of and grieving for a loved one.

So, to start, it is important that people consider personal finances. As most of us know, we have many passwords and accounts, and many times people pay bills either through online banking or through automatic payments. It is really important to speak to a lawyer and have a drafted living will so that when the time comes, your loved ones can easily access what has been left behind.[186] Setting up the living will alleviates much stress for those you love. People don't realize that if they haven't identified someone to take care of their financial matters after they die, it makes it much harder. Yes, *you* have to decide who that one person (most likely a family member) is whom you trust is responsible and clear-minded and who can carry out the objectives you have set for yourself and your assets. If you appoint a clearly defined executor in a legal document, your family will be best able to manage the most emotionally ridden landscapes with end-of-life matters, financial assets (including insurance policies and Social Security payments), and possessions. It is necessary to think about who you'd want to have what you can't take with you, draft it in a legal document, and choose a person as your power of attorney for finances. This type of "living" legal document may also be necessary if you are very much alive but can no longer handle your daily living expenses—you will need someone to manage them for you.

Next, you also need to think about that one person you know who will carry out your health care wishes. This designated person will have a durable power of attorney—for health care, different from the power of attorney for finances just mentioned. You should also have an advanced directive document in place. This means you have to think about the medical procedures you'd prefer (or not prefer) to have in the event of a disabling or catastrophic injurious event happening to you, like an accident, and you were rendered unable to make your own health care decisions. The prominent example is what kinds of lifesaving interventions would you want? This should be discussed with a health care provider who can explain to you choices and options. You alleviate a huge burden (and what could be a major family fight) if you have your own wishes clearly written out in a legal document and you have the person selected to carry out those wishes. If you let them know what you want, they won't be ridden with fear, guilt, or anxiety on what to do because you have decided and it was communicated.

Banks need proper legal documentation (usually a living will) for family members to access your funds on your behalf. This will ensure that those you love, who may rely on your income and assets for their support, will have a way to carry on. Emily has seen (far too many times) families that cannot access their loved one's finances easily. It is enough to go through health scares and stresses, let alone to have to think about how the bills will get paid.

Another thing to think about is what you'd want to have happen to your body when that time comes. Do you want to be buried in the ground or at sea?[187] Do you want to be cremated?[188] Indeed, in his fascinating 2018 book, *Is the Cemetery Dead?*,[189] David C. Sloane puts forth some of these same questions of what people want done with their bodies when they die. How do you want people to honor you? It is really important to consider all of this, too. Mortuaries are businesses. It is better to have conversations about things when you are alive and well than when your family is bogged down with the sadness of your loss. Countless people in Emily's grief support groups have shared their disbelief, upset, outrage, and utter sadness by having to handle the business aspects of a family member's death, especially when grieving.

In an ideal world, you'd make all these decisions and arrangements while in a clear state of mind. You would have a family meeting and discuss it together. This is a great time to have those discussions and air out those unresolved feelings—so everyone can actually hear what others think and feel before a family member's death. You might have a professional facilitate the discussion for you if you do not feel comfortable doing it yourself.

DEATH: A UNIVERSAL HUMAN EXPERIENCE

Not everyone dies while in hospice. Horrible accidents, natural disasters, homicides, suicides, drug overdoses, or fast-acting diseases (heart attacks, strokes, and COVID-19) all take their toll and can bring a sudden demise. However, for many people death is a slower process. And this leads us to a discussion of both palliative and hospice care.

When someone has been diagnosed with a terminal illness, they have some options. Some people will fight and try everything to get more time with family and friends, and to even rid themselves of the disease. If they reach the end of the line, they can choose hospice. When someone is in hospice, they have a lot of support, which can help smooth the path to death, and often their loved ones are around to move with them through the process.

Palliative Care

What is palliative care? It is a program of care that is provided by a medical team to help alleviate stress, symptoms, and emotions that can hinder the quality of one's life. Usually, someone has been diagnosed with a life-threatening illness and has been given one year or less to live, with the potential to cure the disease. Usually, when someone enters palliative care they are on a trajectory of receiving medical care to rid them of their disease and or slow the process down. This is a great resource to utilize when facing illness.

Hospice Care

Many people hate to hear the word hospice. At least in California, there are two reasons why this is so. First, it is completely understandable because that means they have been given an estimated time left to live, six months or less, and this estimate is based on the research and data from disease progression and the individual patient's condition. Second, particularly as the demand for hospice has exploded in California, it has brought with it apparent widespread fraud and abuse in licensing practices. Two bills have been signed into law in that state placing a moratorium on the issuance of new licenses.[190]

According to the most recent data, Medicare hospice care has been growing steadily from 1.43 million users in 2016 to 1.72 million in 2020.[191] Medicare supports about one-half of all hospice care delivered in the U.S., with the rest being supported by private and charitable organizations. The average length of stay in hospice varies by ailment—see table 16.1.

TABLE 16.1. AVERAGE LENGTH OF STAY BEFORE DEATH, 2020

	DAYS
All	106
Chronic kidney disease/kidney failure	35
Cancers	55
Heart disease (including congestive heart failure)	129
Lung (COPD and pneumonias)	146
Cerebrovascular event/stroke	148
Alzheimer's, other dementia, Parkinson's	181
COVID-19	28

Source: NHPCO Facts and Figures, 2020.

At the federal level (Medicare), after the age of sixty-five, hospice is a Medicare-paid-for program. Before age sixty-five it must be paid for by personal health insurance. When someone enters hospice they have available to them a team of providers that includes a doctor, a nurse (case manager), a social worker, therapists, a chaplain, spiritual and bereavement counselors, and a bath aid, as well as volunteers. Four levels of care are provided: routine home care (about 93 percent of cases), continuous home care (about 6 percent), and both inpatient respite care and general inpatient care (rare).

At this time, most people have decided that they want nature to take its course, however long that may be. They no longer wish to have medical interventions. Instead, they seek help to alleviate pain, discomfort, stress, and symptoms that hinder the quality of life.

Hospice care in the home provides weekly visits from the nurse, social worker, chaplain, or bath aides. All medical equipment, medications, and supplies related to managing the diagnosed condition are paid for by Medicare.

In some locations, there are actually hospice facilities where people can spend their remaining time being cared for. More often, people are at their own homes with family and caregivers helping them through the process. Contrary to what many folks think, hospice isn't necessarily a place people go. Indeed, most prefer the services be delivered at home.

It is important for people to understand that you don't have to be on death's door to enter the program. Actually, it is much more supportive to start on the hospice program whether you feel ready for death or not. The purpose of the program is to help walk the journey with you; you don't have to do it alone. The resources available can act as the special pillow you lay your head on.

When someone is dying, what it can look like to the observer is that somehow they are suffering. Hospice care is in place to help alleviate that. In Western medicine, usually pharmaceuticals are used. Pharmaceuticals that are highly regulated and used in strict medical settings to ease pain during end of life include morphine. In addition, there are some medications to alleviate anxiety and other symptoms.

A great majority of the time toward the actively dying state, you will see many of the same physical behaviors: People usually sleep a lot more. They usually withdraw from activities and people they loved and enjoyed. They usually stop eating and drinking and move into a nonresponsive sleep state that may appear as a coma. The patient's systems can start to shut down and stop working. There can be times where they have congestion and fluids building up in their lungs. This can sound really scary to family and those providing care. The alkaloid atropine is used to dry up the secretions that are building up in their lungs so it isn't so difficult to witness.

In her career, Emily has witnessed these experiences countless times. She has seen people go into this active-dying state and somehow wait until their last loved one arrives to see them one more time. It is most advantageous for family members to make their visits to the patient sooner than later, especially if they have been put on the hospice program. That means they have been given six months or less to live. It is much better to show up early on and have the conversations and say what you want to say before they move into the actively dying phase of death. It isn't easy, but it helps people so much to have that option. Quite honestly, it seems that hospice is really the only "death experience" that can allow for those conversations, saying things to each other, planning if it hasn't happened, and reflecting with each other. Other types of deaths, like accidents or sudden deaths, don't allow for that loving process.

Many people in the end of life industry have their own experiences and thoughts about the final days and hours. Some people feel that there is a significant amount of mental processing that goes on for the dying, and even though they are nonresponsive, they can still hear. Some people feel they are halfway between life and death and may even believe that they are out of their body and viewing things from another vantage point. Others feel like during the late stages of the process, the patient has no idea what is going on around them.

In her experience, Emily has seen far too many people hold on until their last child arrives, even when they are in the so-called coma state. Others have waited until everyone leaves the room and then they let go. Emily says, "To me, it is the bravest time for anyone. To consider letting go of this world and not having any idea what is beyond life, is the great big question."

The journey is so personal, and yet one we will all take. Whatever your beliefs or attitudes are, it is *your* experience. It doesn't have to be painful—physically or emotionally—especially if the terminally ill utilize the hospice program to help them along the way. There are resources and support that hospice can offer to all involved.

THE WILLFUL END-OF-LIFE LAWS

We feel obligated to include information on this very controversial new free-dom to die when one chooses.[192] This topic (known as medical aid in dying, death with dignity, the right-to-die, euthanasia, and assisted suicide) is particu-larly appropriate to address because elders are a high-risk category for this path.

Legislation allowing medically assisted aid in dying now exists in several states (Washington, California, Oregon, Vermont,[193] and Montana), and doz-ens of countries around the world. The view we the authors take is that now, in some states, people have options for managing their life-taking illnesses and can make their decisions based on their own experiences, wishes, and desires.

The laws vary and are changing fast around the country,[194] and for that matter around the world.[195] Many of Emily's patients have gone through the process to get the end-of-life medications available to them and never use them. She has also had patients that have said to her, "Why am I still here, this is crazy, I'm ready." In California, you have to be diagnosed with a terminal illness and that must be certified by a licensed medical doctor. Recognizing that approval processes and restrictions are changing fast everywhere, we highly recommend the documentary *Last Plane Home* as an accurate depiction of the legal and medical processes required in California in 2022. We are particularly impressed with the involvement of the extended family as portrayed in the film.

The state of Oregon published a report on the Oregon Death with Dignity Act, providing statistics for 2015 regarding patient usage of the new freedoms provided there (the report is available at Oregon.gov):

During 2015, there were 218 people in the state who were approved and received the lethal drugs to end their own lives. One hundred and thirty-two terminally ill patients ultimately made the decision to ingest drugs. Seventy-eight percent were elders and 72 percent were diagnosed with terminal cancers. When asked for their reasons for their participation in the medical-aid-in-dying program, the top responses in order were: 96.2 percent mentioned the loss of the ability to participate in activities that once made them enjoy life, 92.4 per-cent mentioned the loss of autonomy, or their independence of their own thoughts or actions, and 75.4 percent stated loss of their dignity.

The numbers participating in these legalized programs remain relatively small but are at the same time growing fast.

GRIEVING AND THE FAMILY

As is death, grief is also a universal experience. We all at one point will lose someone we love. And feelings of grief can also be associated with other kinds of losses as well—jobs, homes, pets, friendships, and so on. Recently, CNN news anchor Anderson Cooper launched a podcast, *Facing What's Left Behind*, on the subject of grief and loss—it went to the number one listened-to podcast within days. Clearly, there is a deep desire to understand grief—to hear about how others move through it, to learn what to do with it.

Emily, through her years as a licensed clinical social worker for those placed on hospice or palliative care, has witnessed hundreds of families losing a loved one. She also spent much time afterward with those willing to seek help for their feelings about the loss, how to relate to it, what to do with it, what is normal, etc. Those who have walked through such an experience have a personal understanding of how it is a leveling of sorts on all fronts. Depending on the degree of the relationship in a person's life—the amount of care and love for someone—that person will experience a "dismantling," going from being grounded to shaken at the core. Grieving—the task at hand—is to reintegrate back to having your feet planted on the ground, having now realized the ground can fall out from underneath you.

Grief is a full-bodied experience. It is mental, spiritual, emotional, and physical. It hits everyone in their own way. It demands people to come into some sort of alignment and acceptance of a new reality.

In her 1969 book *On Death and Dying*, Swiss psychiatrist Elisabeth Kübler Ross introduced the five stages of grief model, with respect to the acceptance of one's own death. That is, humans faced with their impending death follow a predictable process of denial, anger, bargaining, depression, and acceptance. Her ideas have widely been generalized to the broader experiences of grief, particularly related to the loss of a loved one. We are not in any way saying these stages aren't a reality or applicable to those losing someone. We are just pointing out that her model was originally developed through her research on a somewhat different topic.

Emily's own experiences suggest grieving can follow different sequences of feelings, and sometimes more than one at a time. That is, denial can follow depression, or anger can be mixed with bargaining. As Emily describes it, "I have witnessed people having multiple feelings and at times two stages at once, and bouncing around from stage to stage."

The most devastating grief is experienced by those who have been partnered for a long time, are in their elder years, and are losing the person they love most. This is where multigenerational living situations can really assist the family in helping their surviving loved one adjust.

Emily also reports that some family members seem to avoid sharing or asking how others are feeling, so as not to upset others. The truth is, when a family loses someone, it impacts the functioning of the whole. Everyone is grieving. Everyone is having feelings unfamiliar to them. Everyone is upset. Most people want to speak about their loved one, talk about them, and reminisce about them. Our deceased loved ones remain in our hearts through this sharing of stories, traits, and memories with one another. Sharing may cause crying, yes. But, it is a healthy sort of interaction, creating bonding and connection. Grieving alone makes loss and healing much more difficult.

It also seems there is some sort of cultural expectation that one year is a long enough time to grieve. But, love and loss cannot be neatly measured in time or strength of feelings. The more we allow people their feelings and processes, the better it is for everyone. Relationships are plentiful and have multiple roles in our lives: sisters, brothers friends, colleagues, all kinds of relationships, and those can be impactful losses, too. Additionally, loss and grief isn't strictly a result of a death. It can be of an activity, a job, and even something that never came to fruition which was a heartfelt desire. My hope is that by sharing what is going on with people, it begins to provide a culture of care and understanding when somebody has a loss, not pressures to get it together, or even to buck up for a job. Ideally, it is there as an ebb and flow; so if you pick up the slack for somebody at work during their process of mourning, that may be just what you need one day done for you.

Now, not all people have complications from a loss. Most people are able to utilize their own family system, their own community and supports to move through it. On the other hand, some people really need assistance. So, our encouragement is to attune to what it is you need and seek the space, people, solitude, or support to assist you. Support groups where peers share experiences and stories which help uplift and normalize the experience can be tremendously helpful. Professional counseling can also be helpful.

Lastly, losses create a lot of change. It becomes apparent slowly, not overnight. Maybe somebody in a marriage always put out the trash, got the mail, or paid the bills. The person left behind is faced with taking on new jobs and roles while they are down-and-out and may need someone to help them manage that, learn that, or do that for them for a bit. So the key is to check on your loved ones—give them a call. Offer a hand. Stick together.

Like Anderson Cooper, we are interested in facing loss, talking about it, sharing about the ones we love, and somehow finding a way to the love that can last your lifetime and beyond.

Finally, John and his coauthors of *Inventive Negotiation* explain the importance of the interrogative, "And?"[196]

"And?" When spoken with a rising tone and emphasis, this simplest of sentences represents the essence of inventive negotiations in two fundamental ways. First, it recognizes that invention is a social activity involving you and me, and sometimes even Dick and Jane and Yoshi and Mario. Second, this simplest of questions asks, "What's next?" after an agreement and beyond that old "getting to yes." It also avoids the creativity-killing "Yeah, but . . ." It implies a long-term relationship among partners where synergy pertains. Our book is about a new way of thinking about human exchange and about how to conduct inventive negotiations in all aspects of your life—personal, commercial, political, and global.

Thus, the answer to the key question we posed at the beginning of this last chapter, *"And?"* is, in fact, *the family. The family is forever!*

APPENDIX

HOW THE ECONOMISTS WERE BLINDSIDED BY THE GREAT RECESSION: THE VIEW FROM 1997, THEN 2011

John L. Graham, "2020 is 23 Years from Now,"
UCInsight Magazine (Spring 1997), 4, 23.

Predictions about 2020? Two are easy. First, Tiger Woods will have won more green blazers and more green in general than any athlete in history. Second, we'll all be about 23 years older. Both things will rivet the attention of the nation. Woods will make us happy. Retirement-age baby boomers will not.

The math is pretty simple. In 1953 there weren't enough first-grade teachers. 1956 brought us the Schwinn bicycle shortage. In 1964, it was college classrooms; 1960, jobs; 1978, houses; and now in 1997, we have the shortage of sure investment opportunities. Baby boomers' fear of the future is now driving the current boom in stock market investment. Fast approaching their fifties, retirement planning is now the rage.

The problem is, even the best investments only produce money. And money is nothing. I'm not saying it isn't important. Like motor oil is to your car engine, money is the lubricant of society. You don't trade your 70 hours a week or your creativity for money. Rather, your hard work and good ideas are actually traded for a nice place to live, nice schools for your kids, and nice vacations. The money just makes the trade a little more efficient. Now I know this isn't what you learned in your finance classes. Money can actually disappear—in a stock market crash or in hyperinflation, for example. Remember 1987? Or, just ask your Japanese friends about the relationship between money, stocks, and real estate. Simply stated, money isn't stronger than demographics. That's why in trying to understand the past and the future, cultural anthropologists focus on people, not money.

Culture's primary impact is that it makes us all imitate our parents, the generation ahead of us. As strange as the Generation-Xers' behavior (tattoos and cigars) looks to their parents today, the Xers will be driving minivans in the next millennium, too. And boomers' parents are now showing us all how to party. In most cultures, throughout history, old folks have lived with and been supported by their kids. Not our folks. They've all had their babies paying into Social Security and such. And that boom crop can afford a lot. 3.5 kids can support a nice house and nice vacations for 1.5 parents pretty easily. Boomers' parents are enjoying the biggest binge in history.

But, in 2020, it will be 1.5 kids supporting 2.0 parents. That simple ratio will be far more salient than any price/earnings ratio. The breakthroughs in biotech (info tech will be passé) will serve to lengthen life. Cancer, AIDS, and heart disease won't kill, bodies and minds will just wear down. And the costs of the worn down baby-boom generation of 2020 will simply not be supported by their 1990s investments in stocks, no matter how red-hot or blue-chip.

I guess I can see three ways to defeat this destined demographic demon. First, of course, culture can change. For example, think how profoundly birth control has changed our values and everyday lives. In 2020, when baby boomers are forced back into the homes and care of their kids, everyone may see it as a positive thing. Indeed, haven't we all decried the decline in family strength? In 2020 we may see the rejoining of young and old in the household as the best kind of family reunion. When old and young are living together again, the fierce independence and political power of the AARP will have gone the same way as other vestiges of culture, like communism and Cabbage Patch dolls.

Globalism is the second way out. While we share this nationwide graying with places like Japan and Western Europe, things are much different in places like Mexico and the Mekong River Delta. The question is, Can we invest in the legions of young people in the latter lands fast enough now, so they will be willing to return the favor in 2020? Let's for a moment focus on the example of our NAFTA neighbors to the south. The free trade agreement with Mexico passed in 1995 was more than Ross Perot's Waterloo. It was the single most important event in U.S.-Mexico relations since the U.S. Marines marched into the Halls of Montezuma (in Mexico City) in the 1840s. For the first time in history we have treated Mexico as an equal. Most Americans have missed this significance, but no Mexican did.

Yes, American jobs have migrated south. But, isn't that better than Mexican workers migrating north? Yes, the peso crash landed. But, now in 1997, the key part of the term is "landed." Indeed, this year they repaid us the billions we loaned them, and they did it early! Yes, cocaine corruption is king in places like Tijuana. But, whose fault is that? The trade in illicit drugs is, and always will be, demand-driven. The Latin American drug lords supply, but they don't advertise.

If we manage our Mexican marriage right, the fruits of the relationship will be a wonderful wealth for both countries in 2020. We need to focus our cross-border investments now in factories and young people's brains. That will enable them to make the cars, televisions, computers, and medical equipment for us. And we'll supply the engineering, financial, healthcare, consulting, and management services and software to them. Immigration won't be an issue. Economic integration will mean open borders in the 2020s like we had in the 1920s, like the Europeans have now. If we can genuinely embrace globalism, the young people of Mexico and the other developing countries we support will help to abate the baby-boomer bomb of the next millennium. Indeed, this is the best of the three approaches to the crisis of gray coming in 2020.

Finally, as I mentioned, there is a third solution, a xenophobic one. You've heard the story of the two hikers who ran into a grizzly bear. One hiker stopped to slip on his running shoes. The other asked, "What are you doing? You can't outrun a grizzly!" His friend replied, "I don't need to outrun the bear, I just need to outrun you!" Yes, a short-sighted Adam Smithian selfishness may lead to better stock-market gambling than your "friends." But, even the biggest fish, with 20-20 vision, can't see very far in a putrid pond.

John L. Graham, "Solution to US Debt Woes Isn't Economic. It's Social." *Christian Science Monitor*, July 27, 2011, https://www.csmonitor.com/Business/new-economy/2011/0727/Solution-to-US-debt-woes-isn-t-economic.-It-s-social.

Economic problems like the housing debacle, Social Security and Medicare shortfalls have a social solution: stronger extended families.

The clock is ticking loudly in Washington over the debt ceiling and long-term funding problems like Medicare and Social Security. Economists have blamed America's current economic malaise on (take your pick): overspending, greed, government regulation, government deregulation, subprime home mortgages, executive incentives, efficient markets theory, the business cycle, the Chinese, Alan Greenspan—the list goes on.

But what if the economists have it completely wrong? Suppose for a minute or 10 that the so-called economic decline is simply a severe symptom of a deeper disease, a cultural shift.

The longest view of the progress of humankind suggests that governments have always been unfaithful to humans. The current example, our crumbling Social Security system, has really only succeeded in dividing families. In 1940, over 60 percent of elderly widows lived with their children. By 1990, that number had dropped to less than 20 percent.

Margaret Mead long ago pointed out that the family is the only institution that persistently supports us. What the economists are calling an economic problem is best understood as a cultural reversion to older living patterns. The reason? Our 20th century experiment with nuclear families has failed.

That's the problem. Here's the fix: Many Americans are rediscovering the importance of the extended family.

RETURN TO THE EMPTY NEST

Consider the phenomenon known as "boomerang kids." Estimates vary, but according to the US Census Bureau, more than one-third of all Americans ages 20 to 34 are now living with their parents. That's some 18 million young adults.

Not everybody is happy about this renewed family closeness, if headlines are anything to go by:

"Adult Children Moving Back Home: Don't Let Them Derail Your Goals"

"The Coddling Crisis: Why Americans Think Childhood Begins at Age 26"

"The PermaParent Trap" (perhaps the scariest headline of all)

The negative headlines get attention, but they also cause angst for all of us, particularly the kids. And it's not clear that they represent reality.

Three in four parents did not report being happier once their children moved out, according to a 2004 survey (available on .pdf) conducted for retirement-community developer Pulte Homes. Even among the 1 in 4 baby boomers who did report themselves being happier as empty nesters, that feeling seemed to decline with the length of time that the nest was actually empty:

0-5 years since the children left: 27 percent feel happier

6-10 years: 11 percent

11+ years: 5 percent

Too bad the kids themselves missed the news that they're missed.

Moreover, when you step back and look at the big picture and the moving picture, it's clear that boomerang kids are just another symptom of the greater cultural change affecting American society as we enter the 21st century: that is, the reunification of the extended family.

Grandparents are also moving back in with their children. Three-generation households are on the rise in America, according to the Census Bureau. The Pew Research Center estimates that 16 percent of the population—49 million Americans—lived in multigenerational housing in 2008, up from 28 million in 1980. The fundamental point is that people are moving back together again because the grand experiment of the World War II generation hasn't worked. Three generations belong together, and not just for financial reasons.

Fundamentally, humans are psychologically and physiologically designed and have evolved to live this way. We've survived by living in such extended family arrangements. We are happiest in such groups. And, we are now quickly learning that other institutions (companies, unions, governments, religious organizations, etc.) ultimately cannot take care of us. Only our families can and will.

Up until the 1950s in this country and in northern Europe, three (sometimes even four) generations lived together in multigeneration families. It's still that way in almost all of the rest of the world.

In prehistoric times these family groupings included all the living descendants in either the male or female line. Each family was practically self-sufficient with men providing most of the food, and women taking care of household duties, children, and elderly parents. The whole family had to cooperate in order to survive. Eventually, families organized themselves into clans and, still later, into cooperative tribes for protection. Even when people began depending on local, state, and national governments for protection, and on persons outside the family for food and education, multigenerational living survived.

The Industrial Revolution began to shift these patterns. People moved from farms to cities where new factories were being built. In the cities, people no longer worked together in extended family units. New kinds of jobs called for individual skills. This meant that workers frequently moved away from their local communities and kinship groupings to live near their places of employment. Extended families began to dissipate in favor of nuclear families consisting of married couples and their children.

Women still stayed at home to raise the children. However, with the new mobility, multigenerational households declined, along with the expectation that children cared for elderly parents in their own homes. In the 20th century, this led to assisted-living and skilled-nursing facilities as new living arrangements to serve the needs of the infirm elderly.

The housing debacle—revisited: Housing also evolved. Single-family homes sprung up to accommodate the new and independent family unit. This tradition of single-family dwellings accelerated in the United States after the end of World War II. Since then, America's residential landscape has shifted from city or small-town to suburban living. A general prosperity, cheap land rendered from new agricultural technologies, easier building techniques, and access to automobiles all combined to initiate the development of suburban tracts of single-family homes for nuclear families. Americans value these homes for the space, security, status, and privacy they provide.

The single-family suburban home did work for a time, while mothers stayed at home to raise children and life spans were shorter. However, with the advent of extended life expectancy, and with both parents working, the single-family home for nuclear families is no longer meeting the needs of our changing population.

It's no wonder that the current so-called economic malaise began with housing in 2007. That's about the time the economic system began to realize that the American housing stock is actually worth less because it doesn't fit the coming needs of the marketplace.

America's elderly population is now growing at a moderate rate. But soon into this century, the rate will accelerate. According to census projections, the elderly population will double between now and the year 2050, to close to 79 million. By then, as many as 1 in 5 Americans could be elderly.

In order to adjust the housing stock of the country to reflect the baby boomers' retirement and the associated growth in multigenerational living arrangements, changes will be required in long-existing and mostly local housing and building codes and associated ordinances. The main battle line in this political fight is over accessory apartments, popularly called "granny flats." Built adjacent to larger houses, they can provide living spaces for adult children or grandparents. They offer both proximity and privacy. Public debate and political battles are being fought, won, and lost around the country over making changes in codes that not only allow for, but actually promote, the construction of accessory apartments in existing neighborhoods and in new developments.

Accessory apartments produce two kinds of complaints. First, physical impacts, such as increased parking and traffic and architectural changes in buildings, are often seen as disruptive to neighborhoods. The second sort relates to social and cultural issues. That is, accessory apartments deviate from the traditional ways of looking at housing, family, and the neighborhood. It stands for a change in the way the single-family house is used, a departure from the conventional meanings connected to residential zoning categories.

While builders and architects do complain about zoning constraints and such, their own practices are often obstacles to housing appropriate for the new century. They talk more about features that will sell to consumers, but won't really serve them. For example, consider a ritzy Newport Beach, California, neighborhood where folks have been sold $2 million homes with granny flats at the tops of stairs! How's granny going to navigate those steep steps?

WHAT AMERICA MUST DO

Fast-rising life expectancies, the growing costs of elder care, the increasing need for child care, the frustrating lack of affordable housing, and the new disconnectedness—all are producing unfamiliar challenges for families all around America. Fortunately, our aforementioned 20th century dalliance with nuclear families and white-picket-fence suburbia is fast winding down. The "social avalanche" of elderly baby boomers will force Americans back to the familiar family form of multigenerational households.

America must spur the comeback of accessory apartments and the flexibility of mixed neighborhoods with respect to size, value, and use. Now that the housing market has crashed, there's some time to reflect on the future and to design communities and homes that will accommodate a fast-graying America in innovative ways.

NOTES

1. For the best evidence of this demographic catastrophe currently overwhelming our central social institutions in the United States, see Charles Goodhart and Manoj Pradhan's *The Great Demographic Reversal: Ageing Societies, Waning Inequality, and an Inflation Revival* (New York: Palgrave Macmillan, 2020).
2. To be precise, the "stereotactic resection of his left frontal temporal lesion was complicated by postoperative bleeding in the right occipitoparietal region, perhaps in the hypothalamus, and pulmonary edema."
3. Trudy Lieberman and Consumer Reports Editors, *Consumer Reports Complete Guide to Health Services for Seniors* (New York: Three Rivers Press: 2000).
4. Joe Mozingo, "Nursing home infamous for high number of COVID deaths to close," *Los Angeles Times*, February 8, 2022. See also Robert Gebeloff, Katie Thomas, and Jessica Silver-Greenberg, "How Nursing Homes Hide Their Most Serious Lapses," *New York Times*, December 21, 2021, https://static01.nyt.com/images/2021/12/10/nytfrontpage/ scan.pdf. See also Samantha Young, "California Aims to Tighten Licensing of Nursing Homes after Pandemic Exposes Deadly Lapses," *Los Angeles Times*, May 13, 2022, https:// www.latimes.com/california/story/2022-05-13/california-aim-to-tighten-rules-on- nursing-homes-after-pandemic-exposed-deadly-lapses.
5. Christopher Rowland, "Seniors Are Flooding Homeless Shelters that Can't Care for Them," *Washington Post*, May 22, 2023, https://www.washingtonpost.com/ business/2023/05/22/seniors-homeless-baby-boomers/.
6. The Economist (2011c), "World population: Now we are seven billion–persuading women to have fewer babies would help in some places. But it is no answer to scarce resources," *The Economist*, October 22, 2011, https://www.economist.com/ leaders/2011/10/22/now-we-are-seven-billion.
7. Laurence Darmiento, "Are California's Public Pension Funds Headed for Another Crisis?," *Los Angeles Times*, September 29, 2022, https://www.latimes.com/business/ story/2022-09-29/are-calpers-calstrs-other-pension-plans-headed-for-crisis.
8. Jim Tankersley, "As Lawmakers Spar over Social Security, Its Costs Are Rising Fast," *New York Times*, February 15, 2023, https://www.nytimes.com/2023/02/15/us/politics/ social-security-costs-biden-republicans.html. See also Paul Krugman, "How Not to Panic about Social Security," *New York Times*, February 28, 2023, https://www.nytimes. com/2023/02/28/opinion/social-security-retirement-age.html.

9. Ricardo Nulla, "American Health Care Is Dying. This Hospital Could Cure It," *New York Times*, March 9, 2023, https://www.nytimes.com/2023/03/09/opinion/american-health-care-hospitals.html.

10. Aurelien Breeden, "Why So Many People in France Are Protesting over Pensions," *New York Times*, April 13, 2023, https://www.nytimes.com/article/france-pension-strikes-macron-explainer.html. See also David Luhnow and Max Colchester, "The U.K.'s Government-Run Healthcare Service Is in Crisis," *Wall Street Journal*, February 6, 2023, https://www.wsj.com/articles/nhs-uk-national-health-service-strike-costs-11675693883.

11. Kathleen McGarry and Robert F. Schoeni, *National Bureau of Economic Research.* Working Paper: *Social Security, Economic Growth, and the Rise of Independence of Elder Widows in the 20th Century*, No. 6511 (April 1998).

12. Richard Fry, Jeffrey S. Passel, and D'Vera Cohn, "A Majority of Young Adults in the U.S. Live with Their Parents for the First Time Since the Great Depression," Pew Research Center, September 4, 2020, https://www.pewresearch.org/short-reads/2020/09/04/a-majority-of-young-adults-in-the-u-s-live-with-their-parents-for-the-first-time-since-the-great-depression/.

13. As far as we know, Seth Crone invented the use of the term "moving picture" in this context, as it connotes that seeing the big picture is not good enough. You also need to see how things change through time as well for true enlightenment.

14. D'Vera Cohn, Juliana Menasce Horowitz, Rachel Minkin, Richard Fry, and Kiley Hurst, "The Demographics of Multigenerational Households," Pew Research Center, March 24, 2022, https://www.pewresearch.org/social-trends/2022/03/24/the-demographics-of-multigenerational-households/. Moreover, Generations United, based on their own surveys, estimates that 26 percent of Americans were living in multigenerational households in 2022.

15. Florence Williams, "Heartbreak Hurts, in Part because Our Cells 'Listen for Loneliness,'" *Los Angeles Times*, February 6, 2022, https://www.latimes.com/opinion/story/2022-02-06/loneliness-white-blood-cells-inflammation-chronic-disease-neurogenomics.

16. Paula Span, "Senior Housing That Seniors Actually Like," *New York Times*, January 29, 2023, https://www.nytimes.com/2023/01/29/health/elderly-housing-adu.html. See also Julie Lasky, "Are Tiny Homes a Solution to the Housing Crisis?" *New York Times*, February 10, 2023, https://www.nytimes.com/2023/02/10/realestate/tiny-homes-housing-market-trends.html.

17. See www.riverparkhomes.com for examples.

18. The Times Editorial Board, "Editorial: California Should Prioritize Housing People, Not Cars," *Los Angeles Times*, July 17, 2022, https://www.latimes.com/opinion/story/2022-07-17/editorial-california-should-prioritize-housing-people-not-cars.

19. Harold T. Christensen, "Family," in *The World Book Encyclopedia* (Westlake, Ohio: Scott Fetzer Company: Berkshire Hathaway, 1976).

20. These figures are based on data supplied from the World Bank Group website, accessed in 2022, https://www.worldbank.org/en/home.

21. Julie Wernau and Jon Kamp, "U.S. Life Expectancy Fell to Lowest Level Since 1996," *Wall Street Journal*, December 22, 2022, https://www.wsj.com/articles/u-s-life-expectancy-fell-to-lowest-level-since-1996-11671667059#:~:text=Covid%2D19%20

and%20opioid%20overdoses,in%20death%20rate%20last%20year&text=Life%20
expectancy%20in%20the%20U.S.,up%20the%20number%20of%20deaths.

22. The "some 50%" estimate varies substantially as different agencies define kinds and degrees of disability differently.

23. U.S. Department of Labor—Bureau of Labor Statistics, "News Release: Employment Characteristics of Families—2022," https://www.bls.gov/news.release/pdf/famee.pdf.

24. Maureen Coffey and Rose Khattar, "The Childcare Sector Will Continue to Struggle Hiring Staff Unless It Creates Good Jobs," Report, at Center for American Progress, September 2, 2022, https://www.americanprogress.org/article/the-child-care-sector-will-continue-to-struggle-hiring-staff-unless-it-creates-good-jobs/.

25. Lisa Boone, "A Sleek Take on a Granny Flat," *Los Angeles Times*, October 16, 2021, F4.

26. Sherry Turkle, *Alone Together: Why We Expect More from Technology and Less from Each Other* (New York: Basic Books, 2011).

27. Robert D. Putnam, *Bowling Alone: The Collapse and Revival of American Community* (New York: Simon & Schuster, 2000).

28. Jean Hanff Korelitz, "All in the Family," *Real Simple* magazine, n.d., n.p.

29. Ellen Graham, "Two Generations, One Nursing Home," *Wall Street Journal,* May 13, 1998.

30. Barbara Lovenheim, "Child's Support," *AARP The Magazine* (March/April 2006).

31. "Generations United, "Family Matters: Multigenerational Living Is on the Rise and Here to Stay," an electronic publications report at gu.org, April 21, 2021, https://www.gu.org/app/uploads/2021/04/21-MG-Family-Report-WEB.pdf.

32. Neale Donald Walsch, *Conversations with God: An Uncommon Dialogue*, book 3 (Charlottesville, VA: Hampton Roads Publishing Company Inc., 1998).

33. Nancy Hooyman and H. Asuman Kiyak, *Social Gerontology: A Multidisciplinary Perspective*, 5th ed. (Boston: Allyn and Bacon, 1998).

34. Hooyman and Kiyak, 269.

35. George Witkin, PhD, "When Families Live Together: A Survival Guide," Grandparents.com, https://www.scribd.com/document/466368890/When-Families-Live-Together#.

36. CNN.com, "Car Plows through Market, Killing 9," July 17, 2003, https://www.cnn.com/2003/US/West/07/16/farmers.market.crash/.

37. That is, if it already hasn't!

38. In chapter 12 we go into some detail about how "mainstream" American culture is really kind of an odd notion. But, please bear with our simplification of things for this chapter.

39. Philip Moeller, "How to Make Multigenerational Living Work," *U.S. News & World Report*, January 14, 2011, https://money.usnews.com/money/blogs/the-best-life/2011/01/14/how-to-make-multigenerational-living-work.

40. Mary Pipher, *Another Country: Navigating the Emotional Terrain of Our Elders* (New York: Riverhead Books, 1999).

41. Pipher, *Another Country*.

42. Virginia Morris, *How to Care for Aging Parents* (New York: Workman, 1996), 192–96.

43. Kathleen A. Hughes, "He Says Maine. She Says Florida," *Wall Street Journal*, March 21, 2011, https://www.wsj.com/articles/SB10001424052748704254304576116471507613288.

44. Pat Curry, "Make Room for Everyone," *Builder* magazine (December 2005), 63–64.
45. Andres Duany, Elizabeth Plater-Zyberk, and Jeff Speck, *Suburban Nation: The Rise of Sprawl and the Decline of the American Dream* (New York: North Point Press, 2000), 52.
46. No author, "Home, Sweet Manufactured Home," *Reader's Digest* (September 2005), 30.
47. Hannah Wiley, "A New California Law Has Done Little to Encourage Building, Report Says," *Los Angeles Times*, January 18, 2023, https://www.latimes.com/california/story/2023-01-18/new-california-duplex-law-housing-sb9-homeowners.
48. Steve Lopez, "For Seniors, Social Isolation Is a Debilitating Burden," *Los Angeles Times*, January 25, 2023, B1–B4.
49. Paula Span, "Who Will Care for 'Kinless' Seniors?" *New York Times*, December 3, 2022, https://www.nytimes.com/2022/12/03/health/elderly-living-alone.html.
50. Angela Escobar, "More 65+ Adults Are Getting Roommates. Should You Join Them?," Clearmatch Medicare Retirement Blog, September 29, 2021, https://clearmatchmedicare.com/blog/retirement/how-and-why-to-get-a-roommate-when-youre-over-65.
51. Margaret Mead and Ken Heyman, *Family* (New York: MacMillan,1965), 80.
52. Dana Goldstein and Robert Gebeloff, "As Gen X and Boomers Age, They Confront Living Alone," *New York Times*, November 27, 2022, https://www.nytimes.com/2022/11/27/us/living-alone-aging.html.
53. William Strauss and Neil Howe, *Generations* (New York: William Morrow, 1991).
54. James A. Michener, *The Covenant* (New York: Fawcett Crest, 1980), 22–25.
55. James A. Michener, *Chesapeake: A Novel* (New York: Fawcett Books, 1978).
56. Michener, *Chesapeake*, 602–03.
57. Laura Esquivel, *Like Water for Chocolate* (New York: Anchor Books, 1989), 10–12.
58. Blanche Weisen Cook, *Eleanor Roosevelt, Volume 1: The Early Years, 1884–1933* (New York: Viking, 1992), 183.
59. Sean Mitchell, "The Interior Landscape—Space," *Los Angeles Times*, April 28, 2005, sec. F1. Used with permission.
60. Ben Dooley and Hisako Ueno, "Japan Looks to Surveillance to Keep an Eye on the Elderly," *New York Times*, February 8, 2022, B1.
61. No author, *Parade* magazine (December 28, 2003), 12.
62. Adam Gopnik, *Paris to the Moon* (New York: Random House, 2001), 71–73.
63. Peter Hessler, *River Town: Two Years on the Yangtze* (New York: HarperCollins, 2001), 90.
64. Edward T. Hall, *The Hidden Dimension* (Garden City, NY: Anchor Doubleday, 1966), n.p.
65. Philippe Ariès, *Centuries of Childhood: A Social History of Family Life* (New York: Vintage, 1965), n.p.
66. Frederik Balfor with Natasha Khan, "China's 'Demographic Tsunami,'" *Bloomberg BusinessWeek*, January 9, 2012.
67. Schumpeter Blog, "Land of Wasted Talent," *The Economist*, November 5, 2011.
68. Patrick H. Hare, "Survey of Installations of Accessory Units" in *Report IV—Accessory Units: The State of the Art* (Washington, DC: Patrick H. Hare Planning and Design, 1989), 6.
69. Hare, Survey 1.

70. Jeannie Matteucci, "Backyard Cottage Industry: Space for Aging Parents"—special to *San Francisco Chronicle* on SFgate, October 9, 2011, https://www.sfgate.com/homeandgarden/article/Backyard-cottage-industry-space-for-aging-parents-2328231.php.

71. Norma J. Shattuck, "Behind the Big Door"—special to *San Francisco Chronicle* on SFgate, October 20, 2004, https://www.sfgate.com/homeandgarden/article/BEHIND-THE-BIG-DOOR-Garages-are-for-cars-our-2641902.php.

72. Charles Smith, "Family Hopes to Add a Room When Rebuilding 1920s Two-Car Garage"—special to *San Francisco Chronicle* on SFgate, October 12, 2005, https://www.sfgate.com/homeandgarden/article/Family-hopes-to-add-a-room-when-rebuilding-1920s-2602717.php.

73. Shattuck, "Behind the Big Door."

74. Smith, "Family Hopes."

75. Smith, "Family Hopes."

76. Charles Smith, "Please, Don't Park Guests in the Garage"—special to *San Francisco Chronicle* on SFgate, May 11, 2005, https://www.sfgate.com/homeandgarden/article/Please-don-t-park-guests-in-the-garage-2672164.php.

77. Lou Manfredini, "Going the Rental Route," *USA Weekend* (September 2003), 17.

78. DIY Doctor: The Home Improvement Hub, http://www.diydoctor.org.uk/projects/barn_conversion.htm.

79. Patricia Bass, "Show Me the Green," *Palo Alto Weekly* in Home and Real Estate sec., October 14, 2005.

80. Bass, "Show Me."

81. Carolyn Said, "White House Picks Up Conservation Mantra"—special to *San Francisco Chronicle* on SFgate, October 9, 2005, https://www.sfgate.com/green/article/QUEST-FOR-CONSERVATION-White-House-picks-up-2602831.php.

82. Bass, "Show Me."

83. Bass, "Show Me."

84. Jane Knoerle, "Affordable Green: Sunset's Idea House Is Rich with Energy-Saving Innovations," *The Almanac* (October 19, 2005), 16, https://www.almanacnews.com/morgue/2005/2005_10_19.sunset.shtml.

85. Knoerle, "Affordable Green."

86. Penny Doherty, "When Adding a Second Unit, Consider These Factors," *Wall Street Journal* in Real Estate Journal sec., 2004.

87. Lynn Comeskey, "Experience Counts," *Palo Alto Weekly* in Home and Real Estate sec., October 21, 2005, 17.

88. Leo L. Cram, "Accessory Apartments," University of Missouri Extension—Missouri Gerontology Institute, October 1993, https://extension.missouri.edu/publications/gg14.

89. Courtney Rosen, *How to Do Just about Everything* (New York: Free Press, 2000). Rosen's tip No. 252 is "hire a builder."

90. Molly Tanenbaum, "Get It in Writing," *The Almanac: Fall Real Estate* (October 10, 2005), 26, 28.

91. Rosen, *How to Do Just about Everything.*

92. Jon Healey, "What to Know Before Bu ilding an ADU," *Los Angeles Times*, March 14, 2022, A9, https://anyflip.com/xizbi/ftst.

93. Conor Dougherty, "It's Been a Home for Decades, But Legal Only a Few Months," *New York Times*, December 18, 2021, https://www.nytimes.com/2021/12/18/business/economy/california-housing.html. See also Doug Smith and Dakota Smith, "Bass Issues Sweeping Directive to Fast Track Affordable Housing," *Los Angeles Times*, December 16, 2022, https://www.latimes.com/california/story/2022-12-16/bass-executive-order-on-housing.

94. The Times Editorial Board, "Here's a Warning, Pasadena: Don't Even Think About Trying to Evade SB 9," *Los Angeles Times*, March 20, 2022, https://www.latimes.com/opinion/story/2022-03-20/editorial-pasadena-sb9-density-historic.

95. This estimate is based on the fact that nationwide, circa 2005, approximately 6 percent of existing housing units are sold in a given year.

96. U.S. Census Bureau data.

97. Andrea Coombes, "Relative Proximity," *Retirement Living Blog—CBS MarketWatch.com*, October 7, 2004, https://www.marketwatch.com/story/as-boomers-parents-age-in-law-units-gain-favor.

98. William Strauss and Neil Howe, *Generations* (New York: Perennial, 1991), 391.

99. Andrea Gross, "Making a Big Move," *Time*, October 20, 2003, https://content.time.com/time/subscriber/article/0,33009,1005962,00.html.

100. Richard Paoli, "Americans Favor Family as Neighbors," *San Francisco Chronicle*, October 5, 2003, G3.

101. Curry, "Make Room for Everyone."

102. Carol Lloyd, "The Fab New World of Prefab Houses,"—special to SFGate.com, May 11, 2004, https://www.sfgate.com/entertainment/article/The-Fab-New-World-of-Prefab-Houses-SF-architect-3303951.php.

103. Judy Richter, "A Full Table," *San Francisco Chronicle*, September 10, 2005, sec. F. Used with permission.

104. Brittany Mejia, Liam Dillon, Gabrielle LaMarr Le Mee, and Sanhya Kambhampati, "L.A.'s love of sprawl made it America's most overcrowded place. Poor people pay a deadly price," *Los Angeles Times*, October 19, 2022, https://www.yahoo.com/now/l-love-sprawl-made-americas-120055651.html.

105. The information in this section is based on the comments of Martin Gellen, in *ADUs in Single-Family Housing* (New Brunswick, NJ: Rutgers CUPE Press 1986), 103–4.

106. "Small Solutions: Second Units as Affordable Housing," in *The Evaluation of the Double Unit Opportunity Program of San Francisco Development Fund, 1985–1988* (The San Francisco Development Fund, 1988).

107. Binyamin Appelbaum, "California Is Actually Making Progress on Building More Housing," *New York Times*, October 4, 2022, https://www.nytimes.com/2022/10/04/opinion/california-housing-crisis.html.

108. Personal interview with Jim Berson by authors, August 22, 2000.

109. Marion Softky, "Woodside Tackles New Rules for Extra Living Units," *The Almanac* (September 27, 2000), https://www.almanacnews.com/morgue/2000/2000_09_27.wsunit1.html.

110. Patrick H. Hare, "The Suburban Frailty Boom," *Aging Network News*, August 1991, 10.

111. The 1990 America with Disabilities Act (ADA) provides rules for construction in public and commercial facilities, even those located in private homes.

112. Iris Harrell and Lisa Sten, "Universal Design," *San Jose Magazine* in supplement *San Jose Home and Garden Program*, June 2003.

113. Ronald L. Mace, Graeme J. Hardie, and Jaine P. Place, "Accessible Environments: Toward Universal Design," in *Design Intervention: Toward a More Humane Architecture*, revised ed. (Raleigh, NC: Center for Universal Design, 1991).

114. S. Mitra Kalita, "Blueprint for a New American Home," *Wall Street Journal*, November 2, 2011, https://www.wsj.com/articles/SB10001424052970204644504576651152960 249150.

115. Personal interview by authors with Jerrine Barrett, January 23, 2001.

116. Mace et al., "Accessible Environments."

117. "Certified Aging-in-Place Specialist (CAPS)," Education-Designations Page, National Association of Home Builders, https://www.nahb.org/education-and-events/education/ designations/certified-aging-in-place-specialist-caps.

118. Roseann Henry, "6 Ideas for Elder-Friendly Design," Home Safety Page, This Old House, https://www.thisoldhouse.com/home-safety/21015178/6-ideas-for-elder-friendly-design.

119. No author, "Helping Older Homeowners," *San Francisco Chronicle*, March 13, 2004, section F.10.

120. Henry, "6 Ideas."

121. Grab Bars á la Mode, AARP—"Grab Bars, Bathroom, Aging in Place, Safety" web page, https://www.aarp.org/home-garden/home-improvement/info-02-2004/bathroom_ grabbars.html.

122. "Grab Bars," AARP.

123. Much of the material in this part comes from an excellent article, cited here: Cindy Gackle, "Home Accessibility = Greater Independence," Fairview-University Medical Center—Consortium of Multiple Sclerosis Centers, n.d., https://cdn.ymaws.com/www. mscare.org/resource/resmgr/Articles/Article0015_HmAccEqGrInd.pdf.

124. Premier Bathrooms advertisement, *AARP Bulletin* 47 no. 5 (2006), 31.

125. Gackle, "Home Accessibility."

126. Premier Bathrooms advertisement, *AARP Bulletin*.

127. Premier Bathrooms advertisement, *AARP Bulletin*.

128. Gackle, "Home Accessibility."

129. Paul J. Donio, "Tailor-Fit Kitchens," www.thisoldhouse.com/toh/knowhowskitchen/ article/0,16417,214601,00.html.

130. Donio, "Tailor-Fit."

131. Gackle, "Home Accessibility."

132. Donio, "Tailor-Fit."

133. Gackle, "Home Accessibility."

134. Harrell and Sten, "Universal Design."

135. Federal Trade Commission, "Making the Home Senior-Friendly," a resource from the American Occupational Therapy Association.

136. "5 Steps," CNNMoney.

137. Gackle, "Home Accessibility."

138. Henry, "6 Ideas."

139. Gackle, "Home Accessibility."

140. "5 Steps," CNNMoney.
141. Gackle, "Home Accessibility."
142. Gackle, "Home Accessibility."
143. Susan Fornoff, "Making Room for Mom and Dad," *San Francisco Chronicle* on SFGate. com, September 18, 2004, https://www.sfgate.com/homeandgarden/article/Making-room-for-Mom-and-Dad-More-Baby-Boomers-2724388.php/.
144. Benny Evangelista, "Public Gets Firsthand View of the Future," *San Francisco Chronicle* on SFGate.com, May 17, 2004, https://www.sfgate.com/business/article/Public-gets-firsthand-view-of-the-future-2758531.php.
145. James Brooke, "Robotic Elder-Care Products Gaining in Popularity in Japan," *San Francisco Chronicle*, March 5, 2004. Also see Jason Horowitz, "Who Will Take Care of Italy's Older People? Maybe Robots," *New York Times*, March 25, 2023, https://www.nytimes.com/2023/03/25/world/europe/who-will-take-care-of-italys-older-people-robots-maybe.html.
146. Brooke, "Robotic Elder-Care."
147. Brooke, "Robotic Elder-Care."
148. James Wright, "Inside Japan's Long Experiment with Automating Elder Care," *MIT Technology Review*, January 29, 2023, https://www.technologyreview.com/2023/01/09/1065135/japan-automating-eldercare-robots/.
149. Elder Cottage Housing Opportunities (ECHO), www.aging.state.va.us.
150. Gail Hand, "The Joys and Pitfalls of Inter-Generational Living: One Family's Success Story," www.the-homestore.com.
151. While we don't recommend this awful book, we must cite it: Josh Hawley, *Manhood: The Masculine Virtue America Needs* (Washington, DC: Regnery Publishing, 2023).
152. Isabella Simonetti, "Living with Mom and Dad while Figuring Out a Financial Exit Plan," *New York Times*, March 1, 2023, https://www.nytimes.com/2023/03/01/business/adults-living-home-parents-saving.html.
153. Teresa Toguchi Swartz, Minzee Kim, Mayumi Uno, Jeylan Mortimer, and Kirsten Bengtson O'Brien, "Safety Nets and Scaffolds: Parental Support in the Transition to Adulthood," *Journal of Marriage and Family* 73 (2), April 2011.
154. Alissa Quart, "Can We Put an End to America's Most Dangerous Myth (That Is, Independence)?" *New York Times*, March 9, 2023, https://www.nytimes.com/2023/03/09/opinion/art-of-dependence.html.
155. Bill George, *Authentic Leadership* (San Francisco: Jossey-Bass, 2003).
156. Perhaps the French noticed our omission when after their own revolution they based the design of their new government on "liberty, fraternity, and equality." The "fraternity" recognizes the missing "ter".
157. Philip Cateora, Bruce Money, Mary Gilly, John Graham, and Graham Cateora, *International Marketing*, 19th ed. (New York: McGraw-Hill, 2023).
158. Richard E. Nisbett, *The Geography of Thought: How Asians and Westerners Think Differently . . . and Why* (New York: Free Press, 2003).
159. Adam Smith, *The Wealth of Nations: Book IV* (New York: Modern Library, 1994), 485.
160. Lyrics of "Little Boxes," words and music by Malvina Reynolds. ©1962 Schroder Music Co. (ASCAP), Renewed 1990. Used with permission.

161. Edward T. Hall, *The Silent Language* (New York: Anchor Books, 1981), 179.
162. Hall, *The Silent Language*, 163–165.
163. Edward T. Hall, "The Silent Language of Overseas Business," *Harvard Business Review* (May-June 1960), 92–96.
164. Mike Dang, "Their Children Are Their Retirement Plans," *New York Times*, January 21, 2023, https://www.nytimes.com/2023/01/21/business/retirement-immigrant-families.html.
165. Kathy Chen, "China's Growth Places Strains on a Family's Ties," *Wall Street Journal*, April 13, 2005, A1.
166. Ralph Warner, *Get a Life*, 3rd ed. (Berkeley, CA: Nolo, 2000), 76.
167. Ken Budd, "The Deep Rewards—and Tangled Legal History—of Living with Extended Family," *Washington Post* magazine (December 5, 2022), https://www.washingtonpost.com/magazine/interactive/2022/family-zoning-moore-city-east-cleveland/.
168. See cobrands.business.findlaw.com and click on "Family Partnerships."
169. Rachel Emma Silverman, "Who Will Mind Mom? Check Her Contract," *Wall Street Journal*, September 7, 2006, https://www.wsj.com/articles/SB115759786200356055.
170. Ron Huxley, "Steps of a Family Meeting," *Parenting Toolbox* online resource, June 26, 2004. Web page not found.
171. Kimberly K. Money and R. Bruce Money, *Creating a Functional Family in a Dysfunctional World* (Dallas: Taylor Trade Publishing, 1999), 169.
172. Gail Hand, "The Joys and Pitfalls of Inter-generational Living: One Family's Success Story with Building an In-Law Addition," on The Home Store web page, n.d., https://www.the-homestore.com/about-us/in-the-news/aarp-joys/.
173. Hand, "Joys and Pitfalls."
174. Hand, "Joys and Pitfalls."
175. Ron Huxley, "Steps to Running a Family Meeting," in Family Healer blog, January 31, 2017, https://ronhuxley.com/2017/01/31/a-family-meeting-gives-every-member-of-the-family/.
176. George L. Maddox, ed., *The Encyclopedia of Aging* (New York: Singer Publishing Company, 1987), 248.
177. Steven Ross Johnson, "Staff Shortages Choking U.S. Health Care System," *U.S. News & World Report*, July 28, 2022, https://www.usnews.com/news/health-news/articles/2022-07-28/staff-shortages-choking-u-s-health-care-system.
178. Emily Alpert Reyes, "We'll End Up on the Streets: L.A. Caregivers for Elderly, Disabled Push for Higher Pay," *Los Angeles Times*, November 27, 2022, https://www.latimes.com/california/story/2022-11-27/la-caregivers-for-elderly-disabled-push-for-higher-pay.
179. Ai-jen Poo and Ilana Berger, "Home Care Workers Deserve a Living Wage," *New York Times*, April 2, 2022, https://www.nytimes.com/2022/03/30/opinion/home-care-aides-industry.html. See also Tammy La Gorce, "An 'Aggressive Love for Life' Regardless of Life's Challenges," *New York Times*, October 28, 2022, https://www.nytimes.com/2022/10/28/style/barbara-torasso-bradley-carbone-wedding.html. And see Heidi De Marco, "Inflation Adds to the Pain of Families Coping with Diabetes and Other Medical Needs," *Los Angeles Times*, August 12, 2022, https://www.latimes.com/california/story/2022-08-12/inflation-families-diabetes-medical-needs.

180. Clare Ansberry, "These Self-Care Strategies Can Help Caregivers Cope with Burnout," *Wall Street Journal*, December 29, 2021, https://www.wsj.com/articles/these-self-care-strategies-can-help-caregivers-cope-with-burnout-11640782803.

181. Partnership for Quality Home Health Care, "Home Health Leaders Urge Lawmakers to Pass Choose Home Care Act of 2021," press release, January 10, 2002, https://pqhh.org/article/home-health-leaders-urge-lawmakers-to-pass-choose-home-care-act-of-2021/#:~:text=WASHINGTON%20–%20The%20Partnership%20for%20Quality,for%20Medicare%20beneficiaries%20following%20hospitalization.

182. Melanie Mason, "Bill Steps toward Single-Payer Healthcare," *Los Angeles Times*, n.d., https://enewspaper.latimes.com/infinity/article_share.aspx?guid=22ce4c07-ece6-4c6d-97db-3c914709d88e.

183. Preyas S. Desai, Devavrat Purohit, and Bo Zhou, "Allowing Consumers to Bundle Themselves: The Profitability of Family Plans," *Marketing Science* 37 (6), November 2018, https://www.researchgate.net/publication/329107431_Allowing_Consumers_to_Bundle_Themselves_The_Profitability_of_Family_Plans.

184. AARP Press Room, "New Report Highlights Increasing Cost of Family Caregiving in the U.S.," March 8, 2023, https://press.aarp.org/2023-03-08-New-Report-Highlights-Increasing-Cost-of-Family-Caregiving-in-the-US#:~:text=WASHINGTON%20—%20The%20unpaid%20work%20provided,report%20was%20released%20in%202019.

185. Nicholas Goldberg, "Column: What's So Great about Living to 100?," *Los Angeles Times*, December 11, 2022, https://www.latimes.com/opinion/story/2022-12-11/longevity-centenarian-living-to-be-100.

186. Deborah Nason, "Your Loved Ones Will Already Be in a State of Trauma: The Ramifications of Dying without a Living Will," CNBC Life Changes web page, October 29, 2022, https://www.cnbc.com/2022/10/29/here-are-the-legal-and-personal-ramifications-of-dying-without-a-will.html.

187. Deborah Netburn, "A Final Rest in Neptune's Realm," *Los Angeles Times*, n.d., https://enewspaper.latimes.com/infinity/article_share.aspx?guid=873d3a5b-baad-4e25-badd-0ca0ffb8015a.

188. Michael Waters, "Cremation Borrows the Direct-to-Consumer Playbook," *New York Times*, February 3, 2022, https://www.nytimes.com/2022/02/03/business/cremation-startups-direct-to-consumer.html.

189. David C. Sloane, *Is the Cemetery Dead?* (Chicago: University of Chicago Press, 2018).

190. Kim Christensen and Ben Poston, "Hospice Reforms to Become Law after *Times* Investigation," *Los Angeles Times*, October 4, 2021, https://www.latimes.com/california/story/2021-10-04/hospice-reforms-law-fraud-abuse-times-investigation.

191. National Hospice and Palliative Care Organization, *Facts and Figures* online resource 2022 edition, December 2022, https://www.nhpco.org/wp-content/uploads/NHPCO-Facts-Figures-2022.pdf.

192. Nicholas Goldberg, "Column: Should Our Aid in Dying Laws Be Expanded, Or Are We Moving Too Far, Too Fast?," *Los Angeles Times*, September 19, 2022, https://www.latimes.com/opinion/story/2022-09-19/aid-in-dying-assisted-suicide.

193. Lola Fadulu, "To Die on Her Own Terms, A Connecticut Woman Turns to Vermont," *New York Times*, March 29, 2023, https://www.nytimes.com/2023/03/29/nyregion/connecticut-vermont-medical-assisted-death.html.

194. Patrick McGreevy, "State Lawmakers OK Simplifying Aid-in-Dying Law," *Los Angeles Times*, September 12, 2021, https://www.pressreader.com/usa/los-angeles-times-sund ay/20210912/281891596398632.

195. Maria Cheng, "Canada's Euthanasia Laws Trouble Experts," *Los Angeles Times*, August 29, 2022, https://www.pressreader.com/usa/los-angeles-times/20220829/281586654409208. See also Motoko Rich and Hikari Hida, "A Yale Professor Suggested Mass Suicide for Old People in Japan. What Did He Mean?," *New York Times*, February 12, 2023, https://www.nytimes.com/2023/02/12/world/asia/japan-elderly-mass-suicide.html.

196. John L. Graham, Lynda Lawrence, and William Hernández Requejo, *AND? How to Build Relationships through Inventive Negotiation* (Palgrave Macmillan and Amazon Services, 2020).

INDEX

ABOUT THE AUTHORS

EMILY K. GRAHAM

Emily is a licensed clinical social worker (LCSW) in the state of California and has a master's in spiritual psychology from the University of Santa Monica, where she also obtained a certificate in program development and facilitation. Currently, she is working part-time for a mental health crisis hotline, has her own counseling private practice, and is doing some consulting in various health care settings after nearly a decade working in the hospice/palliative home care settings. She makes time to enjoy the outdoors, nature, and animals while fostering creative projects in songwriting, fashion, and art.

ANGEL L. VARGAS

Angel Vargas is a health care executive with over nineteen years of experience in the ambulatory and care-at-home settings. As a strategic and operational leader in one of the largest health care delivery systems in the United States, Angel is charged with overseeing service delivery in the at-home setting for thousands of patients. A former military officer, Angel led hundreds of caregivers and staff through the COVID-19 pandemic and set the stage for future growth in the industry. Angel holds a master's degree in business administration and a master's degree in health administration from Baylor University, Texas. Finally, Angel is a board-certified fellow in the American College of Healthcare Executives and currently serves as a senior administrator in the U.S. Air Force Reserve at Travis Air Force Base California.

JOHN L. GRAHAM

John L. Graham also has a deep understanding of multigenerational living through his work with a variety of cultures and their practices. John is a Berkeley PhD and an emeritus professor of marketing and international business in the Merage Business School at the University of California, Irvine. He currently has nine other books in print, including the most popular textbook in the world on international marketing, the last now in its 19th edition. His three fiction books also promote extended family collaboration: *Imagine Everywhere*, *The Great Squirrel Burglar*, and *Charlotte's War*. John also writes for the *New York Times*, *Los Angeles Times*, the *Harvard Business Review*, and several other publications, and has been interviewed on NBC, Fox News, NPR, and the BBC. He lives in Irvine, California.

Made in the USA
Columbia, SC
12 February 2025

53752039R00250